# STEPHEN KING

## STORM
OF
THE
## CENTURY

Book-of-the-Month Club
New York

All interior photographs are provided with the kind permission of ABC, Inc. and include the work of Bruce Macaulay, Michael Courtney, Michael Ginsburg, and Troy Aossey.

This edition was especially created for Book-of-the-Month Club in 1999 by arrangement with the author. This edition copyright © 1999 by Book-of-the-Month Club, Inc. All rights reserved.

Printed in the United States of America

## Screenwriter's Note

The "reach" is a coastal New England term that refers to the stretch of open water between an island and the mainland. A bay is open on one end; a reach is open on two. The reach between Little Tall Island (fictional) and Machias (real) can be supposed to be about two miles wide.

# Introduction

In most cases—three or four out of every five, let's say—I know where I was when I got the idea for a certain story, what combination of events (usually mundane) set that story off. The genesis of *It*, for example, was my crossing a wooden bridge, listening to the hollow thump of my bootheels, and thinking of "The Three Billy Goats Gruff." In the case of *Cujo* it was an actual encounter with an ill-tempered Saint Bernard. *Pet Sematary* arose from my daughter's grief when her beloved pet cat, Smucky, was run over on the highway near our house.

Sometimes, however, I just can't remember how I arrived at a particular novel or story. In these cases the seed of the story seems to be an image rather than an idea, a mental snapshot so powerful it eventually calls characters and incidents the way some ultrasonic whistles supposedly call every dog in the neighborhood. These are, to me, at least, the true creative mysteries: stories that have no real antecedents, that come on their own. *The Green Mile* began with an image of a huge black man standing in his jail cell and watching the approach of a trusty selling candy and cigarettes from an old metal cart with a squeaky wheel. *Storm of the Century* also started with a jailhouse image: that of a man (white, not black) sitting on the bunk in his cell, heels drawn up, arms resting on knees, eyes *unblinking*. This was not a gentle man or a good man, as John Coffey in *The Green Mile* turned out to be; this was an extremely evil man. Maybe not a man at all. Every time my mind turned back to him—while driving, while sitting in the optometrist's office and waiting to get my eyes dilated, or worst of all while lying awake in bed at night with the lights out—he looked a little scarier. Still just sitting there on his bunk and not moving, but a little scarier. A little less like a man and a little more like . . . well, a little more like what was underneath.

Gradually, the story started to spin out from the man . . . or whatever he was. The man sat on a bunk. The bunk was in a cell. The cell was in the back of the general store on Little Tall Island, which I sometimes think of as "Dolores Claiborne's island." Why in the back of the general store? Because a community as small as the one on Little Tall wouldn't need a police station, only a part-time constable to take care of the occasional bit of ugliness—an obstreperous drunk, let us say, or a bad-tempered fisherman who sometimes puts his fists on his wife. Who would that constable be? Why, Mike Anderson, of course, owner and operator of the Anderson's General Store. A nice enough guy, and good with the drunks and the bad-tempered fishermen . . . but suppose something *really* bad came along? Something as bad, perhaps, as the malignant demon that invaded Regan in *The Exorcist?* Something that would just sit there in Mike Anderson's home-welded cell, looking out, waiting . . .

Waiting for what?

Why, the storm of course. The storm of the century. A storm big enough to cut Little Tall Island off from the mainland, to throw it entirely upon its own resources. Snow is beautiful; snow is deadly; snow is also a veil, like the one the magician uses to hide his sleight of hand. Cut off from the world, hidden by the snow, my boogeyman in the jail cell (by then I was already thinking of him by his stated name, Andre Linoge) could do great damage. The worst of it, perhaps, without ever leaving that bunk where he sat with his heels up and his arms on his knees.

I had reached this point in my thinking by October or November of 1996; a bad man (or perhaps a monster masquerading as a man) in a jail cell, a storm even bigger than the one that totally paralyzed the northeast corridor in the mid-1970s, a community cast on its own resources. I was daunted by the prospect of creating an entire community (I had done such a thing in two novels, *'Salem's Lot* and *Needful Things,* and it's an enormous challenge), but enticed by the possibilities. I also knew I had reached the point where I must write or lose my chance. Ideas that are more complete—the majority of them, in other words—will keep a fair length of time, but a story that rises from a single image, one that exists mostly as potential, seems to be a much more perishable item.

I thought the chances that *Storm of the Century* would collapse of its own weight were fairly high, but in December of 1996 I began to write, anyway. The final impetus was provided by the realization that if I set my story on Little Tall Island, I had a chance to say some interesting and provocative things about the very nature of community . . . because there is no community in America as tightly knit as the island communities off the coast of Maine. The people in them are bound together by situation, tradition, common interests, common religious practices, and work that is difficult and sometimes dangerous. They are also blood-bound and clannish, the populations of most islands composed of half a dozen old families that overlap at the cousins and nephews and inlaws like patchwork quilts.* If you're a tourist (or one of the "summah people"), they will be friendly to you, but you mustn't expect to see inside their lives. You can come back to your cottage on the headland overlooking the reach for sixty years, and you will still be an outsider. Because life on the island is different.

I write about small towns because I'm a small-town boy (although not an *island* boy, I hasten to add; when I write about Little Tall, I write as an outsider), and most of my small-town tales—those of Jerusalem's Lot, those of Castle Rock, those of Little Tall Island—owe a debt to Mark Twain ("The Man That Corrupted Hadleyburg") and Nathaniel Hawthorne ("Young Goodman Brown"). Yet all of them, it seemed to me, had a certain unexamined postulate at their center: that a malevolent encroachment must always shatter the community, driving the individuals apart and turning them into enemies. But that has been my experience more as a reader than as a community member; as a community member, I've seen towns pull together every time disaster strikes.†

Still the question remains: is the result of pulling together always the common good? Does the idea of "community" always warm the cockles of the heart, or does it on occasion chill the blood? It was at

---

*In eastern Maine, basketball teams play their season-ending tourney at the Bangor Auditorium, and normal life comes pretty much to a complete stop as folks all over the region listen to the radio broadcasts. One year when the Jonesport-Beals girls' team was in the Class D (Small School) tourney, the radio announcers referred to all five of the starters by their first names. They had to, because all the girls were either sisters or cousins. Every one was a Beals.

†In the ice storm of January 1998, for instance, when some communities went without power for two weeks or more.

that point that I imagined Mike Anderson's wife hugging him, and at the same moment whispering, "Make [Linoge] have an accident" in his ear. Man, what a chill that gave me! And I knew I would have to at least try to write the story.

The question of form remained to be answered. I don't worry about it, ever—no more than I worry about the question of voice. The voice of a story (usually third person, sometimes first person) always comes with the package. So does the form an idea will take. I feel most comfortable writing novels, but I also write short stories, screenplays, and the occasional poem. The idea always dictates the form. You can't make a novel be a short story, you can't make a short story be a poem, and you can't stop a short story that decides it wants to be a novel instead (unless you want to kill it, that is).

I assumed that if I wrote *Storm of the Century*, it would be a novel. Yet as I prepared to sit down to it, the idea kept insisting that it was a movie. Every image of the story seemed to be a movie image rather than a book image: the killer's yellow gloves, Davey Hopewell's bloodstained basketball, the kids flying with Mr. Linoge, Molly Anderson whispering "Make him have an accident" in her husband's ear, and most of all, Linoge in the cell, heels up, hands dangling, orchestrating it all.

It would be too long for a theatrical movie, but I thought I saw a way around that. I had developed a wonderful working relationship with ABC over the years, providing material (and sometimes teleplays) for half a dozen so-called miniseries that had done quite well in the ratings. I got in touch with Mark Carliner (who produced the new version of *The Shining)* and Maura Dunbar (who has been my creative contact at ABC since the early nineties). Would either of them, I asked, be interested in a *real* novel for television, one that existed as its own thing rather than being based on a preexisting novel?

Both of them said yes with hardly a pause, and when I finished the three two-hour scripts that follow, the project went into preproduction and then to film with no creative dithering or executive megrims at all. It is fashionable to shit on television if you're an intellectual (and for God's sake, never admit that you watch *Frasier*, let alone *Jerry Springer)*, but I have worked as a writer in both TV and the movies, and I subscribe to the adage that in Hollywood, TV people want to make shows and movie people want to make lunch reservations. This isn't sour grapes; the movies have been pretty good to me, by and large (let's just ignore such films as *Graveyard Shift* and *Silver Bullet*). But in television, they let you work . . . plus if you have a history of some success with multipart dramas, they let you spread a little, too. And I like to spread. It's a beautiful thing. ABC committed thirty-three million dollars to this project on the basis of three first-draft scripts, which were never significantly changed. That was also a beautiful thing.

I wrote *Storm of the Century* exactly as I would a novel, keeping a list of characters but no other notes, working a set schedule of three or four hours every day, hauling along my Mac PowerBook and working in hotel rooms when my wife and I went on our regular expeditions to watch the Maine women's basketball team play their away games in Boston, New York, and Philadelphia. The only real difference was that I used a Final Draft screenwriting program rather than the Word 6 program I use for ordinary prose (and every now and then the damned program would crash and the screen would freeze—the new Final Draft program is blessedly bug-free). And I would argue that what follows (and what you'll see on your TV screen if you watch *Storm* when it airs) isn't really a "TV drama" or a "miniseries" at all. It is a genuine novel, one that exists in a different medium.

The work was not without its problems. The main drawback to doing network TV is the censorship question (ABC is the one major network that still maintains an actual Standards and Practices arm; they read scripts and tell you what you *absolutely cannot show in the living rooms of America*). I had struggled mightily with this issue in the course of developing *The Stand* (the world's population strangles to death on its own snot) and *The Shining* (talented but clearly troubled young writer beats wife within an inch of her life with a croquet mallet, then attempts to bludgeon son to death with the same implement), and it was the absolute worst part of the process, the creative equivalent of Chinese foot-binding.

Happily for me (the self-appointed guardians of America's morality are probably a lot less happy about it), network television has broadened its spectrum of acceptability quite a bit since the days when the producers of *The Dick Van Dyke Show* were forbidden to show a double bed in the master bedroom (dear God, what if the youth of America began indulging fantasies of Dick and Mary lying there at night *with their legs touching?*). In the last ten years the changes have been even more sweeping. A good deal of this has been in response to the cable-TV revolution, but much of it is the result of general viewer attrition, particularly in the coveted eighteen to twenty-five age group.

I have been asked why bother with network TV at all when there are cable outlets like Home Box Office and Showtime, where the censorship issue is negligible. There are two reasons. The first is that, for all the critical sound and fury surrounding such original cable shows as *Oz* and *The Real World,* the potential cable-TV audience is still pretty small. Doing a mini on HBO would be like publishing a major novel with a small press. I have nothing at all against either small presses or cable TV, but if I work hard over a long period of time, I'd like a shot at the largest possible audience. Part of that audience may elect to switch away on Thursday night to watch *ER,* but that's the chance you take. If I do my job and people want to see how matters turn out, they'll tape *ER* and hang in there with me. "The exciting part is when you've got some competish," my mother used to say.

The second reason to stick with a major network is that a little footbinding can be good for you. When you know your story is going under the gaze of people who are watching for dead folks with open eyes (a no-no on network TV), children who utter bad words (another no-no), or large amounts of spilled blood (a *gigantic* no-no), you begin to think of alternative ways of getting your point across. In the horror and the suspense genres, laziness almost always translates into some graphic crudity: the popped eyeball, the slashed throat, the decaying zombie. When the TV censor takes those easy scares away it becomes necessary to think of other routes to the same goal. The filmmaker becomes subversive, and sometimes the filmmaker becomes actually elegant, as Val *(Cat People)* Lewton's films are often elegant.

The above probably sounds like a justification, but it's not. I am, after all, the guy who once said I wanted to terrify my audience, but would horrify it if I couldn't achieve terror . . . and if I couldn't achieve horror, I'd go for the gross-out. What the fuck, I'd say, I'm not proud. Network TV has, in a manner of speaking, taken away that ultimate fallback position.

There are some visceral moments in *Storm of the Century*—Lloyd Wishman with the axe and Peter Godsoe with his rope are just two examples—but we had to fight for every one of them, and some (where five-year-old Pippa scratches her mother's face and screams "Let me go, you bitch!" for example) are still under strenuous discussion. I'm not the most popular person at Standards and Practices these days—I keep calling people and whining, threatening to tell my big brother if they don't stop teasing me (in this case the part of my big brother is most frequently played by Bob Iger, who is ABC's top guy). Working with Standards and Practices on such a level is okay, I think; to get along really well with them would make me feel like Tokyo Rose. If you want to know who ends up winning most of the battles, compare the original teleplay (which is what I'm publishing here), with the finished TV program (which is in edit as I write this).

And remember, please, that not all the changes which take place between original script and final film are made to satisfy Standards and Practices. Them you can argue with; TV timing is beyond argument. Each finished segment must run ninety-one minutes, give or take a few seconds, and be divided into seven "acts," in order to allow all those wonderful commercials which pay the bills. There are tricks that can get you a little extra time in that time—one is a form of electronic compression I don't understand—but mostly you just whittle your stick until it fits in the hole. It's a pain in the ass but not a gigantic one; no worse, say, than having to wear a school uniform or a tie to work.

Struggling with network TV's arbitrary rules was often annoying and sometimes dispiriting with *The Stand* and *The Shining* (and what the producers of *It* must have gone through I shudder to think of, since one stringent Standards and Practices rule is that TV dramas must not be built upon the premise of children in mortal jeopardy, let alone dying), but both of those shows were based on novels that were written with no regard for network TV's rules of propriety. And that's the way novels should be written, of course. When people ask me if I write books with the movies in mind, I always feel a little irritated . . . even insulted. It's not quite like asking a girl "Do you ever do it for money?" although I used to think so; it's the assumption of calculation which is unpleasant. That kind of ledger-sheet thinking has no business in the writing of stories. Writing stories is only about writing stories. Business and ledger-sheet thinking comes after, and is best left to people who understand how to do it.

This was the sort of attitude I adopted while working on *Storm of the Century*. I wrote it as a TV script because that's how the story *wanted* to be written . . . but with no actual belief that it would ever be *on* TV. I knew enough about filmmaking by December of 1996 to know I would be writing a special-effects nightmare into my script—a snowstorm bigger than any that had been previously attempted on television. I was also creating an enormous cast of characters—only, once the writing is done and the business of actually *making* a show begins, the writer's characters become the casting director's speaking parts. I went ahead with the script anyway, because you don't do the budget while you're writing the book. The budget is someone else's problem. Plus, if the script is good enough, love will find a way. It always does.* And because *Storm* was *written* as a TV miniseries, I found myself able to push the envelope without tearing it. I think it's the most frightening story I've ever written for film, and in most cases I was able to build in the scares without allowing Standards and Practices cause to scream at me too much.†

I have worked with director Mick Garris three times—first on the theatrical film *Sleepwalkers,* then on the miniseries of *The Stand* and *The Shining.* I sometimes joke that we're in danger of becoming the Billy Wilder and I.A.L. Diamond of the horror genre. He was my first choice to direct *Storm of the Century,* because I like him, respect him,

---

*And, I thought, what the hell—if *Storm* is never made because it budgets out at too high a number, I'll do it as a book after all. I found the idea of novelizing my own unproduced screenplay quite amusing.

†In the end, S & P were reduced to screaming about some fairly petty shit. In Part One, for instance, a fisherman says that the approaching bad weather is apt to be "one mother of a storm." S & P insisted the line be changed, perhaps believing this was my sly way of implying "one motherfucker of a storm," thus further corrupting American morals, causing more schoolyard shootings, etc. I immediately made one of my whining calls, pointing out the phrase "the mother of all . . ." had been originated by Saddam Hussein and had since passed into popular usage. After some consideration, Standards and Practices allowed the phrase, only insisting "the dialogue not be delivered in a salacious way." Absolutely not. Salacious dialogue on network TV is reserved for shows like *3rd Rock from the Sun* and *Dharma and Greg.*

and know what he can do. Mick had other fish to fry, however (the world would be a much simpler place if people would just drop everything and come running when I need them), and so Mark Carliner and I went hunting for a director.

Around this time I had snagged a direct-to-video film called *The Twilight Man* from the rental place down the street from my house. I'd never heard of it, but it looked atmospheric and starred the always reliable Dean Stockwell. It seemed like the perfect Tuesday evening time-passer, in other words. I also grabbed *Rambo*, a proven commodity, in case *The Twilight Man* should prove to be a lemon, but *Rambo* never got out of the box that night. *Twilight Man* was low-budget (it was an original made for the Starz cable network, I found out later), but it was nifty as hell just the same. Tim Matheson also starred, and he projected some of the qualities I hoped to see in *Storm*'s Mike Anderson: goodness and decency, yes . . . but with a sense of latent violence twisting through the character like a streak of iron. Even better, Dean Stockwell played a wonderfully quirky villain: a soft-spoken, courtly southerner who uses his computer savvy to ruin a stranger's life . . . all because the stranger has asked him to put out his cigar!

The lighting was moody and blue, the computer gimmickry was smartly executed, the pace was deftly maintained, and the performance levels were very high. I reran the credits and made a note of the director's name, Craig R. Baxley. I knew it from two other things: a good cable-TV movie about Brigham Young starring Charlton Heston as Young, and a not-so-good SF movie, *I Come in Peace*, starring Dolph Lundgren. (The most memorable thing about that film was the protagonist's final line to the cyborg: "You go in pieces.")

I talked with Mark Carliner, who looked at *The Twilight Man*, liked it, and discovered Baxley was available. I followed up with a call of my own and sent Craig the three hundred-page script of *Storm*. Craig called back, excited and full of ideas. I liked his ideas and I liked his enthusiasm; what I liked most of all was that the sheer size of the project didn't seem to faze him. The three of us met in Portland, Maine, in February of 1997, had dinner at my daughter's restaurant, and pretty much closed the deal.

Craig Baxley is a tall, broad-shouldered man, handsome, prone to Hawaiian shirts, and probably a few years older than he looks (at a glance you'd guess he was about forty, but his first theatrical work was *Action Jackson,* starring Carl Weathers, and so he's got to be older than that). He has the laid-back, "no problem, man" attitude of a California surfer (which he once was; he has also worked as a Hollywood stunt-player) and a sense of humor drier than an Errol Flynn foreign legion flick. The low-key attitude and the *nah, I'm just fuckin' with you* sense of humor tend to obscure the real Craig Baxley, who is focused, dedicated, imaginative, and a touch autocratic (show me a director without at least a dash of Stalin and I'll show you a bad director). What impressed me most about the dailies as *Storm of the Century* began its long march in February of 1998 was where Craig called "Cut!" At first it's unsettling, and then you realize he's doing what only the most visually gifted directors are capable of: cutting in the camera. As I write this I have begun to see the first "outputs"—sequences of cut footage on videotape—and thanks to Craig's direction, the show seems almost to be assembling itself. It's risky to assume too much too soon (remember the old newspaper headline "DEWEY DEFEATS TRUMAN"), but based on early returns, I'd say that what you're about to read bears an eerie resemblance to what you will see when ABC telecasts *Storm of the Century.* My fingers are still crossed, but I think it works. I think it may even be extraordinary. I hope so, but it's best to be realistic. Huge amounts of work go into the making of most films, including those made for television, and very few are extraordinary; given the number of people involved, I suppose it's amazing that any of them work at all. Still, you can't shoot me for hoping, can you?

The teleplay of *Storm* was written between December of 1996 and February of 1997. By March of 1997, Mark and Craig and I were sitting at dinner in my daughter Naomi's restaurant (closed now, alas; she's studying for the ministry). By June I was looking at sketches of Andre Linoge's wolf's head cane, and by July I was looking at storyboards. See what I mean about TV people wanting to make shows instead of lunch reservations?

Exteriors were filmed in Southwest Harbor, Maine, and in San Francisco. Exteriors were also filmed in Canada, about twenty miles north of Toronto, where Little Tall Island's main street was re-created inside an abandoned sugar-refining factory. For a month or two that factory in the town of Oshawa became one of the world's largest soundstages. Little Tall's studio main street went through three carefully designed stages of snow-dressing, from a few inches to total burial.* When a group of Southwest Harbor natives on a bus trip visited the Oshawa stage, they were visibly staggered by what they saw when they were escorted through the defunct factory's tall metal doors. It must have been like going home again in the blink of an eye. There are days when making movies has all the glamour of bolting together the rides at a county fair . . . but there are other days when the magic is so rich it dazzles you. The day the people from Southwest Harbor visited the set was one of those days.

Filming commenced in late February of 1998, on a snowy day in Down East Maine. It finished in San Francisco about eighty shooting days later. As I write this in mid-July, the cutting and editing processes—what's known as postproduction—has just begun. Optical effects and CGI (computer graphic imaging) effects are being built up one layer at a time. I'm looking at footage with temporary music tracks (many of them lifted from Frank Darabont's film *The Shawshank Redemption)*, and so is composer Gary Chang, who will do the show's actual score. Mark Carliner is jousting with ABC in the matter of telecast dates—February of 1999, a sweeps period, seems the most probable—and I'm watching the cut footage with a contentment that is very rare for me.

The script that follows makes a complete story, one that's been overlaid with marks—we call them "scenes" and "fades" and "inserts"—showing the director where to cut the whole into pieces . . . because, unless you're Alfred Hitchcock filming *Rope*, films are always piecework. Between March and June of this year, Craig Baxley filmed the script as scripts are usually filmed—out of sequence, often with tired actors working in the middle of the night, always under pressure—and finished up with a box of pieces called "the dailies." I can turn from where I'm sitting and look at my own set of those dailies—roughly sixty cassettes in red cardboard cases. But here is the odd thing: putting the dailies back together again to create the finished show isn't like putting a jigsaw puzzle back together. It

---

*Our snow consisted of potato flakes and shredded plastic blown in front of giant fans. The effect isn't perfect . . . but it's the best I've ever seen during my time in the film business. It *should* look good, dammit; the total cost of the snow was two million dollars.

should be, but it isn't . . . because, like most books, most movies are living things with breath and a heartbeat. Usually the putting-together results in something less than the sum of the parts. In rare and wonderful cases it results in more. This time it might be more. I hope it will be.

One final matter: what about people who say movies (especially TV movies) are a lesser medium than books, as instantly disposable as Kleenex? Well, that's no longer exactly true, is it? The script, thanks to the good people at Pocket Books, is here anytime you want to take it down and look at it. And the show itself, I'd guess, will eventually be available on videotape or videodisc, just as many hardcover books are eventually available in paperback. You'll be able to buy it or rent it when (and if) you choose. And, as with a book, you will be able to leaf back to check on things you may have missed or to savor something you particularly enjoyed; you will use the REWIND button on your remote control instead of your finger, that's all. (And if you're one of those awful people who have to peek ahead to the end, there is always FAST FORWARD or SEARCH, I suppose . . . although I tell you, you will be damned for doing such a thing).

I won't argue, either pro or con, that a novel for television is the equal of a novel in a book; I will just say that, once you subtract the distractions (ads for Tampax, ads for Ford cars and trucks, local newsbreaks, and so on), I myself think that is possible. And I would remind you that the man most students of literature believe to be the greatest of English writers worked in an oral and visual medium, and not (at least primarily) in the medium of print. I'm not trying to compare myself to Shakespeare—that would be bizarre—but I think it entirely possible that he would be writing for the movies or for television as well as for Off Broadway if he were alive today. Even possibly calling up Standards and Practices at ABC to try to persuade them that the violence in Act V of *Julius Caesar* is necessary . . . not to mention tastefully done.

In addition to the folks at Pocket Books who undertook to publish this project, I'd like to thank Chuck Verrill, who agented the deal and served as liaison between Pocket Books and ABC-TV. At ABC I'd like to thank Bob Iger, who put such amazing trust in me; also Maura Dunbar, Judd Parkin, and Mark Pedowitz. Also the folks at Standards and Practices, who really aren't that bad (in fact I think it would be fair to say they did one mother of a job on this).

Thanks are due to Craig Baxley for taking on one of the largest film projects ever attempted for network TV; also to Mark Carliner and Tom Brodek, who put it all together. Mark, who won just about all the TV awards there are for *Wallace,* is a great guy to have on your team. I'd also like to thank my wife, Tabby, who has been so supportive over the years. As a writer herself, she understands my foolishness pretty well.

—Stephen King
Bangor, Maine 04401
July 18, 1998

# STORM
### OF
### THE
# CENTURY

# PART 1
## Linoge

## Act 1

FADE IN ON:
1  EXTERIOR: MAIN STREET, LITTLE TALL ISLAND—LATE AFTERNOON.

SNOW is flying past the lens of THE CAMERA, at first so fast and so hard we can't see anything at all. THE WIND IS SHRIEKING. THE CAMERA starts to MOVE FORWARD, and we see a STUTTERY ORANGE LIGHT. It's the blinker at the corner of Main Street and Atlantic Street—Little Tall's only town intersection. The blinker is DANCING WILDLY in the wind. Both streets are deserted, and why not? This is a full-throated blizzard. We can see some dim lights in the buildings, but no human beings. The snow is drifted halfway up the shop windows.

MIKE ANDERSON speaks with a *light* Maine accent.

> MIKE ANDERSON (voice-over)
> My name is Michael Anderson, and I'm not what you'd call a Rhodes scholar. I don't have much in the way of philosophy, either, but I know one thing: in this world, you have to pay as you go. Usually a lot. Sometimes all you have. That's a lesson I thought I learned nine years ago, during what folks in these parts call the Storm of the Century.

The BLINKER LIGHT GOES DEAD. So do all the other brave little lights we saw in the storm. Now there's only the WIND and the BLOWING SNOW.

1

MIKE

I was wrong. I only started learning during the big blow. I
finished just last week.

DISSOLVE TO:

2　EXTERIOR: MAINE WOODS, FROM THE AIR (HELICOPTER)—DAY.

It's the cold season—all the trees except the firs are bare, branches
reaching up like fingers into the white sky. There's snow on the ground,
but only in patches, like bundles of dirty laundry. The ground skims by
below us, the woods broken by the occasional twisty line of two-lane
blacktop or little New England town.

MIKE (voice-over)

I grew up in Maine . . . but in a way, I never really lived in
Maine. I think anyone from my part of the world would say
the same.

All at once we hit the seacoast, land's end, and what he's telling us
maybe makes sense. Suddenly the woods are gone; we get a glimpse of
gray-blue water surging and spuming against rocks and headlands . . .
and then there's just water beneath us until we:

DISSOLVE TO:

3　EXTERIOR: LITTLE TALL ISLAND (HELICOPTER)—DAY.

There's plenty of bustling activity on the docks as the lobster boats are
either secured or boathoused. The smaller craft are being removed by
way of the town's landing slip. People pull them away behind their
four-wheel drives. On the dock, BOYS AND YOUNG MEN are carrying
lobster traps into the long, weather-beaten building with GODSOE FISH
AND LOBSTER printed on the side. There's laughter and excited talk; a
few bottles of something warm are passed around. The storm is
coming. It's always exciting when the storm is coming.

Near Godsoe's is a trim little volunteer fire department firehouse just
big enough for two pumpers. LLOYD WISHMAN and FERD AN-
DREWS are out washing one of the trucks right now.

Atlantic Street runs uphill from the docks to town. The hill is lined with
pretty little New England houses. South of the docks is a wooded
headland, with a ramshackle flight of steps leading down, zigzag, to the
water. North, along the beach, are the homes of the rich folks. At the far

northern point of land is a squatty white lighthouse, maybe forty feet high. The automated light turns constantly, its glow pale but readable in the daylight. On top is a long radio antenna.

> MIKE (voice-over)
> (continues)
> Folks from Little Tall send their taxes to Augusta, same as other folks, and we got either a lobster or a loon on our license plates, same as other folks, and we root for the University of Maine's teams, especially the women's basket-ball team, same as other folks . . .

On the fishing boat *Escape*, SONNY BRAUTIGAN is stuffing nets into a hatch and battening down. Nearby, ALEX HABER is making *Escape* fast with some big-ass ropes.

> JOHNNY HARRIMAN (voice)
> Better double it, Sonny—the weather guy says it's coming on.

JOHNNY comes around the pilothouse, looking at the sky. SONNY turns to him.

> SONNY BRAUTIGAN
> Seen 'em come on every winter, Big John. They howl in, they howl out. July always comes.

SONNY gives the hatch a test and puts his foot up on the rail, watching ALEX finish. Behind them, LUCIEN FOURNIER joins JOHNNY. LUCIEN goes to the live well, flips it open, and looks in as:

> ALEX HABER
> Still . . . they say this one's gonna be somethin' special.

LUCIEN yanks out a lobster and holds it up.

> LUCIEN FOURNIER
> Forgot one, Sonny.

> SONNY BRAUTIGAN
> One for the pot brings good luck.

>              LUCIEN FOURNIER
>               (to the lobster)
> Storm of the Century coming, *mon frere*—so the radio say.


>              (knocks on the shell)
> Good t'ing you got your coat on, hey?

He tosses Bob the lobster back into the live well—SPLASH! The four men leave the boat, and THE CAMERA CONTINUES TO TRACK.

>              MIKE (voice-over)
>               (continues)
> But we ain't the same. Life out on the islands is different. We
> pull together when we have to.

SONNY, JOHNNY, ALEX, and LUCIEN are on the ramp now, maybe carrying gear.

>              SONNY BRAUTIGAN
> We'll get through her.


>              JOHNNY HARRIMAN
> Ayuh, like always.


>              LUCIEN FOURNIER
> When you mind the swell, you mind the boat.


>              ALEX HABER
> What's a Frenchman like you know?

LUCIEN takes a mock swing at him. They all laugh and go on. We watch SONNY, LUCIEN, ALEX, and JOHNNY go into Godsoe's. THE CAMERA starts up Atlantic Street toward the blinker we saw earlier. It then SLIDES RIGHT, showing a piece of the business section and bustling traffic on the street.

>              MIKE (voice-over)
>               (continues)
> And we can keep a secret when we have to. We kept our share
> back in 1989. (pause) And the people who live there keep
> them still.

We come to ANDERSON'S GENERAL STORE. People hurry in and out. Three WOMEN emerge: ANGELA CARVER, MRS. KINGSBURY, and ROBERTA COIGN.

> MIKE (voice-over)
> (continues)

I know.

> ROBERTA COIGN

All right, I've got my canned goods. Let it come.

> MRS. KINGSBURY

I just pray we don't lose the power. I can't cook on a woodstove. I'd burn water on that damned thing. A big storm's only good for one thing—

> ANGELA

Ayuh, and my Jack knows what it is.

The other two look at her, surprised, and then they all GIGGLE LIKE GIRLS and head for their cars.

> MIKE (voice-over)
> (continues)

I stay in touch.

3A   EXTERIOR: THE SIDE OF A FIRE TRUCK.

A HAND polishes the gleaming red hide with a rag, then pulls away. LLOYD WISHMAN looks at his own face, pleased.

> FERD ANDREWS (off-screen)

Radio says it's gonna snow a bitch.

LLOYD turns, and THE CAMERA HINGES to show us FERD, leaning in the door. His hands are plugged into the tops of half a dozen boots, which he begins to arrange by pairs below hooks holding slickers and helmets.

> FERD ANDREWS

If we get in trouble . . . we're in trouble.

LLOYD grins at the younger man, then turns back to his polishing.

> LLOYD
> Easy, Ferd. It's just a cap of snow. Trouble don't cross the reach . . . ain't that why we live out here?

FERD isn't so sure. He goes to the door and looks up at:

4   EXTERIOR: APPROACHING STORM CLOUDS—DAY.

We HOLD a moment, then PAN DOWN to a TRIM WHITE NEW ENGLAND HOME. This house is about halfway up Atlantic Street Hill—that is, between the docks and the center of town. There's a picket fence surrounding a winter-dead lawn (but there's no snow at all, not out here on the island), and a gate that stands open, offering the concrete path to anyone who cares make the trip from the sidewalk to the steep porch steps and the front door. To one side of the gate is a mailbox, amusingly painted and accessorized to turn it into a pink cow. Written on the side is CLARENDON.

> MIKE (voice-over)
> The first person on Little Tall to see Andre Linoge was Martha Clarendon.

In the extreme foreground of the shot, there now appears a SNARLING SILVER WOLF. It is the head of a cane.

5   EXTERIOR: LINOGE, FROM BEHIND—DAY.

Standing on the sidewalk, back to us and before the open CLARENDON gate, is a tall man dressed in jeans, boots, a pea jacket, and a black watch cap snugged down over his ears. And gloves—yellow leather as bright as a sneer. One hand grips the head of his cane, which is black walnut below the silver wolf's head. LINOGE'S own head is lowered between his bulking shoulders. It is a thinking posture. There is something brooding about it, as well.

He raises the cane and taps one side of the gate with it. He pauses, then taps the other side of the gate. This has the feel of a ritual.

MIKE (voice-over)
(continues)
He was the last person she ever saw.

LINOGE begins to walk slowly up the concrete path to the porch steps, idly swinging his cane as he goes. He whistles a tune: "I'm a little teapot."

6   INTERIOR: MARTHA CLARENDON'S LIVING ROOM.

It's neat in the cluttery way only fastidious folks who've lived their whole lives in one place can manage. The furniture is old and nice, not quite antique. The walls are crammed with pictures, most going back to the twenties. There's a piano with yellowing sheet music open on the stand. Seated in the room's most comfortable chair (perhaps its only comfortable chair) is MARTHA CLARENDON, a lady of perhaps eighty years. She has lovely white beauty-shop hair and is wearing a neat housedress. On the table beside her is a cup of tea and a plate of cookies. On her other side is a walker with bicycle-grip handholds jutting out of one side and a carry-tray jutting out from the other.

The only modern items in the room are the large color TV and the cable box on top of it. MARTHA is watching the Weather Network avidly and taking little birdie-sips of tea as she does. Onscreen is a pretty

WEATHER LADY. Behind the WEATHER LADY is a map with two large red *L*'s planted in the middle of two large storm systems. One of these is over Pennsylvania; the other is just off the coast of New York. The WEATHER LADY starts with the western storm.

> ### WEATHER LADY
> This is the storm that's caused so much misery—and fifteen deaths—as it crossed the Great Plains and the Midwest. It's regathered all its original punch and more in crossing the Great Lakes, and you see its track—

The track appears in BRIGHT YELLOW (the same color as LINOGE'S gloves), showing a future course that will carry it straight across New York, Vermont, New Hampshire, and Maine.

> ### WEATHER LADY
> (continues)
> —before you in all its glory. Now look down here, because here comes trouble.

She focuses her attention on the coastal storm.

> ### WEATHER LADY
> (continues)
> This is a very atypical storm, almost a winter hurricane—the sort of knuckle-duster that paralyzed most of the East Coast and *buried* Boston back in 1976. We haven't seen one of comparable power since then . . . until now. Will it give us a break and stay out to sea, as these storms sometimes do? Unfortunately, the Weather Network's Storm-Trak computer says no. So the states east of the Big Indian Waters are getting pounded from one direction—

She taps the first storm.

> ### WEATHER LADY
> (continues)
> —the mid-Atlantic coast is going to get pounded from another direction—

She goes back to the coastal storm.

>               WEATHER LADY
>                (continues)

—and northern New England, if none of this changes, tonight you're going to win the booby prize. Look . . . at . . . this.

A second BRIGHT YELLOW STORM TRACK appears, this one hooking north from the blob of storm off New York. This track makes landfall around Cape Cod, then heads up the coast, where it intersects the first storm track. At the point of intersection, some Weather Network computer genius with too much time on his hands has added a bright red blotch, like an explosion graphic on a news broadcast.

>               WEATHER LADY
>                (continues)

If neither of these two systems veer, they are going to collide and merge over the state of Maine. That's bad news for our friends in Yankee land, but not the worst news. The worst news is that they may temporarily cancel each other out.

>               MARTHA
>              (sipping tea)

Oh, dear.

>               WEATHER LADY

The result? A once-in-a-lifetime supersystem which may stall over central and coastal Maine for at least twenty-four hours and perhaps as long as forty-eight. We're talking hurricane-force winds and phenomenal amounts of snow, combining to create the sort of drifting you normally only see on the Arctic tundra. To this you can add region-wide blackouts.

>               MARTHA

Oh, *dear!*

>               WEATHER LADY

No one wants to scare viewers, least of all me, but folks in the New England area, especially those on the Maine coast and the offshore islands, need to take this situation very seriously. You've had an almost completely brown winter up your way, but over the next two to three days, you're apt to be getting a whole winter's worth of snow.

SOUND: DOORBELL.

MARTHA looks in that direction, then back at the TV. She'd like to stay and watch the WEATHER LADY, but nevertheless sets her teacup down, pulls over her walker, and struggles erect.

> WEATHER LADY
> We sometimes overuse the phrase "storm of the century," but if these two storm tracks converge, as we now think they will, the phrase will be no exaggeration, believe me. Judd Parkin's in next to talk about storm preparations—no panic, just practicalities. But first, this.

An ad comes on—it's a mail-order disaster video called *Punishments of God*—as MARTHA begins working her way across the living room toward the hall, clutching the bicycle-grip handles of her walker and clumping along.

> MARTHA
> When they tell you the world's ending, they want to sell cereal. When they tell you not to panic, it's serious.

SOUND: DOORBELL.

> MARTHA
> I'm coming fast's I can!

7   INTERIOR: THE FRONT HALL OF MARTHA'S HOUSE—DAY.

She makes her way down the hall, holding tight to the walker. On the walls are quaint photographs and drawings of Little Tall as it was early in the twentieth century. At the corridor's end is a closed door with a graceful glass oval in its upper half. This has been covered by a sheer curtain, probably so the sun won't fade the carpet. On the sheer is the silhouette of LINOGE'S head and shoulders.

> MARTHA
> (puffing a little)
> Hold on . . . almost there . . . I broke my hip last summer and I'm still just as slow as cold molasses . . .

And the WEATHER LADY is continuing:

WEATHER LADY (voice-over)
Folks in Maine and the Maritimes saw one heck of a storm in
January of 1987, but that was a freezing-rain event. This one
is going to be a very different kettle of chowder. Don't even
think about the snow shovel until the plows have come by.

MARTHA reaches the door, looks curiously at the shape of the man's
head on the sheer curtain, then opens it. There stands LINOGE. His
face is as handsome as that of a Greek statue, and a statue is sort of
what he looks like. His eyes are closed. His hands are folded over the
wolf's head at the top of his cane.

WEATHER LADY (voice-over)
(continues)
As I've said before and will say again, there's no cause for
panic; northern New Englanders have seen big storms before
and will again. But even veteran weather forecasters are a
little stunned by the sheer size of these converging systems.

MARTHA is puzzled—of course—by the appearance of this stranger
but not really uneasy. This is the island, after all, and bad things don't
happen on the island. Except for the occasional storm, of course. The
other thing at work here is that the man is a stranger to her, and
strangers on the island are rare once the fleeting summer is over.

MARTHA
Can I help you?

LINOGE
(eyes closed)
Born in lust, turn to dust. Born in sin, come on in.

MARTHA
I beg pardon?

He opens his eyes . . . except there are no eyes there. The sockets are
filled with BLACKNESS. His lips peel back from HUGE, CROOKED
TEETH—they look like teeth in a child's drawing of a monster.

WEATHER LADY (voice-over)
(continues)
These are *monster* low-pressure areas. And are they really
coming? Yes, I'm afraid they are.

MARTHA'S intrigued interest is replaced by stark terror. She opens her mouth to scream and staggers backward, losing hold of the walker's handles. She is going to fall.

LINOGE raises his cane, the SNARLING WOLF'S HEAD JUTTING FORWARD. He grabs the walker, which is between him and the old woman, and throws it out the door behind him, where it lands on the porch, near the steps.

8    INTERIOR: HALLWAY, WITH MARTHA.

She falls heavily and SCREAMS, raising her hands, looking up at:

9    INTERIOR: LINOGE, FROM MARTHA'S POINT OF VIEW.

A SNARLING MONSTER, hardly human, with the cane upraised. Behind him, we see the porch and the white sky that signals the oncoming storm.

10   INTERIOR: MARTHA, ON THE FLOOR.

> MARTHA
> Please don't hurt me!

11   INTERIOR: MARTHA'S LIVING ROOM.

On the TV now is JUDD PARKIN, standing in front of a table. On it are: a flashlight, batteries, candles, matches, prepared foods, stacks of warm clothing, portable radio, a cellular phone, other supplies. Beside him is the WEATHER LADY, looking bewitched by these goods.

> JUDD
> But a storm doesn't need to be a disaster, Maura, and a disaster doesn't have to be a tragedy. Given that philosophy to start with, I think we can give our New England viewers some tips which will help them prepare for what, from all indications, is apt to be a pretty extraordinary weather-maker.

> WEATHER LADY
> What have you got there, Judd?

JUDD

Well, to begin with, warm clothing. That's number one. And you want to say to yourself, "How are my batteries? Have I got enough to keep a portable radio going? Possibly a small TV?" And if you've got a generator, the time to check your gasoline supplies—or your diesel or your propane—is before, not after. If you wait until it's too late . . .

During all this, THE CAMERA MOVES AWAY from the TV, as if losing interest. It is drawn back toward the hall. As we begin to lose the dialogue, we begin to hear far less pleasant SOUNDS: THE STEADY WHACK-WHACK-WHACK of LINOGE'S cane. At last it stops. There is SILENCE for a little bit, then FOOTSTEPS. Accompanying them is a CURIOUS DRAGGING SOUND, almost as if someone were pulling a chair or a stool slowly across a wood floor.

JUDD (voice-over)
(continues)

. . . it'll be too late.

LINOGE comes into the doorway. His eyes aren't ordinary—a distant and somehow unsettling blue—but they aren't that HIDEOUS BLACK EMPTINESS that MARTHA saw, either. His cheeks, brow, and the bridge of his nose are covered with FINE STIPPLES OF BLOOD. He comes to EXTREME CLOSE-UP, eyes focused on something. A look of interest begins to warm his face up a little.

WEATHER LADY (voice-over)

Thanks, Judd. Words of wisdom our northern New England viewers have probably heard before, but when it comes to storms this size, some things bear repeating.

12  INTERIOR: THE LIVING ROOM, FROM OVER LINOGE'S SHOULDER.

It's the TV he's looking at.

WEATHER LADY

Your local forecast is next, right after this.

She is replaced by an ad for *Punishments of God 2*—all the volcanoes, fires, and earthquakes you could ever want for $19.95. Slowly, back to us again, LINOGE crosses the room to MARTHA'S chair. The

DRAGGING SOUND recommences, and as he approaches the chair and his lower half comes into the frame, we see it's the tip of his cane. It's leaving a thin trail of blood along the rug. More blood is oozing through the fingers of the fist clamped over the wolf's head. That's mostly what he hit her with, the head of that wolf, and we probably wouldn't want to see what it looks like now.

LINOGE stands, looking down at the TV, where a forest is going up in flames.

LINOGE
(sings)

"I'm a little teapot, short and stout. . . .
Here is my handle, here is my spout."

He sits down in MARTHA'S chair. Grasps her teacup with a gory hand that smears the handle. Drinks. Then takes a cookie with his bloody hand and gobbles it down.

LINOGE settles back to watch JUDD and MAURA talk disaster on the Weather Network.

13   EXTERIOR: MIKE ANDERSON'S STORE—DAY.

This is an old-fashioned general store with a long front porch. If it were summer, there would be rockers lined up out here and lots of old-timers to fill them. As it is, there is a line of snowblowers and snow shovels, marked with a neat handmade sign: SUPERSTORM SPECIAL! LET'S TALK PRICE!

The steps are flanked by a couple of lobster traps, and more hang from the underside of the porch roof. We may also see a whimsical display of clamming gear. By the door stands a mannequin wearing galoshes, a yellow rain slicker, goggle eyes on springs, and a beanie with a propeller (the propeller now still) on his head. Someone has stuffed a pillow under the slicker, creating a fairly prominent potbelly. In one plastic hand is a blue University of Maine pennant. In the other is a can of beer. Around the dummy's neck is a sign: GENUINE "ROBBIE BEALS BRAND" LOBSTERIN' GEAH SOLD HEAH, DEAH.

In the windows are signs for meat specials, fish specials, videotape rentals (WE RENT OLD 'UNS THREE FOR $1), church suppers, a volunteer fire department blood drive. The biggest sign is on the door. It reads: STORM EMERGENCY POSSIBLE NEXT 3 DAYS! "TAKE SHELTER" SIGNAL IS 2 SHORTS, 1 LONG. Above the display windows, now rolled up, are slatted wooden STORM SHUTTERS. Above the door is a lovely old-fashioned sign, black with gold gilt letters: ANDERSON'S MARKET•ISLAND POST OFFICE•ISLAND CONSTABLE'S OFFICE.

There are several WOMEN going in, and a couple more—OCTAVIA GODSOE and JOANNA STANHOPE—coming out. TAVIA (forty-five-ish) and JOANNA (late forties or early fifties) are clutching full grocery bags and chatting animatedly. TAVIA looks at the ROBBIE BEALS dummy and elbows JOANNA. They both laugh as they go down the steps.

14   INTERIOR: ANDERSON'S MARKET—DAY.

This is a very well equipped grocery store, and in many ways a charming throwback to the groceries of the 1950s. The floors are wood and creak comfortably underfoot. The lights are globes hanging on chains. There's a tin ceiling. Yet there are signs of our modern age; two new cash registers with digital price-readers beside them, a radio scanner on a shelf behind the checkout counter, a wall of rental videos, and security cameras mounted high in the corners.

At the rear is a meat cooler running nearly the length of the store. To its left, below a convex mirror, is a door marked simply TOWN CONSTABLE.

The store is very crowded. Everybody is stocking up for the oncoming storm.

15   INTERIOR: MEAT COUNTER.

MIKE ANDERSON COMES out of the door leading to the meat locker (it is at the other end of the rear from the constable's office). He is a good-looking man of about thirty-five. Right now he also looks harried half to death . . . although the little smile never leaves his eyes and the corners of his mouth. This guy likes life, likes it a lot, and usually finds something in it to amuse him.

He's wearing butcher's whites right now and pushing a shopping cart filled with wrapped cuts of meat. Three WOMEN and one MAN converge on him almost at once. The MAN, dressed in a red sport coat and black shirt with turned-around collar, is first to reach him.

> REV. BOB RIGGINS

Don't forget the bean supper next Wednesday-week, Michael—I'm going to need every deacon I can lay my hands on.

> MIKE

I'll be there . . . if we get through the next three days, that is.

> REV. BOB RIGGINS

I'm sure we will; God takes care of his own.

Off he goes. Behind him is a cute little muffin named JILL ROBI-CHAUX, and she apparently has less trust in God. She starts pawing over the packages and reading the labels before MIKE can even begin to distribute them.

> JILL

Are there pork chops, Michael? I thought for sure you'd still have pork chops.

He gives her a wrapped package. JILL looks at it, then puts it in her heaped-up shopping cart. The other two women, CARLA BRIGHT and LINDA ST. PIERRE, are already going through the other wrapped cuts. CARLA looks at something, almost takes it, then drops it back into one of the trays of the meat-display cabinet.

> CARLA

Ground chuck's too dear! Don't you have plain old ham-burger, Michael Anderson?

> MIKE

Right—

She snatches the package he's holding out before he can finish.

> MIKE
> (continues)

—here.

More folks now, picking the stuff over as fast as he can get it out of his cart. MIKE bears this for a moment, then decides to put on his constable's hat. Or try.

MIKE

Folks, listen. It's a storm, that's all. We've gotten through plenty before this, and we'll get through plenty after. Calm down and stop acting like mainlanders!

That gets them a little. They stand back, and MIKE begins distributing the meat again.

LINDA

Don't be smart, Michael Anderson.

She says it the way islanders do—"sma'aat." And when CARLA says "dear," it comes out "deah."

MIKE
(smiles)
No, Mrs. St. Pierre. I won't be smart.

Behind him, ALTON "HATCH" HATCHER comes out of the cold room pushing a second cart of wrapped meat. HATCH is about thirty, portly and pleasant. He's MIKE'S second-in-command at the market, and in the constabulary, as well. He is also wearing butcher's whites, and a white hard hat for good measure. Printed on the hard hat is "A. HATCHER."

CAT (over the market loudspeaker)
Mike! Hey, Mike! Got a phone call!

16    INTERIOR: THE COUNTER, WITH KATRINA "CAT" WITHERS.

She's about nineteen, very pretty, and handling one of the cash registers. She ignores the line of customers and holds the PA microphone in one hand. In the other is the receiver of the telephone hanging on the wall by the CB radio.

CAT

It's your wife. She says she's got a little problem down to the day care.

17    INTERIOR: RESUME MIKE, HATCH, SHOPPERS AT MEAT CABINET.

The customers are interested and diverted. Life on the island is like a soap opera where you know all the characters.

> MIKE
She hot under the collar?

18   INTERIOR: RESUME COUNTER, WITH CAT.

> CAT
How do I know where she's hot? She's your wife.

Smiles and chuckles from the CUSTOMERS. In island parlance, that was "a good 'un." A man of about forty grins at MIKE.

> KIRK FREEMAN
You better go see about that, Mike.

19   INTERIOR: RESUME MIKE AND HATCH AT MEAT CABINET.

> MIKE
Can you take over here a bit?

> HATCH
Can I borrow your whip and chair?

MIKE laughs, knocks on the top of HATCH'S hard hat, and hurries on down front to see what his wife wants.

20   INTERIOR: AT THE COUNTER.

MIKE arrives and takes the phone from CAT. He speaks to his wife, oblivious of the watching, interested audience.

> MIKE
Hey, Moll, what's up?

> MOLLY (phone voice)
I've got a little problem here—can you come?

MIKE eyes his store, which is full of pre-storm shoppers.

> MIKE
I've got a few little problems of my own, hon. What's yours?

21   INTERIOR: PIPPA HATCHER, CLOSE-UP.

PIPPA is a child of about three years old. Right now she fills the whole screen with her SCREAMING, TERRIFIED FACE. There are RED SMEARS AND BLOTCHES all over it. Maybe we at first take these for blood.

THE CAMERA DRAWS BACK and we see the problem. PIPPA is halfway up a flight of stairs, and has poked her head between two of the posts supporting the banister. Now she can't get it back through. She's still holding on to a piece of bread and jam, though, and we see that what we first took for blood is actually strawberry preserves.

Standing at the foot of the stairs below her, looking solemn, is a group of SEVEN SMALL CHILDREN, ranging in age from three to five. One of the four-year-olds is RALPH ANDERSON, son of MIKE and MOLLY. Although we may not notice it at once (right now we're more interested in PIPPA'S plight), RALPHIE has a birthmark on the bridge of his nose. It's not hugely disfiguring or anything, but it's there, like a tiny saddle.

> RALPHIE
> Pippa, can I have your bread, if you're not going to eat it?

> PIPPA
> (shrieks)
> NO-OOO-OO!

She begins to yank backward, trying to free herself, still holding on to her snack. It's disappearing into her chubby little fist now, and she appears to be sweating strawberry jam.

22   INTERIOR: THE HALLWAY AND STAIRWELL OF THE ANDERSON HOUSE.

The phone is here, placed on a hallway table halfway between the stairs and the door. Using it is MOLLY ANDERSON, MIKE'S wife. She's about thirty, pretty, and right now vacillating between amusement and fright.

> MOLLY
> Pippa, don't do that, honey . . . just hold still . . .

> MIKE (phone voice)
> Pippa? What about Pippa?

23   INTERIOR: BEHIND THE MEAT COUNTER, FEATURING HATCH.

His head snaps up in a hurry.

> **LINDA ST. PIERRE**
> Something about *Pippa?*

HATCH starts around the counter.

24   INTERIOR: RESUME HALLWAY, WITH MOLLY.

> **MOLLY**
> Be quiet! The last thing in the world I want is Alton Hatcher
> down on me.

25   INTERIOR: RESUME MARKET.

Steaming down Aisle 3, still wearing his hard hat, comes HATCH. All
the smiling good humor has gone out of his face. He's completely
intent, a father back to front and top to bottom.

> **MIKE**
> Too late, babe. What's up?

26   INTERIOR: THE HALLWAY, WITH MOLLY.

She closes her eyes and GROANS.

> **MOLLY**
> Pippa's got her head stuck in the stairs. It's not serious—I
> don't think—but I can't deal with a big storm and a crazed
> daddy all on the same day. If Hatch comes, you be with him.

She hangs up the phone and heads back to the stairs.

> **MOLLY**
> Pippa . . . honey . . . don't pull that way. It'll hurt your ears.

27   INTERIOR: THE STORE COUNTER, WITH MIKE, HATCH, CUSTOMERS.

MIKE looks at the phone, bemused, then hangs it up again. As he does,
HATCH comes shouldering through the CUSTOMERS, looking worried.

> HATCH

Pippa! What about Pippa?

> MIKE

Got a little stuck-itis, I hear. Why don't we go see?

28   EXTERIOR: MAIN STREET, IN FRONT OF THE STORE.

There's slant parking here. The vehicle in the slot handiest to the store is a forest-green four-wheel drive with ISLAND SERVICES painted on the doors, and a police flasher-bar on the roof.

MIKE and HATCH come out of the store and hurry down the steps. As they approach:

> HATCH

How upset did she sound, Mike?

> MIKE

Molly? Point five on a scale of one to ten. Don't worry.

A gust of wind strikes them, rocking them back on their heels. They look toward the ocean. We can't see it, but we can hear the POUNDING WAVES.

> HATCH

This is going to be one bad mother of a storm, isn't it?

MIKE doesn't answer. He doesn't have to. They get into the Island Services truck and drive off.

29   EXTERIOR: THE MANNEQUIN ON THE STORE'S PORCH.

There's another GUST OF WIND. The hanging lobster traps click together . . . and the beanie propeller on "ROBBIE BEALS'S" head slowly BEGINS TO TURN.

30   INTERIOR: THE STAIRWELL OF THE ANDERSON HOUSE.

PIPPA is still stuck with her head through the posts, but MOLLY is sitting beside her on the stairs and has her calmed down quite a bit. The CHILDREN still cluster around, watching her. MOLLY strokes

PIPPA'S hair with one hand. In her other, MOLLY is holding PIPPA'S bread and jam.

> MOLLY
>
> You're okay, Pippa. Mike and your daddy will be here in another minute. Mike will get you out.

> PIPPA
>
> How can he?

> MOLLY
>
> I don't know. He's just magic that way.

> PIPPA
>
> I'm hungry.

MOLLY gets her arm through the bars and maneuvers the bread to PIPPA'S mouth. PIPPA eats. The other KIDS watch this with fascination. One, a boy of five, is JILL ROBICHAUX'S son.

> HARRY ROBICHAUX
>
> Can I feed her, Missus Anderson? I fed a monkey once, at the Bangor Fair.

The other kids laugh. PIPPA is not amused.

> PIPPA
>
> I'm not a monkey, Harry! I'm a *child,* not a monkey!

> DON BEALS
>
> Look, you guys, I'm a monkey!

He starts leaping around at the foot of the stairs, scratching under his armpits and being foolish as only a four-year-old can be. At once, the others start imitating him.

> PIPPA
>
> I am not a monkey!

And begins to cry. MOLLY strokes her hair, but can't talk her out of this one. Getting your head stuck between the bars is bad; being called a monkey is even worse.

MOLLY

You kids, stop that! Stop it right now! It's not nice, and it's making Pippa sad!

Most of them stop, but DON BEALS, a little booger of the purest ray serene, goes on prancing and scratching.

MOLLY

Don, you stop. It's mean.

RALPHIE

Momma says it's mean.

He tries to grab hold of DON. DON shakes him off.

DON BEALS

I'm bein' a monkey!

DON does the monkey thing twice as hard, just to spite RALPHIE . . . and RALPHIE'S mother, of course. The hall door opens. MIKE and HATCH come in. HATCH sees the problem at once and reacts with a mixture of fright and relief.

PIPPA

Daddee!

She starts yanking backward again, trying to free herself.

HATCH

Pippa! Hold still! You want to yank your ears right off your head?

RALPHIE
(runs to MIKE)

Daddy! Pippa got her head stuck and Don won't stop being a monkey!

RALPHIE leaps into his father's arms. HATCH climbs to where his daughter has been caught by the incredible girl-eating stairs and kneels by her. MOLLY looks over her back at her husband and sends a message with her eyes: "Please fix this!"

A CUTE LITTLE BLONDE GIRL with pigtails pulls at the pocket of MIKE'S white butcher's pants. She is wearing most of her own strawberry jam treat on the front of her shirt.

> SALLY GODSOE
>
> Mr. Anderson? I stopped being a monkey. As soon as she said.

SALLY points to MOLLY. MIKE gently disengages her. SALLY, another four-year-old, promptly pops her thumb into her mouth.

> MIKE
>
> That's good, Sally. Ralphie, got to put you down now.

He puts RALPHIE down. DON BEALS promptly pushes him.

> RALPHIE
>
> Ow, hey! Why'd you do that?

> DON BEALS
>
> For acting smart!

It comes out "sma'aat." MIKE picks DON BEALS up and raises him to eye level. DON isn't afraid a bit, the little craphead.

> DON BEALS
>
> I ain't afraid of you! My dad's town manager! He pays your salary!

He sticks out his tongue and BLOWS A RASPBERRY right in MIKE'S face. MIKE isn't the slightest put out of countenance.

> MIKE
>
> Pushers get pushed, Donnie Beals. You want to remember that, because it's a true fact of this sad life. Pushers get pushed.

DON doesn't understand, but reacts to the tone. He'll get up to more dickens eventually, but he's been put in his place for the time being. MIKE puts DON down and goes to the side of the stairs. Behind him we see a half-open door marked WEE FOLKS. In the room beyond the door are little tables and chairs. Happy, colorful mobiles hang from the ceiling. It's the classroom of MOLLY'S day-care center.

HATCH is pushing at the top of his daughter's head. This isn't accomplishing anything, and she's consequently growing panicky again, thinking she'll be stuck forever.

> HATCH
> Honey, why did you do this?

> PIPPA
> Heidi St. Pierre dared me.

MIKE puts his hands over HATCH'S and moves HATCH aside. HATCH looks at MIKE hopefully.

31   INTERIOR: THE CHILDREN AT THE FOOT OF THE STAIRS.

HEIDI ST. PIERRE, the five-year-old daughter of LINDA ST. PIERRE, is a carrottop wearing thick glasses.

> HEIDI
> Did not.

> PIPPA
> Did so!

> HEIDI ST. PIERRE
> Liar, liar, pants on fire!

> MOLLY
> Stop it, both of you.

> PIPPA
> (to MIKE)
> It was easy going out, but now I can't get back in. I think my head must be bigger on this side.

> MIKE
> It is . . . but I'm going to make it smaller. Do you know how?

> PIPPA
> (fascinated)

No . . . how?

> MIKE

I'm just going to push the smaller button. And when I do, your head will get smaller and you'll slide right back where you were. Just as easy as you slid in. Do you understand, Pippa?

He speaks in slow, soothing tones. He's engaged in something that's almost hypnosis.

> HATCH

What kind of—

> MOLLY

Shhh!

> MIKE

Are you ready for me to push the button?

> PIPPA

Yes.

MIKE reaches up and pushes the end of her nose with the tip of his finger.

> MIKE

Beep! There it goes! Smaller! Quick, Pippa, before it gets big again!

PIPPA pulls her head out easily from between the posts. The kids clap and cheer. DON BEALS hops around like a monkey. One of the other boys, FRANK BRIGHT, hops around a little, too, then sees RALPHIE giving him a disgusted look and quits it.

HATCH gathers his daughter in for a hug. PIPPA hugs back, but eats her bread and jam at the same time. She stopped being scared when MIKE started talking to her. MOLLY smiles at MIKE gratefully and puts her hand through the stairwell posts where PIPPA was stuck. MIKE takes it on his side and kisses each finger extravagantly. The

KIDS GIGGLE. One of them, BUSTER CARVER (BUSTER, the last of MOLLY'S day-care pupils, is about five), puts his hands over his eyes.

> BUSTER
> (moaning)
> Finger-kissin'! Oh, no!

MOLLY laughs and pulls her hand back.

> MOLLY
> Thank you. Really.

> HATCH
> Yeah—thanks, boss.

> MIKE
> No problem.

> PIPPA
> Dad, is my head still little? I felt it get little when Mr. Anderson said. Is it still little?

> HATCH
> No, honey, just the right size.

MIKE walks to the foot of the stairs. MOLLY meets him. RALPHIE is there, too; MIKE picks him up and kisses the red mark on the bridge of the little boy's nose. MOLLY kisses MIKE'S cheek.

> MOLLY
> I'm sorry if I pulled you away at a bad time. I saw her head that way and when I couldn't get it to come out on my own, I just . . . freaked.

> MIKE
> It's okay. I needed a break, anyway.

> MOLLY
> Is it bad down at the store?

> HATCH
> Bad enough. You know how it is when there's a storm

coming . . . and this is no ordinary storm. (to PIPPA) Got to
go back, sweet girl. You be good.

DON BLOWS ANOTHER RASPBERRY.

> MIKE
> (low)

Gee, I love Robbie's kid.

MOLLY says nothing, but rolls her eyes in agreement.

> MIKE

What do you say, Hatch?

> HATCH

Let's roll while we still can. If they're right, we're all apt to be
cooped up for the next three days. (pause) Like Pippa, with
her head caught in the stairs.

None of them laugh. There's too much truth in what he says.

32   EXTERIOR: THE ANDERSON HOUSE ON LOWER MAIN STREET—DAY.

The Island Services four-wheel drive is parked at the curb. In the
foreground, by the walk, is a sign reading WEE FOLKS DAY-CARE CENTER.
It's on a chain, and swinging back and forth in the wind. The sky
overhead is grayer than ever. The ocean, visible here in the background, is full of gray chop.

The door opens. MIKE and HATCH come out, pulling down their hats
to keep the wind from tearing them off, raising the collars of their
jackets. As they approach the car, MIKE stops and looks up at the sky.
It's coming, all right. A big one. MIKE'S anxious face says he knows
that. Or thinks he does. No one knows how big *this* baby is going to be.

He gets into the car behind the wheel, waving to MOLLY, who stands
on the porch with her sweater over her shoulders. HATCH waves, too.
She waves back. The four-wheel drive pulls around in a U-turn, headed
back to the market.

33   INTERIOR: THE ISLAND SERVICES VEHICLE, WITH MIKE AND HATCH.

HATCH
(quite amused)
The "smaller button," huh?


MIKE
Everyone's got one. You gonna tell Melinda?


HATCH
No . . . but Pippa will. Did you notice, through the whole thing, she never lost sight of her bread.

The two men look at each other and grin.

34   EXTERIOR: ATLANTIC STREET—DAY.

Coming up the center of the street, oblivious of the impending storm and rising wind, is a boy of about fourteen—DAVEY HOPEWELL. He's dressed in a heavy coat and gloves with the fingers cut off. This makes it easier to handle a basketball. He weaves from side to side, dribbling and talking to himself. Doing play-by-play, in fact.


DAVEY
Davey Hopewell in transition . . . he avoids the press . . . Stockton tries to steal the ball, but he doesn't have a chance . . . It's Davey Hopewell at the top of the key . . . clock running out . . . Davey Hopewell's the Celtics' only hope . . . he shakes and bakes . . . he—

DAVEY HOPEWELL stops. Holds the ball and looks at:

35   EXTERIOR: MARTHA CLARENDON'S HOUSE, FROM DAVEY'S POINT OF VIEW.

The door is open in spite of the cold, and the overturned walker is lying by the porch steps, where LINOGE threw it.

36   EXTERIOR: RESUME DAVEY.

He tucks his basketball under his arm and goes slowly to MARTHA'S gate. He stands there for a moment, then sees something black on the white paint. There are CHAR MARKS where LINOGE tapped his cane. DAVEY touches one with a couple of bare fingers (cutoff gloves, remember) and then snatches them away.

> DAVEY

Owww!

Still hot, those marks. But he loses interest in them as he looks at the overturned walker and the open door—that door shouldn't be open, not in this weather. He starts up the path; climbs the steps. He bends, moves the walker aside.

> WEATHER LADY (voice)

What part does global warming play in such storms? The fact is, we just don't know . . .

> DAVEY
> (calls)

Mrs. Clarendon? You all right?

37   INTERIOR: MARTHA'S LIVING ROOM, WITH LINOGE.

The weather is still playing. The storm graphics have moved closer toward their eventual point of impact. LINOGE sits in MARTHA'S chair, with his bloody cane drawn across his lap. His eyes are closed. His face has that look of meditation.

> WEATHER LADY

One thing we do know is that the jet stream has taken on a pattern which is very typical for this time of year, although the upper flow is even stronger than usual, helping to account for the terrific strength of this western storm.

> DAVEY (off-screen)
> (calls)

Mrs. Clarendon? It's Davey! Davey Hopewell! Are you all right?

LINOGE opens his eyes. Once again they are BLACK . . . but now the black is shot through with TWISTS OF RED . . . like FIRE. HE GRINS, showing those AWFUL TEETH. We hold on this, then:

FADE OUT. THIS ENDS ACT 1.

# Act 2

38  EXTERIOR: THE PORCH OF MARTHA'S HOUSE—DAY.

We are looking out through the open door at DAVEY HOPEWELL, who is approaching the door slowly and with growing unease. He's still got his basketball under his arm.

> DAVEY
> Mrs. Clarendon? Mrs.—

> WEATHER LADY (voice-over)
> Large windows should be taped to improve their integrity in the face of strong wind gusts.

He stops suddenly, his eyes widening, as he sees:

39  INTERIOR: THE HALLWAY, FROM DAVEY'S POINT OF VIEW.

Sticking out of the shadows are two old-lady shoes, and the hem of an old-lady dress.

> WEATHER LADY (voice-over)
> Gusts in this storm may range into . . .

40  EXTERIOR: THE PORCH, WITH DAVEY.

His fears temporarily forgotten—he thinks he knows the worst, that she's fainted, or had a stroke, or something—DAVEY drops to one knee and leans forward to examine her . . . then FREEZES. His basketball slips out from under his arm and rolls across the porch as his eyes fill up with horror. We don't need to see. We know.

> WEATHER LADY (voice-over)
> . . . speeds we normally associate with hurricanes. Check the dampers on stoves and fireplace chimneys! This is very important . . .

DAVEY pulls in breath, and at first can't get it out. We see him struggle. He is trying to scream. He touches one of MARTHA'S shoes and makes a little wheezing noise.

> LINOGE (voice)
> Forget the NBA, Davey—you'll never even play first string in high school. You're slow, and you couldn't throw it in the ocean.

DAVEY looks down the shadowy hall, realizing that MARTHA'S killer is likely still in MARTHA'S house. His paralysis breaks. He lets out a SHRIEK, bolts to his feet, turns, and pelts down the steps. He stumbles on the last one and sprawls on the walk.

> LINOGE (voice)
> (calling)
> Also, you're short. You're a *dwarf*. Why don't you come on in here, Davey? I'll do you a favor. Save you a lot of grief.

DAVEY scrambles to his feet and flees, flinging terrified glances back over his shoulder as he buttonhooks out of the CLARENDON gate, across the sidewalk, and into the street. He pelts down Atlantic toward the docks.

> DAVEY
> (screaming)
> Help! Missus Clarendon's dead! Someone's killed her! Blood! Help! Oh, God, somebody help!

41   INTERIOR: MARTHA'S LIVING ROOM, WITH LINOGE.

His eyes are back to normal . . . if you can call that cool, unsettling blue normal. He raises one hand, and makes a beckoning gesture with his index finger.

> WEATHER LADY
> The best way to sum up what we're saying to you is "prepare for the worst, because this is going to be a bad one."

42   EXTERIOR: MARTHA'S FRONT PORCH.

Faintly, we can still hear DAVEY HOPEWELL bawling for help. His basketball, which came to rest against the porch rail, rolls across the boards—slowly at first, then gathering speed—to the front door. It bounces up over the doorstoop and inside.

43   INTERIOR: MARTHA'S HALL, LOOKING BACK TOWARD THE PORCH.

In the background is MARTHA'S body, just a dark lump of shadow. DAVEY'S basketball bounces past it, leaving great big smacks of blood every time in lands.

> WEATHER LADY
> Another piece of advice? Make sure you've got plenty of Smile-Boy all-beef bologna on hand. When the weather turns nasty, nothing warms you up . . .

44   INTERIOR: THE LIVING ROOM, WITH LINOGE.

The ball rolls across the floor, weaving between the furniture. When it reaches MARTHA'S chair, where LINOGE now sits, it bounces itself twice, gaining altitude. On the third bounce, it lands in his lap. He picks it up.

> WEATHER LADY
> (holds sandwich)
> . . . like a good old fried bologna sandwich! Especially if the bologna is Smile-Boy all-beef bologna!

> LINOGE
> He shoots . . .

He throws the ball with SUPERHUMAN FORCE at the TV. It hits the screen dead center, sending the WEATHER LADY, her sandwich, and her two enormous storm systems into electronic limbo. Sparks fly.

> LINOGE
> . . . he scores!

45   EXTERIOR: ATLANTIC STREET, WITH DAVEY.

He's still running down the center of the street, still screaming at the top of his lungs.

DAVEY

Mrs. Clarendon! Someone killed Mrs. Clarendon! There's blood all over! One of her eyes is out! It's on her cheek! Oh, God, one of her eyeballs is right out on her cheek!

People are coming to windows and opening front doors to look. They all know DAVEY, of course, but before anyone can grab him and calm him down, a big green Lincoln pulls in front of him, like a cop cutting off a speeder. Written on the side is ISLAND-ATLANTIC REALTY. A portly gentleman in a suit, tie, and topcoat (the only business garb on Little Tall Island, quite likely) gets out. We may or may not see a resemblance to the absurd mannequin on the store's porch. This is ROBBIE BEALS, the local big deal, the unpleasant DON BEALS'S even more unpleasant father. Now he grabs DAVEY by the shoulders of his jacket and gives him a hard shake.

ROBBIE

Davey! Stop it! Stop that right now!

DAVEY stops it and begins to get himself under control.

ROBBIE

Why are you running down the middle of Atlantic Street, making a spectacle of yourself?

DAVEY

Someone killed Mrs. Clarendon.

ROBBIE

Nonsense, what are you talking about?

DAVEY

There's blood everywhere. And her eye's out. It's . . . it's on her cheek.

DAVEY begins to weep. Other people are gathering now, looking at the man and the boy. Slowly, ROBBIE releases DAVEY. Something is going on here, something that may be serious, and if so, there's only one man to check it out. We see this realization dawning on ROBBIE'S face.

He looks around at a middle-aged woman with a sweater hastily pulled around her shoulders and a bowl of cake batter still in one hand.

> ROBBIE

Mrs. Kingsbury. Look after him. Get him a hot tea . . .
> (reconsiders)

No, give him a little whiskey, if you've got some.


> MRS. KINGSBURY

Are you going to call Mike Anderson?


ROBBIE looks sour. There's no love lost between him and MIKE.


> ROBBIE

Not until I take a look for myself.


> DAVEY

Be careful, Mr. Beals. She's dead . . . but there's someone in
the house, I think . . .


ROBBIE looks at him impatiently. The boy is clearly hysterical. An old
man with a craggy New England face steps forward.


> GEORGE KIRBY

You want help, Robbie Beals?


> ROBBIE

Not necessary, George. I'll be fine.


He gets back into his car. It's too big to U-turn in the street, so he uses a
neighboring driveway.


> DAVEY

He shouldn't go up there alone.


The group in the street (which is still growing) watches ROBBIE drive
up to MRS. CLARENDON'S with troubled eyes.


> MRS. KINGSBURY

Come on inside, Davey. I'm not giving whiskey to a child, but
I can put the teapot on.


She puts an arm around him and leads him toward the house.

46  EXTERIOR: MARTHA CLARENDON'S HOUSE.

ROBBIE'S Lincoln pulls up in front. He gets out. Surveys the path, the overturned walker, the open door. His face suggests that this might be a little more serious than he at first thought. But he starts up the path, anyway. Leave it to that know-all MIKE ANDERSON? Not likely!

47  EXTERIOR: LITTLE TALL ISLAND TOWN HALL—DAY.

This is a white wooden building, stark in the New England style, and the center of the town's public life. In front of it is a little cupola with a largish bell inside—a bell the size of an apple basket, say. The Island Services four-wheel drive pulls up in front, using a slot marked RESERVED FOR TOWN BUSINESS.

48  INTERIOR: THE ISLAND SERVICES VEHICLE, WITH MIKE AND HATCH.

HATCH has got a pamphlet called *Storm Preparedness: State of Maine Guidelines.* He's deep in it.

> MIKE
>
> You want to come in?

> HATCH
> (doesn't look up)
>
> Nope. I'm fine.

As MIKE opens the door, HATCH does look up . . . and gives MIKE a sweet, open smile.

> HATCH
>
> Thanks for seeing after my little girl, boss.

> MIKE
> (smiles back)
>
> My pleasure.

49  EXTERIOR: ANGLE ON THE ISLAND SERVICES FOUR-WHEEL DRIVE.

MIKE gets out, once more settling his hat so it won't blow off. As he does this, he takes another small measuring glance at the sky.

50  EXTERIOR: MIKE, ON THE WALK.

He stops at the cupola. Now that we're closer, we can read the plaque in front. There is a list of war dead on it: ten from the Civil War, one from the Spanish-American, a couple each from I, II, and Korea, and six from Vietnam, the po' folks' war. Among the names we see lots of BEALSES, GODSOES, HATCHERS, AND ROBICHAUXES. Above the list, in big letters, is this: WHEN WE RING FOR THE LIVING, WE HONOR OUR DEAD.

MIKE brushes the bell's clapper with a gloved forefinger. It rings faintly. Then he goes on inside.

51    INTERIOR: THE LITTLE TALL ISLAND TOWN OFFICE.

It's your usual cluttered secretarial bullpen, dominated by an aerial photo of the island on one wall. A single woman is running the whole show—plump and pretty URSULA GODSOE (she has a plaque with her name on it beside the in/out basket on her desk). Behind her, through a number of glass windows along the main corridor, we see the actual town meeting hall. This consists of many straight-backed benches, like Puritan pews, and a bare wood lectern with a microphone. Looks more like church than government. Nobody's out there right now.

Prominent on the wall of URSULA'S office is the same sign we saw on the door of the market: STORM EMERGENCY POSSIBLE NEXT 3 DAYS! "TAKE SHELTER" SIGNAL IS 2 SHORTS, 1 LONG. MIKE strolls over and looks at this, waiting for URSULA. She is on the phone, speaking to someone in tones of forced patience.

> URSULA
> No, Betty, I haven't heard any more than you have . . . we're all dealing with the same forecast . . . No, not the memorial bell, not with the winds we're expecting . . . It'll be the siren, comes to that. Two shorts and one long, that's right . . . Mike Anderson, of course . . . those are decisions we pay him to make, aren't they, dear?

URSULA winks broadly at MIKE and gives him a one-moment gesture. MIKE raises his own hand and claps his fingers against his thumb several times, miming a talking mouth. URSULA grins and nods.

> URSULA
> Yes . . . I'll be praying, too . . . of course we all will. Thanks for calling, Betty.

She hangs up and closes her eyes for a moment.

> MIKE
>
> Tough day?

> URSULA
>
> Betty Soames seems to think we have access to some secret forecast.

> MIKE
>
> Kind of a Jeane Dixon forecast? Psychic weather?

> URSULA
>
> I guess.

MIKE taps the STORM EMERGENCY placard.

> MIKE
>
> Most people in town have seen this?

> URSULA
>
> If they're not blind, they've seen it. You need to relax, Mike Anderson. How's little Pippa Hatcher?

> MIKE
>
> Whoa, that was fast.

> URSULA
>
> Ayuh. No secrets on the island.

> MIKE
>
> She's fine. Got her head stuck in the stairs. Her dad's out in the car, doing his homework for the Big Blow of '89.

> URSULA
> (laughing)
> Ain't that just like Alton and Melinda Hatcher's daughter. Perfect.
> (grows serious)
> People know this one's bad, and if they hear the siren, they'll come. You needn't worry about that. Now—you came to look at the emergency shelter setup, didn't you?

MIKE

Thought it might not be a bad idea.

URSULA
(gets up)

We can handle three hundred for three days, a hundred and fifty for a week. And if what I'm hearing on the radio's right, we may have to. Come on, let's look.

They start out of the room, URSULA leading.

52   INTERIOR: ROBBIE BEALS, CLOSE-UP.

His face is HORRIFIED, UNBELIEVING.

ROBBIE

Oh, my God.

WEATHER LADY (voice-over)

So enough doom and gloom, already! Let's talk SUNSHINE!

THE CAMERA PULLS BACK and we see he is kneeling beside MARTHA in her hall, performing the useless ritual of trying to take her pulse. We can see her wrist and the bloodstained cuff of her dress, but that's all. ROBBIE looks around, unbelieving.

In the background, the WEATHER LADY is spieling on. LINOGE broke the TV, but she's there, just the same.

WEATHER LADY (voice-over)

The finest weather in the U.S. today? Well, there's no question about that; the Big Island of Hawaii! Temperatures in the high seventies to low eighties, plus an onshore breeze to cool things off. And things ain't too shabby in Florida, either. Last week's chill there is a thing of the past. In Miami temperatures are in the mid-seventies, and how about San-ibel Island and beautiful Captiva? If you're down that way, you'll be picking up shells with plenty of sunshine to show you the way and temps in the high eighties.

ROBBIE

Is anybody here?

He gets to his feet. He looks first at the walls, where some of MARTHA'S nice old pictures are now dotted with a fine spray of blood. Then he looks at the floor and sees more blood: the thin line drawn by LINOGE'S cane and those big, dark smacks that were left by DAVEY'S bouncing ball.

ROBBIE

Is anybody here?

He pauses, undecided, then starts down the hall.

53   BLACK.

A BANK OF OVERHEAD FLUORESCENTS SNAPS ON, revealing the spacious basement room of the town hall. This room is ordinarily used for dances, Bingo, and various town functions. Signs on the pine-paneled walls remind visitors of the volunteer fire department blood drive, which will be held right here. Now the room is filled with cots, each with a small pillow at its head and a folded blanket at its foot. At the far end are stacks of coolers, cartons of bottled water, and a big radio with its digital readout flashing.

URSULA and MIKE stand looking at this.

URSULA

Good?

MIKE

You know it is.
(she smiles)
How's the supply closet?

URSULA

Full, just like you wanted. Concentrates, mostly—pour the water over the powder and then gag it down—but nobody'll starve.

MIKE

You did all this yourself?

>                    URSULA
> Me and Pete's sister, Tavia. Be discreet, you said. Don't panic
> anyone.

>                    MIKE
> Ayuh, that's what I said. How many people know we're
> stocked for World War III?

>                    URSULA
>               (perfectly serene)
> Everyone.

MIKE winces but doesn't look too surprised.

>                    MIKE
> No secrets on the island.

>                    URSULA
>               (a bit defensive)
> I didn't talk, Mike Anderson, and neither did Tavia. Mostly it
> was Robbie Beals who spread the tattle. Madder than a wet
> hen about all this, he is. Claims you're costing the town
> money for no reason.

>                    MIKE
> Well . . . we'll see. (pause) Tell you one thing, his kid makes a
> hell of a good monkey.

>                    URSULA
> What?

>                    MIKE
> Never mind.

>                    URSULA
> Want to look in the storage?

>                    MIKE
> I think I'll trust you. Let's go back up.

She reaches for the switch, then pauses. Her face is troubled.

URSULA
How serious is this, Mike?

MIKE
I don't know. I hope Robbie Beals can kick my ass for being an alarmist, come town meeting next month. Come on. Let's go.

URSULA flicks the switch and the room GOES BLACK.

54   INTERIOR: MARTHA CLARENDON'S LIVING ROOM.

We're looking toward the hall door. The TV is louder. It's an ad for a litigation law firm. Have you been injured in an accident? Can't work? Lost your mind?

TV ANNOUNCER (voice-over)
You feel hopeless. You may even feel that the whole world is against you. But the firm of Macintosh and Redding will stand with you and see that you get your day in court. Don't make a bad situation worse! When life hands you a bag of lemons, we can help you make lemonade! Stick it to them before they can stick it to you! If you have been injured in an accident, you may have thousands, even tens of thousands of dollars waiting for you. So don't wait. Call now. Pick up the phone and dial 1-800-1-STIK-EM. That's 1 . . . 800 . . .

ROBBIE comes into the doorway. His arrogance and authority have gone. He looks rumpled, nauseated, and scared to death.

55   INTERIOR: THE LIVING ROOM, FROM ROBBIE'S POINT OF VIEW.

The TV is smashed to hell, smoking . . . but still the TV AD blares on.

TV ANNOUNCER (voice-over)
(continues)
One-STIK-EM. Get what's coming to you. Haven't you been through enough?

We can see the top of LINOGE'S head over the back of the chair. There is a SLURP as he sips tea.

56   INTERIOR: THE LIVING ROOM, A WIDER ANGLE.

We're mostly over ROBBIE'S shoulder, here, looking at the smashed but still talking TV and the top of LINOGE'S head.

> **ROBBIE**
> Who are you?

The TV falls silent. Outside, we hear the WIND OF THE RISING STORM. Slowly, slowly, the SNARLING SILVER WOLF rises above the back of the chair, pointed at ROBBIE like a sinister puppet. Its eyes and muzzle seem to DRIP BLOOD. It wags slowly back and forth like a pendulum.

> **LINOGE** (voice)
> Born in sin, come on in.

ROBBIE flinches, opens his mouth, then closes it again. What do you say to a remark like that? But LINOGE isn't finished.

> **LINOGE** (voice)
> You were with a whore in Boston when your mother died in Machias. Ma was in that crappy nursing home they closed down last fall, the one where they found the rats in the pantry, right? She choked to death calling your name. Isn't that sweet? Other than a good slice of processed yellow cheese, there's nothing on earth like a mother's love!

57   INTERIOR: ROBBIE.

Big reaction here. How would any of us react, if told one of our darkest secrets by a murderous stranger we could not properly see?

> **LINOGE** (voice)
> But that's all right, Robbie.

Another big reaction from ROBBIE—the stranger knows his name!

58   INTERIOR: MARTHA'S CHAIR.

LINOGE peeks around the chair's left-side wing, almost coyly. His eyes are more or less normal, but he is almost as blood-streaked as the head of his silver bludgeon.

> LINOGE

She's waiting for you in hell. And she's turned cannibal. When you get there, she's going to eat you alive. Over and over and over again. Because that's what hell's about—repetition. I think in our hearts, most of us know that. CATCH!

He heaves DAVEY'S basketball.

59    INTERIOR: THE LIVING ROOM DOORWAY, WITH ROBBIE.

The ball hits him in the chest, leaving a blood mark. ROBBIE'S had enough. He turns and FLEES, SCREAMING.

60    INTERIOR: MARTHA'S LIVING ROOM, ANGLE ON CHAIR AND TV.

Once again, we can just see the top of LINOGE'S head. Then his hand appears, rolled into a fist. It hovers in the air for a moment, then one finger POPS OUT, pointed at the TV. The WEATHER LADY resumes immediately.

> WEATHER LADY (voice-over)

Let's check the area apt to be most severely affected by the oncoming storm.

LINOGE reaches for another cookie.

61    EXTERIOR: IN FRONT OF MARTHA'S.

ROBBIE bolts down the steps to his car, as fast as his chubby little legs will carry him. His face is a mask of horror and bewilderment.

62    INTERIOR: MARTHA'S LIVING ROOM, FEATURING THE TV.

THE CAMERA MOVES IN SLOWLY on the SHATTERED PICTURE TUBE and SMOKING INNARDS as the WEATHER LADY talks.

> WEATHER LADY (voice-over)

The forecast calls for destruction tonight, death tomorrow, and Armageddon by the weekend. In fact, this could be the end of life as we know it.

63   INTERIOR: LINOGE.

LINOGE
Seems unlikely . . . but we can always hope.

He takes another bite of cookie.

FADE OUT. THIS ENDS ACT 2.

# Act 3

EXTERIOR: ROBBIE'S LINCOLN, WITH ROBBIE—DAY.

He claws at the driver's side door. Down the street, a number of TOWNSFOLK are watching him curiously.

### GEORGE KIRBY
Everything all right up there, Beals?

ROBBIE doesn't answer the old guy. He gets his car door open and dives inside. He has a CB radio under the dash, and now he yanks the mike off its prong. He punches the power button, punches in channel 19, and speaks. All during this, he keeps casting panicky glances at the open door of the CLARENDON house, in terror that MARTHA'S killer will show up.

### ROBBIE
This is Robbie Beals for Constable Anderson! Come back, Anderson! This is an emergency!

65    INTERIOR: ANDERSON'S MARKET—DAY.

The market is as crowded as ever. CAT and TESS MARCHANT, a motherly looking woman in her mid- to late-forties, have been checking folks out just as fast as they can, but now everyone freezes as the radio spews out its EXCITED BABBLE.

### ROBBIE (voice)
Come back, dammit! Anderson! We've got a murder over here! Martha Clarendon's been beaten to death!

A DISMAYED, DISBELIEVING MURMUR goes through the shoppers at that. Their eyes get big.

### ROBBIE (voice)
The guy who did it is still in the house! Anderson! *Anderson!*

You come back, do you hear me? You're always around when it comes to unwanted advice, where are you when—

TESS MARCHANT takes the microphone from the radio like a woman in a dream.

TESS

Robbie? This is Tess Marchant. Mike's not—

ROBBIE (voice)

I don't want you! I want Anderson! I can't do his job and mine, too!

CAT<br>(takes the mike)

He had an emergency at home. Alton went with him. It was his little g—

Just then, MIKE and HATCH come in through the door. CAT and TESS look incredibly relieved. A LOW MURMUR runs through the crowd. MIKE makes about three steps into the room, then stops, realizing something very much out of the ordinary is going on here.

MIKE

What? What is it?

Nobody in the market will answer him. Meantime, the RADIO continues to SQUAWK.

ROBBIE (voice)

What do you mean, an emergency at home? There's an emergency right here! An old woman murdered! A lunatic in Martha Clarendon's living room! I want the town constable!

MIKE walks quickly to the counter. CAT gives him the mike as if glad to be rid of it.

MIKE

What's he talking about? Who's murdered?

TESS

Martha. He says.

ANOTHER, LOUDER MURMUR this time.

> MIKE
> (pushes TRANSMIT button)
> I'm here, Robbie. Just a minute—

> ROBBIE (voice)
> Never mind just a minute, dammit! I could be in a life-threatening situation here!

MIKE ignores the man for the moment, holding the mike against his chest and talking to the two dozen or so islanders who have clumped together at the heads of the aisles, staring at him, stunned. There hasn't been a murder on this island for almost seventy years . . . unless you count Dolores Claiborne's husband, Joe, and that was never proved.

> MIKE
> You folks back off, now, and give me a little privacy. I get six thousand a year to be constable; let me do the job you pay me for.

They back off, but are still listening; how can they help it? MIKE, meanwhile, turns so his back is to them and he's facing the radio and the lottery ticket dispensers.

> MIKE
> Where are you, Robbie? Come back.

66   INTERIOR: ROBBIE, IN HIS CAR.

Behind him, we can see TOWNSPEOPLE—probably a dozen of them—standing in the street and watching. They have worked themselves quite a bit closer, but don't dare come all the way. The door to MARTHA'S house still stands ominously open.

> ROBBIE
> Martha Clarendon's house on Atlantic Street! Where did you think I was, Bar Harbor? I'm—
> (a great idea occurs to him)
> I'm keeping the man inside at bay! Now get your ass down here!

He racks the mike, then fumbles in the glove compartment. Under the jumble of maps, town documents, and Whopper wrappers, he finds a little pistol. He gets out of his car.

67  EXTERIOR: ROBBIE.

> ROBBIE
> (calls down to the cluster of folks)
> You stay where you are!

With his authority thus exerted, ROBBIE turns toward the house and points his gun at the open door. He's recovered a certain amount of his toadlike savoir faire, but he's not about to go back in there. The man in there didn't just kill MARTHA CLARENDON; he knew where ROBBIE was when ROBBIE'S mother died. He knew ROBBIE'S name.

The WIND GUSTS, blowing ROBBIE'S gray-streaked hair back from his brow . . . and the first few snowflakes of the Storm of the Century go dancing past his face.

68  INTERIOR: ANDERSON'S MARKET, WITH MIKE, HATCH, ONLOOKERS.

MIKE stands with the microphone in his hand, trying to think what to do next. As CAT WITHERS takes the mike and racks it, he makes up his mind.

> MIKE
> (to HATCH)
> Let's take another ride, all right?

> HATCH
> Sure . . .

> MIKE
> Cat, you and Tess're minding the store.
> (raising his voice)
> All you folks just stay and finish your shopping, all right?
> There's nothing you can do on Atlantic Street, and whatever's happened over there, you'll know it soon enough.

As he speaks, he moves behind the cash register. He reaches beneath it.

69 INTERIOR: THE SHELF, CLOSE-UP.

On it are a .38 and a pair of handcuffs. MIKE takes both.

70 INTERIOR: ANGLE ON MIKE.

He puts the handcuffs in one coat pocket and the .38 in the other. This is done quickly and deftly—none of the goggle-eyed customers see. CAT and TESS do, though, and it brings the reality of the situation home to them: crazy as it may be, there could be a dangerous criminal on Little Tall.

>                           CAT
> Do you want me to call your wives?

>                           MIKE
> Absolutely not.

Then he looks at the avidly watching islanders. If CAT doesn't, one of them will, as soon as he or she can reach the nearest phone.

>                           MIKE
> Yeah, I guess you better. But make sure they know the situation is under control.

71 EXTERIOR: ANDERSON'S MARKET.

MIKE and HATCH hurry down the steps, and THE CAMERA TRACKS THEM to the Island Services utility vehicle. The snow is still just flurrying, but we can see that it's thicker now.

>                           HATCH
> Snow's early.

MIKE stops with one hand on the driver's side doorhandle. He takes a deep breath, preparing himself, then lets it out.

>                           MIKE
> Yeah, it is. Let's go.

They get in and drive away. Meantime, people have been drifting out onto the porch, watching them.

72 EXTERIOR: THE ROBBIE BEALS MANNEQUIN.

The propeller on the beanie is now turning briskly.

73 EXTERIOR: THE TOWN DOCK.

The waves CRASH HIGH against the pilings, throwing spray. The work of securing the boats and getting loose gear undercover has progressed quite a bit. We FOCUS IN on GEORGE KIRBY (an older guy—sixtyish), ALEX HABER (thirty-five), and CAL FREESE (a twenty-something). ALEX points west, toward the end of the docks and the reach beyond.

ALEX HABER
Looka there, at the mainland.

74 EXTERIOR: MAINLAND, FROM THE DOCK'S POINT OF VIEW.

The mainland is about two miles away, and quite clear—gray-green woods, mostly.

75 EXTERIOR: RESUME DOCK, WITH SONNY, ALEX, AND CAL.

ALEX HABER
When you can't see over there no more, it's time to get in while you can. And when you can't even see the reach no more, it's time to head down to the town hall, whether you've heard the siren or not.

CAL FREESE
(to GEORGE)
How bad do you think it'll be, Unc?

GEORGE KIRBY
Maybe the worst we ever saw. Come on, help me with the last of these nets. (pause) I wonder if that fool Beals has any slight idear what he's doin up there?

76 EXTERIOR: ATLANTIC STREET, IN FRONT OF MARTHA'S HOUSE.

The fool BEALS is still being the good sentry, standing in front of his Lincoln with his .38 pointed at the open door of the CLARENDON house. Snow is coming down more thickly now; it's scattered across the shoulders of his topcoat like dandruff. He's been here for a while.

Down below, a little gathering of WATCHERS (MRS. KINGSBURY and DAVEY HOPEWELL are back among them) moves aside to allow the Island Services vehicle through. It pulls up beside the Lincoln. MIKE gets out from behind the wheel, HATCH from the passenger seat.

                              HATCH
You want the shotgun?

                              MIKE
I guess we better have it. You just make sure the safety's on, Alton Hatcher.

HATCH leans back into the truck, fumbles, and reappears with the shotgun that is ordinarily kept latched under the dash. HATCH ostentatiously checks the safety, and then they approach ROBBIE. ROBBIE'S attitude toward MIKE all through this is one of confrontation and contempt. The history of these feelings will never be fully explored, but its basis is undoubtedly ROBBIE'S desire to keep all the reins of power in his own hands.

                              ROBBIE
It's about time.

                              MIKE
Put that thing away, Robbie.

                              ROBBIE
No such thing, Constable Anderson. You do your job, I'll do mine.

                              MIKE
Your job is real estate. Would you at least lower it, please? (pause) Come on, Robbie—it's in my face, and I know it's loaded.

ROBBIE grudgingly lowers the .38. HATCH, meanwhile, is looking nervously at the open door and the overturned walker.

                              MIKE
What happened?

ROBBIE

I was driving over to the town office when I saw Davey
Hopewell running down the middle of the street.
(points toward DAVEY)
He said Martha Clarendon was dead—murdered. I didn't
believe him, but it's true. She's . . . awful.

MIKE

You said the person who did it was still inside.

ROBBIE

He spoke to me.

HATCH

And said what?

ROBBIE
(nervous, lying)
Told me to get out. I think he said for me to get out or he'd
kill me, too. I don't know. And this hardly seems like the right
time for an interrogation.

MIKE

What did he look like?

ROBBIE starts to reply, then stops, puzzled.

ROBBIE

I . . . I barely got a look at him.

He got a pretty good one, actually . . . but he doesn't remember.

MIKE
(to HATCH)
Stay on my right. Keep the barrel of that scattergun pointed
down, and keep the safety on unless I tell you to take it off.
(to ROBBIE)
You stay exactly where you are, please.

ROBBIE

You're the constable.

He watches MIKE and HATCH start for the gate, then calls.

> ROBBIE
> The TV's on. Tuned quite loud. If the guy starts moving around, I'm not sure you'll hear him.

MIKE nods, then goes through the gate with HATCH on his right. The TOWNSPEOPLE have crept closer yet; we now see them in the background. The SNOW SWIRLS around them in the HIGH WIND. It's still light, but thickening up.

77   EXTERIOR: MIKE AND HATCH, FROM THE PORCH.

They come up the walk, MIKE tuned tightly (but in control), HATCH scared but trying not to show it.

> HATCH
> Even if there was a guy, he's probably gone out the back by now, don't you think? She ain't got but a five-foot garden fence—

MIKE shakes his head to indicate he doesn't know, then taps his lips with a forefinger, indicating that HATCH should keep quiet. They stop at the foot of the steps. MIKE pulls gloves out of his coat pockets and puts them on. He also takes out his own pistol. He indicates for HATCH to put on gloves, and HATCH hands him the shotgun so he can comply. MIKE takes the opportunity to double-check the safety (still on), then hands it back.

They go up the steps and examine the walker. Then they cross the porch. They see the feet, clad in their old-lady shoes, poking out from the shadows of the hallway, and exchange a dismayed glance. They go in.

78   INTERIOR: THE HALL OF MARTHA'S HOUSE.

Behind them, the WEATHER LADY runs on endlessly.

> WEATHER LADY (voice)
> Conditions along the New England coast are expected to worsen dramatically toward sunset—not that our Down East friends are going to see the sun go down tonight, I'm afraid.

We are expecting gale force winds along the Massachusetts and New Hampshire coasts, and *hurricane*-force wind gusts along the Maine coast and offshore islands. There's going to be significant beach erosion, and once the snow starts to fall, amounts will increase dramatically until . . . well . . . until it's over. At this point it is literally impossible to talk about accumulations. Let's just say that the total fall is going to be enormous. Three feet? That's probable. Five feet? Even that is possible. You'll want to stay tuned for updates, and be assured we'll break into our programming if conditions warrant doing so.

The two men ignore her—they have more immediate problems. They kneel on either side of the dead woman. MIKE ANDERSON is grim— shocked, but holding it in. Already focusing on the job at hand and the ramifications to follow. HATCH, on the other hand, is close to losing it. He looks up at MIKE, face pale, eyes full of tears. He speaks in a BARE WHISPER.

> HATCH
> Mike . . . oh, my God, Mike . . . *she got no face left!* She—

MIKE reaches out and puts a gloved finger across HATCH'S lips. He inclines his head toward the SOUND of the BABBLING TV. Someone might be listening. MIKE leans toward his shaking DEPUTY over the body of the dead woman.

> MIKE
> (very low)
> Are you going to be all right? Because if you're not, I want you to hand me the twelve-gauge and go back to Robbie.

> HATCH
> (low)
> I'm all right.

> MIKE
> Sure?

HATCH nods. MIKE considers him, then decides to believe him. He gets to his feet. HATCH does the same, then sways a little. He puts a hand on the wall to catch his balance, and smears some of that fine blood-spatter. He looks at his gloved hand with amazement and dismay.

MIKE points up the hall to the living room door—and the SOUND of the TV. HATCH gathers his courage and nods. Very slowly, the two men slip up the hallway. (All played for maximum suspense, of course.)

They are three-quarters of the way up the hall when the SOUND OF THE TV ABRUPTLY CUTS OFF. HATCH'S shoulder brushes one of the pictures on the wall and knocks it off. MIKE catches it before it can clatter to the floor . . . mostly by good luck and fast reflexes. He and HATCH exchange a strained glance, then go on.

79    INTERIOR: THE DOORWAY BETWEEN HALL AND LIVING ROOM.

The two men come into the doorway. Looking at them from the living room, as we are, HATCH is on the left and MIKE on the right. They look at:

80    INTERIOR: THE LIVING ROOM, FROM MIKE AND HATCH'S POINT OF VIEW.

We see the BLOWN-OUT TV and MARTHA'S wing chair. Over the top of the chair, we see the top of LINOGE'S head. Very still. It's probably a man's head, but it's impossible to tell if the guy is alive.

81    INTERIOR: RESUME HALL DOORWAY, WITH MIKE AND HATCH.

They exchange a glance, and MIKE nods them forward. CAMERA FOLLOWS as they move in on the back of the chair, very slowly. Three steps into the room, MIKE gestures for HATCH to move out wider. HATCH does so. MIKE moves in a step closer to the chair (we can see it now, as well as the MEN), then stops as a BLOODSTAINED HAND appears. It goes to the table beside the chair and takes a cookie.

> MIKE
> (levels his gun)

Freeze!

The hand does just that—freezes in midair, holding the cookie.

MIKE

Raise your hands. Both hands, up over the chair. I want to see them clear as day. There are two guns pointed at you, and one of 'em's a scatter.

LINOGE raises his hands. He's still holding the cookie in his left one.

MIKE indicates that HATCH should circle the chair to the front on his side. As HATCH does, MIKE circles around on the right.

82   INTERIOR: MARTHA'S LIVING ROOM, ANGLE ON THE CHAIR.

LINOGE sits there, hands raised, face composed. There's no sign of a weapon, but the men react to his bloodstained face and coat. LINOGE'S calm demeanor is in sharp contrast to MIKE and HATCH, who are wound as tight as guitar strings. Maybe we see here how suspects are sometimes shot by accident.

MIKE

Hands together.

LINOGE puts his hands together, wrist to wrist and back to back.

83   OMIT.

84   EXTERIOR: IN FRONT OF MARTHA'S HOUSE.

Several TOWNSFOLK hurry forward as far as the trunk of ROBBIE'S car. One is an older woman named ROBERTA COIGN.

> ROBERTA COIGN
> What's happened to Martha?

> ROBBIE
> (shrill, near hysteria)
> Just stay back! This is under control!

He points his pistol at the house again, and I think we have a real question about what may happen when and if MIKE and HATCH bring their prisoner out. ROBBIE is on a hair trigger.

85   INTERIOR: THE LIVING ROOM OF MARTHA'S HOUSE.

Extreme close-up, cuffs

> MIKE (voice)
> If he moves, shoot him.

CAMERA DRAWS BACK TO INCLUDE LINOGE, MIKE, HATCH

> LINOGE
> (low, pleasant, and composed)
> If he shoots, he'll get us both. That thing's still loaded with buckshot.

Both men react to this. Not because it's true, but because it *could* be true. Hell, HATCH might blow a hole through MIKE in any case; the two men are quite close together.

> LINOGE
> Also, he's still got the safety on.

HATCH reacts with terrified realization: he *has* forgotten to take off the safety. While MIKE inexpertly fumbles the cuffs onto LINOGE'S wrists, HATCH fumbles the safety off. As he does, the gun leaves the vicinity of LINOGE completely. We need to see that LINOGE could take these two courageous but fumbling locals any time he wants . . . but chooses not to do so.

The cuffs are on. MIKE steps back, very relieved. He and HATCH exchange a rather wild look.

> LINOGE
> But you remembered to wear gloves. That was good.

He begins to eat the cookie, oblivious of his blood-streaked hand.

> MIKE
> On your feet.

LINOGE finishes the last bite of cookie and gets obediently to his feet.

86 EXTERIOR: MARTHA CLARENDON'S PORCH.

Beyond it, the snow is now coming hard, with the wind driving it into slanting lines. The houses on the far side of the street are misty, as if seen through a veil.

MIKE and LINOGE come out side by side, LINOGE with his hands cuffed at belt level, a look all of us are familier with from the evening news. HATCH is walking behind them, with the shotgun at port arms.

In the street, there are now about a dozen people clustered by the rear bumper of ROBBIE'S Lincoln. When the men come out, ROBBIE crouches a little, and MIKE sees the man's little glove compartment gun pointed at them.

> MIKE
> *Put that down!*

Looking slightly ashamed, ROBBIE does.

> MIKE
> Hatch, close the door.

> HATCH
> Is that wise? I mean, aren't we supposed to leave stuff pretty much like it is? It being a crime scene, and all—

> MIKE
> We leave the door open and the crime scene's going to be under six feet of fresh powder. Now close the door!

HATCH tries. One of MARTHA'S shoes is in the way. He squats. Grimacing, he moves her foot with one gloved hand. Then he gets up and closes the door. He looks at MIKE, who nods.

MIKE
What's your name, mister?

LINOGE looks at him. There's a beat when we're not sure he's going to answer. Then:

LINOGE
Andre Linoge.

MIKE
Well, come on, Andre Linoge. Let's get walking.

87   EXTERIOR: LINOGE, CLOSE-UP.

For just a moment, LINOGE'S eyes CHANGE. They SWIRL WITH BLACK, the blue irises and the whites disappearing. Then everything goes back to normal.

88   EXTERIOR: RESUME PORCH, WITH MIKE, HATCH, AND LINOGE.

MIKE blinks at the sight like a man trying to cope with a momentary attack of vertigo. HATCH hasn't seen it, but MIKE has. LINOGE smiles at him, as if to say "our little secret." Then we see MIKE'S rationality reasserting itself, and he gives LINOGE a poke.

MIKE
Come on. Move.

They go down the steps.

89   EXTERIOR: ON THE CONCRETE PATH.

The storm blows snow past them, smacking their faces, making them wince. HATCH'S hat BLOWS OFF. As he looks helplessly after it, LINOGE gives MIKE that look again, the one that says they have a secret. MIKE is less able to shake it off this time . . . but he gets LINOGE moving.

FADE OUT. THIS ENDS ACT 3.

# Act 4

90    EXTERIOR: THE LITTLE TALL LIGHTHOUSE—LATE DAY.

The snow flies past it so thickly we can only make out its shape . . . and of course its light, each time it swings around. The waves CRASH HIGH on the rocks of this promontory. THE WIND SHRIEKS.

91    EXTERIOR: GODSOE FISH & LOBSTER—LATE DAY.

This long building—part warehouse, part retail fish market—is far out on the dock. Waves smash into the dock, and foam splatters high, wetting the sides and roof of the building. As we watch, the WIND tears a door free of its latch. It begins to BANG BACK AND FORTH. Nearby, a tarp blows free of the boat it's covering and WHIRLS OFF INTO THE SNOWY DAY.

92    EXTERIOR: THE ANDERSON HOUSE—LATE DAY.

A four-wheel drive is parked at the curb, by the WEE FOLKS sign. Its windshield wipers are clapping back and forth rapidly, but the glass is still snowing up. Its headlights cut twin cones through the snow-choked air. The WEE FOLKS sign swings back and forth on its chain. On the porch, MOLLY ANDERSON is handing over a bundled-up BUSTER CARVER and an equally bundled-up PIPPA HATCHER to their moms, ANGELA and MELINDA. THE CAMERA MOVES IN on the porch. All three women have to shout in order to be heard over the HOWLING WIND.

> MELINDA
> Pip, you sure you're all right?

> PIPPA
> Yes. Don Beals hurt my feelings, but they're better now.

> MOLLY
> I'm sorry I had to call you early, guys . . .

ANGELA CARVER

It's okay. The radio says they're going to keep the bigger kids over in Machias, at least tonight . . . the reach is too choppy to send them back on the water-bus.

MOLLY

Probably for the best.

BUSTER

Mommy, I'm cold.

ANGELA CARVER

Coss you are—but you'll be warm in the car, honey.
(to MOLLY)
Are there more?

MOLLY

Buster and Pippa are the last.
(to PIPPA)
You had an adventure, didn't you?

PIPPA

Yes. Momma, I've got a smaller button!

She honks her own nose. Neither MELINDA nor ANGELA understand, but they laugh. It's cute; they understand that much.

ANGELA CARVER

We'll see you Monday, if the roads are open. Wave a bye, Buster.

BUSTER obediently waves a bye. MOLLY waves one back as the mothers carry their babies down the steps and into the increasing fury of the storm. Then she goes back inside.

93   INTERIOR: THE ANDERSON HOUSE FRONT HALL, WITH MOLLY AND RALPHIE.

There's a mirror about halfway down, by the telephone table. RALPHIE has pulled a chair over and is standing on it so he can look at that red mark on the bridge of his nose. It's a birthmark, but actually more cute than disfiguring.

MOLLY hardly notices him. She's relieved to be in out of the storm, and even more relieved that her little charges have all been packed home for the day. She shakes the snow out of her hair, then takes off her parka and hangs it up. She looks at the stairs, winces at the memory of PIPPA'S misadventure, then snorts laughter.

> MOLLY
> (to herself)

The smaller button!

> RALPHIE
> (still looking in the mirror)

Mommy, why do I have to have this?

MOLLY goes to him, plants her chin on his shoulder, and looks at him in the mirror. They make a rather lovely mother-and-son portrait that way. She reaches around and touches the little red mark on his nose with love.

> MOLLY

Your daddy calls it a fairy saddle. He says it means you were born lucky.

> RALPHIE

Donnie Beals says it's a pimple.

> MOLLY

Donnie Beals is a . . . Donnie Beals is a nut.

She grimaces briefly. "Nut" isn't the word she'd probably use, if given a free choice.

> RALPHIE

I don't like it. Even if it is a fairy saddle.

> MOLLY

Myself, I love it . . . but if you still feel the same way when you're older, we'll take you to Bangor and have it removed. They can do that now. Okay?

> RALPHIE

How much older do I have to be?

>                    MOLLY
> Ten—how's that?

>                    RALPHIE
> Too long to wait. Ten's *old*.

The phone rings. MOLLY picks it up.

>                    MOLLY
> Hello?

94   INTERIOR: THE MARKET, WITH CAT WITHERS.

She's on the phone behind the counter. TESS MARCHANT is running the checkout operation by herself for the time being. There's still quite a line, although with the storm now on the rise, it's thinned a bit. Those people that are left BUZZ EXCITEDLY about the police call to the CLARENDON house.

>                    CAT
> There you are, I've been trying to get you for almost ten
> minutes.

95   INTERIOR: THE ANDERSON HALL, WITH MOLLY AND RALPHIE.

[Through the rest of this conversation, the director will cut back and forth as he/she chooses, but we should see MOLLY almost unconsciously censoring her end, not asking all the questions she'd like to ask, because little pitchers have big ears.]

>                    MOLLY
> I've mostly been out on the porch, handing kids over to their
> parents. I sent them home early. What's up, Katrina?

>                    CAT
> Well . . . I don't want you to be scared or anything, but we
> got word that there's been a murder on the island. Old
> Martha Clarendon. Mike and Hatch have gone over there.

>                    MOLLY
> What?! Are you sure?

> CAT

I'm not sure of anything right now—this place has been a madhouse all day—except that they went over there and Mike asked me to call you and say everything's under control.

> MOLLY

Is it?

> CAT

How do I know? Yeah, probably . . . anyway, he wanted me to call before anyone else did it. If you see Melinda Hatcher—

> MOLLY

She just left here with Angie Carver. They're carpooling. You can get her at home in fifteen minutes or so.

Outside, the WIND RISES IN A SHRIEK. MOLLY looks toward the sound.

> MOLLY

Better give her twenty.

> CAT

Okay.

> MOLLY

There's no chance it's a . . . I don't know, a joke? A prank?

> CAT

Robbie Beals called it in. He doesn't do humor, you know?

> MOLLY

Yeah. I know.

> CAT

He said that the person who did it might still be there. I don't know if Mike would want me to tell you that or not, but I thought you had a right to know.

MOLLY closes her eyes for a moment, as if in pain. Probably she *is* in pain.

> CAT

Molly?

> MOLLY

I'm coming down to the store. If Mike gets there before I do, tell him to stay put.

> CAT

I'm not sure he'd want—

> MOLLY

Thanks, Cat.

She hangs up before CAT can say any more. She turns to RALPHIE, who is still examining his birthmark in the mirror. He's so close to the glass that his eyes are rather charmingly crossed. She gives him a big smile that only a four-year-old could believe in; her eyes are clouded with worry.

> MOLLY

Let's go down to the store and see your daddy, big boy . . . what do you say?

> RALPHIE

Daddy, yay!

He jumps down from his chair, then pauses, looking at her dubiously.

> RALPHIE

What about the storm? We've only got the car. It slides around in the snow.

MOLLY grabs his coat off the tree by the door and starts getting him into it at superspeed. That big, false smile never leaves her face.

> MOLLY

Hey, it's only a quarter of a mile. And we'll come back with Daddy in the truck, because I bet he's going to close the market early. How's that? Sound good?

> RALPHIE

Yeah, excellent!

She zips his jacket up. As she does, we see she is terribly worried.

96   EXTERIOR: IN FRONT OF MARTHA CLARENDON'S HOUSE.

The storm is still getting worse by degrees; people are now having some trouble standing their ground against the wind-driven snow . . . but no one has left. ROBBIE BEALS has joined MIKE and HATCH. His gun is still in his hand, but with the prisoner cuffed, he looks a little more at ease and has pointed the little pistol at the ground.

MIKE has opened the back of the Island Services vehicle. It has been outfitted to transport stray and sick animals. The floor is bare steel. There's a mesh barrier between this storage compartment and the backseat. Mounted on the wall is a plastic water reservoir with a tube.

> HATCH
> You going to put him in *there?*

> MIKE
> Unless you want to sit in the backseat with him and baby-sit.

> HATCH
> (takes the point)
Get in.

LINOGE doesn't, at least not immediately. He looks around at ROB-BIE, instead. ROBBIE doesn't care for that.

> LINOGE
> Remember what I said, Robbie: hell is repetition.

He smiles at ROBBIE. A private smile, like the one he gave MIKE. Then he gets into the back of the Island Services vehicle.

> ROBBIE
> (nervous)
> He talks a lot of nonsense. I think he's crazy

LINOGE has to sit with his legs crossed and his head ducked, but this really doesn't seem to put him out in the least. He is still smiling, his handcuffed hands clasped in his lap, as MIKE swings the doors shut.

MIKE

How does he know your name? Did you tell him?

ROBBIE
(drops his eyes)

I don't know. All I *do* know is that no sane person would want
to kill Martha Clarendon. I'll come down to the store with
you. Help you clear this up. We'll have to get in touch with
the state police—

MIKE

Robbie, I know this goes against your grain, but you have to
let me handle this.

ROBBIE
(bristles)

I'm the town manager here, in case you forgot. I have a
responsibility—

MIKE

So do I, and our responsibilities are clearly divided in the
town charter. Right now Ursula needs you over at the town
hall a lot more than I need you at the constable's. Come on,
Hatch.

MIKE turns away from the furious town manager.

ROBBIE

Listen here—!

He starts to chase them up the side the Island Services vehicle, then
realizes he's being undignified in front of a dozen of his constituents.
MRS. KINGSBURY stands nearby, with her arm around the shoulders
of a frightened-looking DAVEY HOPEWELL. Behind them, ROBERTA
COIGN and her husband, DICK, look at ROBBIE with poker faces that
can't quite mask their contempt.

ROBBIE stops chasing MIKE. He sticks his gun in his topcoat pocket.

ROBBIE
(still furious)

You're getting too big for your britches, Anderson!

MIKE takes no notice. He opens the driver's side door of the Island Services vehicle. ROBBIE, seeing them about to make their getaway, fires the only other arrow in his quiver.

ROBBIE
And get the sign off that damned dummy on your porch! It's not funny!

MRS. KINGSBURY puts a hand over her mouth to hide a snicker. ROBBIE doesn't see—probably lucky for her. The Island Services vehicle starts up, and its lights come on. It heads upstreet, bound for the market and the constable's office contained therein.

ROBBIE stands, slump-shouldered and fuming, then looks around at the cluster of people in the snowy street.

ROBBIE
What are you standing here for? Go on home! Show's over!

He stalks back to his Lincoln.

97    EXTERIOR: LOWER MAIN STREET, IN THE SNOW.

Headlights appear in the SCREAMING WHITE, and a car eventually materializes behind them. It's small, light, and two-wheel drive. It's going slow and slipping back and forth; already there are at least four inches of fresh snow on the road.

98    INTERIOR: THE CAR, WITH MOLLY AND RALPHIE.

Up ahead, we see lights looming out of the snow on the left, plus the long porch and the hanging lobster traps.

RALPHIE
It's the store! Yay!

MOLLY
Yay is right.

She turns into the parking area in front. Now that she's here, MOLLY realizes that coming out was dangerous . . . but who could have guessed the snow would pile up so fast? She turns off the engine and allows herself a small slump over the wheel.

RALPHIE

Mom? You okay?

MOLLY

Fine.

RALPHIE

Get me out of my car seat, 'kay? I want to see Daddy!

MOLLY

You bet.

She opens her door.

99    EXTERIOR: THE ISLAND SERVICES VEHICLE.

It turns left at the blinker and heads toward the market through the thickening snow.

100    INTERIOR: THE ISLAND SERVICES VEHICLE, WITH MIKE AND HATCH.

HATCH

What are we gonna do with him, Mike?

MIKE
(sotto voce)

Keep your voice down.
(HATCH looks guilty)
We'll have to call the state police barracks in Machias—
Robbie was right about that much—but what are the
chances they'll be able to take him off our hands in this?

HATCH looks doubtfully out the window at the pelting snow. This
situation keeps complicating itself, and HATCH isn't a very compli-
cated guy. They continue to talk in low voices, so LINOGE won't
overhear.

MIKE

Robbie said the TV was on, and I heard it when we were in
the hall. Did you?

HATCH

At first, yeah. The weather. Then the guy must have . . .

He trails away, remembering.

HATCH

It was busted. Busted all to hell and gone. He didn't do it
while we were in the hall, either. You bust a TV picture tube,
it makes a noise, like *Boof!* We would have heard.
(MIKE nods)
It must have been the radio . . .

It's almost a question. MIKE doesn't reply. Both of them know it wasn't
the radio.

101   INTERIOR: LINOGE, IN THE ANIMAL TRANSPORT COMPARTMENT.

Smiling. We just see the tips of the fangs in his mouth. LINOGE knows
what they know . . . and in spite of their low tones, he hears them.

102   EXTERIOR: ANGLE ON THE MARKET IN THE SNOW—AFTERNOON.

The Island Services four-wheel drive rolls past the parking lot in the
snow (the little car MOLLY and RALPHIE came in is already wearing a

fresh coat) and then pulls into an alley that runs down the side of the store and around to the back.

103   EXTERIOR: THE ALLEY, FROM THE FAR END.

The Island Services vehicle comes toiling toward us out of the snow, HEADLIGHTS GLARING. THE CAMERA PULLS BACK as it reaches the snowy yard at the rear. There is a loading dock at the back of the market, with a sign that says DELIVERIES ONLY—GO THRU MARKET FOR CONSTABLE BUSINESS. The vehicle pulls up here, backing into place. For this sort of deal, the dock is mighty convenient—and MIKE and HATCH *do* have a delivery to make.

They get out and walk around to the back. HATCH is as nervous as before, but MIKE has got his own nerves under control. As they reach the rear of the vehicle:

> MIKE
>
> Safety off?

HATCH looks first surprised, then guilty. He pushes the shotgun's safety off. MIKE, who has his own gun in his hand, nods in satisfaction.

> MIKE
>
> You're up top.

There are stairs at one end of the loading dock. HATCH climbs them and stands with his shotgun at port arms. MIKE unlocks the back doors of the vehicle, then stands back.

> MIKE
>
> Step out on the dock. Don't approach my . . . partner.

Sounding like a guy on *Adam 12* makes MIKE uncomfortable, but under the circumstances, "partner" is the right word.

LINOGE steps out, still awkwardly bent over but graceful. And still smiling that faint, corners-of-the-mouth smile. HATCH takes a step back to give him room as LINOGE mounts the steps. Their prisoner is cuffed and they have the guns, but HATCH is still scared of LINOGE.

LINOGE stands in the driving snow, as comfortable as a man in his own living room. MIKE climbs the stairs to the loading dock, searching in his pants pocket. He brings out a ring of keys, separates out the one that opens the back door, and gives it to HATCH. MIKE keeps his pistol pointed slightly down but in LINOGE'S direction.

104    EXTERIOR: HATCH, AT THE LOADING DOOR.

He bends and slides the key into the lock.

105    EXTERIOR: LINOGE, CLOSE-UP.

He's watching HATCH very closely . . . and now we see A FLICKER OF BLACKNESS in his eyes.

106    EXTERIOR: MIKE, CLOSE-UP.

He frowns. Did he see something? It was too quick to tell.

107    EXTERIOR: THE LOADING DOCK DOOR, CLOSE-UP.

HATCH twists the key. SOUND: A SNAP. And now HATCH'S hand is holding nothing but the head of the key.

108    EXTERIOR: RESUME LOADING DOCK.

                    HATCH
    Aw, *sugar!* Snapped right off! Must have been the cold!

He begins to HAMMER ON THE DOOR with a gloved fist.

109    INTERIOR: THE ISLAND CONSTABLE'S OFFICE.

This was once part of the market's storage area. Now it boasts a desk, a few filing cabinets, a fax, a CB radio, and a bulletin board on the wall. There is also a jail cell in the corner. The cell looks sturdy enough, but homemade—a kind of do-it-yourself project. It's a strictly temporary facility for weekend drunks and part-time hell-raisers.

SOUND: HAMMERING ON THE DOOR.

                    HATCH (voice-over)
    Hey! Anybody in there? Anybody?

110   EXTERIOR: RESUME LOADING DOCK.

> MIKE
>
> Forget it. Go around and open it from the inside.

> HATCH
>
> You want me to leave you out here alone with him?

> MIKE
> (stress breaking through)
> Unless you happen to see Lois or Superman hanging around
> in the alley.

> HATCH
>
> We could take him—

> MIKE
>
> Through the market? With half the island doing their storm
> shopping? I don't think so. Go on, now.

HATCH gives him a doubtful look, then starts back down the stairs.

111   EXTERIOR: IN FRONT OF THE MARKET.

In snow that's thicker than ever, ROBBIE BEALS'S Lincoln comes SPINNING AND SLEWING into the parking area, almost broadsiding MOLLY'S little car. ROBBIE gets out and goes up the porch steps just as PETER GODSOE comes out of the market. PETER is a ruggedly handsome man in his early forties, father of SALLY, the little girl with the jam on her shirt.

> PETER GODSOE
>
> What happened, Beals? Is Martha really dead?

> ROBBIE
>
> She's dead, all right.

ROBBIE sees the mannequin with the sign around its neck—GENUINE "ROBBIE BEALS BRAND" LOBSTERIN' GEAH—and yanks the sign off with a snarl. He SCOWLS at it. HATCH has slogged around from the back just in time to see and react to this. PETER GODSOE follows ROBBIE back inside, to monitor developments. HATCH follows them both.

112    INTERIOR: THE MARKET—AFTERNOON.

Lots of people milling around. Prominent among them is MOLLY
ANDERSON, talking to CAT but mostly worrying about MIKE. We see
RALPHIE halfway down one of the aisles and mooning over the sugary
cereals.

> MOLLY
> (as HATCH enters)
> Where's Mike? Is he all right?

> HATCH
> Fine. Out back with the prisoner. I just have to let him in.

Other people move in on him.

> PETER GODSOE
> Is he a local?

> HATCH
> I never saw him before in my life.

Lots of relief at this. Others try to grab HATCH'S attention and ask
questions, but MOLLY isn't among them—the sooner HATCH does his
job, the sooner she'll have her husband back. HATCH fights his way up
the center aisle, pausing to ruffle RALPHIE'S hair. RALPHIE gives him
an AFFECTIONATE GRIN.

ROBBIE still has the sign; is tapping it angrily against his thigh.
MOLLY sees it and winces a little.

113    EXTERIOR: ON THE LOADING DOCK, WITH MIKE AND LINOGE.

They stand facing each other in the DRIVING SNOW. There are several
beats of silence. Then:

> LINOGE
> Give me what I want, and I'll go away.

> MIKE
> What is it you want?

That smile shakes MIKE in spite of himself.

114   INTERIOR: THE CONSTABLE'S OFFICE, WITH HATCH.

He comes bustling in and hurries to the loading door. He turns the dead-bolt knob and tries to open it. The door still won't open. He pushes hard, then harder. No luck. As a last resort, he SLAMS HIS SHOULDER against the door. Nothing. The door might as well be dipped in concrete.

>                    HATCH
>   Mike?

>                    MIKE (voice-over)
>   Come on, hurry up! It's freezing out here!

>                    HATCH
>   It won't open! It's stuck!

115   EXTERIOR: RESUME LOADING DOCK, WITH MIKE AND LINOGE.

MIKE is totally EXASPERATED—everything has gone wrong with this piece of work; it's a complete Russian fire drill. LINOGE is still smiling his faint little smile. For him, everything's right on track.

>                    MIKE
>   Did you unlock it?

>                    HATCH
>              (rather hurt by this)
>   Course I did, Mike!

>                    MIKE
>   Then *whale* on it! There's probably ice in the jamb.

116   INTERIOR: RESUME CONSTABLE'S OFFICE, WITH HATCH.

ROBBIE is standing in the door behind HATCH, observing all this with HEAVY CONTEMPT. HATCH rolls his eyes, knowing perfectly well the door isn't frozen; he already whaled on it. Nevertheless, he hits the door another couple of good shots. ROBBIE crosses the room, stopping on the way to drop the joke sign on MIKE'S constable's desk. HATCH turns toward him, startled. ROBBIE (who *is* a physically bigger man) moves HATCH aside, none too gently.

STORM OF THE CENTURY   77

Let me.

He hits the door several more good shots, his look of confidence gradually subsiding. HATCH watches with subtle but understandable satisfaction. ROBBIE gives up, rubbing his shoulder.

ROBBIE
Anderson! You'll have to come around and take him through the store.

117   EXTERIOR: RESUME LOADING DOCK, WITH MIKE AND LINOGE.

MIKE ROLLS HIS EYES IN ANNOYANCE—BEALS in the constable's office, still meddling. Oh, goody, better and better.

MIKE
Hatch!

HATCH (voice-over)
Yeah!

MIKE
Come around. (pointedly) Alone.

HATCH (voice-over)
Right there!

MIKE turns his attention back to LINOGE.

MIKE
Be a little bit longer. Just stand quiet.

LINOGE
Remember what I said, Mr. Anderson. And when the time comes . . . we'll talk.

He smiles.

118   EXTERIOR: MAIN STREET, LITTLE TALL ISLAND—LATE AFTERNOON.

The houses and storefronts are graying out, starting to look like mirages, as THE STORM INTENSIFIES.

119   EXTERIOR: BREAKWATER AND LIGHTHOUSE.

HUGE WAVES CRASH THE ROCKS. FOAM LEAPS INTO THE AIR.
On this image, we:

FADE TO BLACK. THIS ENDS ACT 4.

## Act 5

120    EXTERIOR: THE ISLAND MARKET—LATE AFTERNOON.

In worsening conditions that now make moving a serious problem, MIKE, HATCH, and LINOGE come out of the alley and struggle toward the steps of the market. LINOGE has been made to walk in front of them, and now he LOOKS UPWARD, SMILING.

121    EXTERIOR: ISLAND MARKET'S ROOF.

Here is a little nest of radio antennas that serve the various two-ways inside the store. The tallest of these radio antennas SNAPS OFF and goes rolling down the backslant of the roof.

122    EXTERIOR: FOOT OF THE MARKET STEPS, WITH MIKE, HATCH, LINOGE.

> HATCH
> (with a flinch)
> What was that?

> MIKE
> Antenna, I think. Never mind now. Go on.

HATCH heads up the steps, giving LINOGE a healthy berth.

123    EXTERIOR: THE TOWN HALL.

SOUND: That same TWANGING SNAP.

124    INTERIOR: TOWN OFFICE, WITH URSULA.

She's at her radio, which is on a table below the STORM EMERGENCY/TAKE SHELTER poster. From the RADIO comes the LOUD SOUND OF STATIC.

> URSULA
> Come back? Rodney, are you there? Come back, Rodney!

Nothing. After another moment or two of twiddling, URSULA racks the mike and looks at the useless radio with disgust.

125   INTERIOR: THE MARKET.

HATCH, coated with snow, steps in. The SHOPPERS react to the shotgun. Before, it was under his arm and pointed at the floor. Now he's holding it up against his shoulder and pointed at the ceiling, like Steve McQueen in *Wanted: Dead or Alive*. HATCH looks around at the SHOPPERS.

> HATCH
> Mike wants all you folks to move back on both sides, okay? No one in Aisle 2. We've got us a bad guy, and we can't use the back door to bring him in like we'd like to, so just move back. Give us some room.

> PETER GODSOE
> Why'd he kill her?

> HATCH
> Just move back, Pete, okay? Mike's standing out in the snow, and his feet must be pretty cold by now. Also, we're all gonna feel better when this guy's locked up. Move back, folks, give 'em a clear way up that second aisle.

The customers move aside in two groups, leaving the center of the market clear. PETER GODSOE and ROBBIE BEALS are with one group (the one on the left, as you look toward the back of the market); MOLLY is in the other, standing with CAT and TESS MARCHANT, who has moved away from the cash register.

HATCH surveys this and decides it'll do—it'll have to. He goes to the door and opens it. He beckons.

126   EXTERIOR: THE PORCH, WITH MIKE AND LINOGE.

LINOGE walks ahead, cuffed hands at his waist. MIKE is alert for anything . . . or so he no doubt hopes.

> MIKE
> Not one wrong move, Mr. Linoge. You mind me, now.

127 INTERIOR: THE MARKET, FEATURES HATCH.

He lowers the shotgun to port arms, one hand on the barrel and the other wrapped around the trigger. LINOGE, coated with snow, eyebrows crusted white, comes in. MIKE follows closely, the gun now raised and pointed at LINOGE'S back.

> MIKE
> Right down Aisle 2. Nowhere else.

But MARTHA'S killer stops for a moment and surveys the clusters of frightened islanders. Here is an enormously important moment. LINOGE is like a tiger that has been let out of its cage. The trainer is there (two of them, counting HATCH), but when it comes to tigers only bars—lots of them, strong and thick—are safe. And LINOGE doesn't look like a prisoner, or act like one. He stares at the residents of Little Tall with shining eyes. The residents look back at him with fear and fascination.

> MIKE
> (prods him with the gun)
> Come on. Let's go.

LINOGE starts, then stops. He looks at PETER.

> LINOGE
> Peter Godsoe! My favorite seafood wholesaler standing shoulder to shoulder with my favorite politician!

PETER flinches at being addressed by name.

> MIKE
> (prodding with the gun)
> Come on. *Andale.* Let's just—

> LINOGE
> (ignores him)
> How's the fish business? Not so good, is it? Lucky you've got the marijuana business to fall back on. How many bales have you got in the back of the warehouse right now? Ten? Twenty? Forty?

PETER GODSOE reacts violently. The shot has gone home. ROBBIE BEALS moves away from his friend, as if afraid of catching a flu germ. And for a moment, MIKE is too shocked to shut LINOGE up.

> LINOGE
> Better make sure you've got it wrapped up good, Pete—there's gonna be a hell of a storm surge tonight when the tide comes high.

MIKE reaches out and shoves LINOGE'S shoulder, good and hard. LINOGE stumbles forward, but keeps his balance easily. This time it is CAT WITHERS that his bright eye fixes upon.

> LINOGE
> (as if greeting an old friend)
> Cat *Withers!*

She flinches as if struck. MOLLY puts an arm around her and looks at LINOGE with fear and mistrust.

> LINOGE
> You're looking well . . . but why not? It's just an in-office procedure these days, nothing to it.

> CAT
> (real agony)
> Mike, make him stop!

MIKE pushes LINOGE again, but this time LINOGE won't budge; he's as firm as . . . well, as firm as that troublesome stuck door out back.

> LINOGE
> Went up to Derry to have it taken care of, didn't you? Don't suppose you've told your folks about it yet? . . . or Billy? No? My advice would be to go ahead. What's a little scrape among friends these days?

CAT puts her hands to her face and begins to CRY. Any number of townspeople are looking at her with shock, wonder, and horror. One looks absolutely stunned. BILLY SOAMES, about twenty-three, is wearing a red apron. He's BETTY SOAMES'S son, also the market's produce man and janitor. He's CAT'S steady guy, and this is the first he knows of how CAT got rid of their child.

MIKE places the barrel of his gun against the back of LINOGE'S head and thumbs back the hammer.

> MIKE
>
> Move, or I'll move you.

LINOGE starts up the center aisle. He's not afraid of the gun to his head; he's simply finished with this bit of business.

128    INTERIOR: BY THE CHECKOUT, WITH MOLLY AND CAT.

CAT is SOBBING HYSTERICALLY, and MOLLY has her arms around her. TESS MARCHANT is dividing her attention between the sobbing girl and the incredulous BILLY SOAMES. All at once, MOLLY wakes up to a very important consideration.

> MOLLY
>
> Where's Ralphie?

129    INTERIOR: AISLE 2, WITH LINOGE AND MIKE, HATCH IN BACK-GROUND.

As they approach the end of the aisle, RALPHIE comes tearing around it from the other side with a box of the sweet cereal in his hands.

> RALPHIE
>
> Mom! Mommy! Can I have this one?

With absolutely no hesitation at all, LINOGE bends, picks RALPHIE up by the shoulders, and swings him around. All at once, MIKE'S son is between LINOGE and MIKE'S gun. The kid's a hostage. MIKE reacts first with shock and then with sickening, agonized fear.

> MIKE
>
> Put him down! Or—

> LINOGE
> (smiling; almost laughing)
>
> Or what?

130   INTERIOR: BY THE COUNTER, WITH MOLLY.

She loses all interest in CAT and hurries toward the head of Aisle 2 so she can see what's happening. One of the ISLAND RESIDENTS, KIRK FREEMAN, tries to stop her.

MOLLY

Let me go, Kirk!

She gives a good, hard yank, and he does. When she sees that LINOGE has her son, she GASPS LOUDLY and her hands go to her mouth.

MIKE gestures her to stay where she is without ever taking his eyes from LINOGE. Behind MOLLY, the MARKET CUSTOMERS begin to gather, staring tensely at the confrontation.

131   INTERIOR: AISLE 2, WITH LINOGE AND RALPHIE, CLOSE-UP.

LINOGE puts his forehead to RALPHIE'S, so the two of them can look intimately into each other's eyes. RALPHIE is too young to be scared. He looks into that shining, smiling, interested tiger's gaze with a kind of breathless interest.

LINOGE

I know you.

> RALPHIE

You do?


> LINOGE

You're Ralph Emerick Anderson. And I know something else.

RALPHIE is fascinated, unaware of HATCH RACKING A SHELL into the shotgun, unaware that the market has turned into a powder keg of which he is the fuse. He is fascinated, almost hypnotized, by LINOGE.

> RALPHIE

What?

LINOGE plants a quick, light kiss on the bridge of RALPHIE'S nose.

> LINOGE

You have a fairy saddle!

> RALPHIE
> (smiling, delighted)

That's what my daddy calls it!

> LINOGE
> (returns the smile)

You bet! And speaking of Daddy—

He sets RALPHIE down, but for a moment he's leaning so close that RALPHIE is still, in effect, his hostage. RALPHIE sees the handcuffs.

> RALPHIE

Why're you wearing those?

> LINOGE

Because I choose to. Go on. See your dad.

He turns RALPHIE around and gives him a light swat on the butt. RALPHIE sees his father and lights up in a smile. Before he can take more than a step or two, MIKE grabs him and pulls the boy into his arms. RALPHIE sees the pistol.

> RALPHIE

Daddy, why have you got—

MOLLY

*Ralphie!*

She sprints for him, brushing past HATCH and knocking a bunch of canned goods to the floor. The cans roll everywhere. She pulls RALPHIE out of MIKE'S arms and hugs him frantically. MIKE, flustered and rocky (who wouldn't be?), returns his focus to the faintly smiling LINOGE, who has now had about nine billion chances to get away.

RALPHIE

Why's Daddy pointing a gun at that man?

MIKE

Moll, get him out of here.

MOLLY

What are you—

MIKE

*Get him out of here!*

She FLINCHES at the unaccustomed shout and begins to retreat with RALPHIE in her arms, toward the other people clustering timidly at the foot of the aisle. She steps on a can and it rolls out from under her. Before she can fall, KIRK FREEMAN catches and steadies her. RALPHIE, looking over her shoulder at his daddy, is finally upset.

RALPHIE

Don't shoot him, Daddy, he knows about the fairy saddle.

MIKE
(more to LINOGE than RALPHIE)
I'm not going to shoot him. Not if he goes where he's supposed to.

He looks toward the end of the aisle. LINOGE smiles and nods, as if to say, "Of course, since you insist," and starts that way, hands in front of him again. HATCH catches up to MIKE.

HATCH

What are we going to—?

MIKE
Lock him up! What else?

He's terrified, ashamed, relieved . . . you name it, MIKE is feeling it. HATCH sees enough of MIKE'S emotions to be abashed and retires a bit into the background as MIKE shadows LINOGE to the upper end of the aisle.

132   INTERIOR: ANGLE ON MEAT COUNTER AND CONSTABLE'S OFFICE DOOR.

As LINOGE and MIKE get to the head of the aisle, LINOGE turns left, toward the constable's office, as if he knows where it is. HATCH follows after. And then, from Aisle 1, comes BILLY SOAMES. He's too angry to be scared, and before MIKE can stop him, he grabs LINOGE and THROWS HIM against the meat counter.

BILLY SOAMES
What do you know about Katrina? And how do you know it?

MIKE has had enough. He grabs BILLY by the back of his shirt and HEAVES HIM against a rack of powdered herbs and fish fixin's. BILLY hits it hard and goes spawling.

MIKE
What are you, crazy? This guy's a killer! Stay out of his way! And stay out of mine, Billy Soames!

LINOGE
Also, clean yourself up.

We glimpse that STRANGE, BLACKISH WAVERING in his eyes again.

133   INTERIOR: BILLY, CLOSE-UP.

At first he sits there where he landed, looking question marks at LINOGE. Then his nose GUSHES BLOOD. He feels it, reaches up to catch the flow, and looks unbelievingly at the blood on his palms.

CAT runs up Aisle 1 to where he is and kneels beside him. She wants to help him; she wants to do anything, really, that will take away the awful look of surprise and hurt anger on his face. But BILLY is having none of it. He shoves her back.

#### BILLY SOAMES
Leave me alone!

He lurches to his feet.

134   INTERIOR: BY THE MEAT COUNTER, WIDER.

#### LINOGE
Before he gets too self-righteous, Katrina, ask him how well he knows Jenna Freeman.

BILLY flinches, stunned.

135   INTERIOR: KIRK FREEMAN, IN AISLE 2.

#### KIRK FREEMAN
What do you know about my sister?

136   INTERIOR: RESUME MEAT COUNTER.

#### LINOGE
That horses aren't all she enjoys riding when the weather's hot. Right, Billy?

CAT looks at BILLY, stricken. He wipes at his BLEEDING NOSE with the back of his hand and looks anywhere but at her. His self-righteous, wounded anger has dissolved into a kind of slinking furtiveness. His face says, "lemme outta here." MIKE still looks like he can't believe how screwed up this whole thing has gotten.

#### MIKE
Move away from this man, Cat. You too, Billy.

She doesn't move. Perhaps doesn't hear. There are tears on her cheeks. HATCH uses one hand to push her gently away from the door marked CONSTABLE'S OFFICE. He inadvertently pushes her in BILLY'S direction, and they both shrink back.

#### HATCH
(kindly)
Got to get out of his grabbin' range, darlin'.

This time she goes blundering past BILLY (who makes no move to stop her) toward the front of the store. MIKE, meanwhile, steps forward

and picks a package of plastic bags—the kind you use to save
leftovers—off a display. Then he puts the muzzle of his gun between
LINOGE'S shoulder blades.

                          MIKE
Come on. Move.

137   INTERIOR: THE CONSTABLE'S OFFICE.

The WIND is VERY LOUD, SCARY—shrieking like a train whistle. We
can hear SHINGLES CLAPPING and BOARDS CREAKING.

The door opens. LINOGE comes in, followed by MIKE and HATCH.
LINOGE moves toward the cell, then stops as a PARTICULARLY
HARD GUST OF WIND strikes the building and makes it shudder.
Snow puffs in under the loading dock door.

                          HATCH
I don't like the sound of that.

                          MIKE
Move, Mr. Linoge.

As they pass the desk, MIKE puts down the box of plastic bags and
picks up a large combination padlock. From his pocket he takes his key
ring, looking ruefully at the busted-off loading door key for a second.
He hands the keys and the combination lock to HATCH. He also swaps
weapons, giving HATCH his pistol and taking the shotgun. As they
reach the cell:

                          MIKE
Put your hands up and grab a couple of bars.
              (LINOGE does)
Now spread your legs.
              (LINOGE does)
Wider.
              (LINOGE does)
I'm going to pat you down, and if you move, my good friend
Alton Hatcher is going to save us all a lot of wear and tear.

HATCH gulps, but points the pistol. MIKE sets the shotgun aside.

> MIKE

Don't even twitch, Mr. Linoge. You had your filthy hands on my son, so don't you so much as *twitch*.

MIKE reaches into the pockets of LINOGE'S pea coat and brings out the YELLOW GLOVES. They are BLOTCHED AND STAINED with MARTHA'S blood. MIKE grimaces with distaste and tosses them onto the desk. He rummages in the jacket pockets some more and finds nothing. He reaches into the front pockets of LINOGE'S jeans and pulls them inside out. They're empty. Checks the back pockets. Nothing but a few lint balls. He takes off LINOGE'S watch cap and looks inside it. Nothing. He tosses it on the desk with the gloves.

> MIKE

Where's your wallet?
>> (nothing from LINOGE)

Where's your wallet, huh?

MIKE slaps LINOGE twice on the shoulder, first time sorta friendly, second time sorta hard. Still no response.

> MIKE

Huh?

> HATCH
> (uneasy)

Mike, take it easy.

> MIKE

Guy had his hands on my son, had his face right down in my son's face; guy kissed my son's *nose*—don't tell me to take it easy. Where's your wallet, sir?

MIKE shoves LINOGE, hard. LINOGE crashes into the bars of the cell, but keeps his high grip on the home-welded bars and his legs spread.

> MIKE

Where's your wallet? Where's your bank card? Where's your blood-donor card? Where's your discount card from Valu-Mart? What sewer did you crawl through to get here? Huh? Answer me!

All his frustration, anger, fear, and humiliation are on the verge of coming out. He grabs LINOGE by the hair and SLAMS HIS FACE INTO THE BARS.

> MIKE
>
> Where's your wallet?

> HATCH
>
> Mike—

MIKE SLAMS LINOGE'S FACE INTO THE BARS AGAIN. He'd do it again, too, but HATCH reaches out and grabs his arm.

> HATCH
>
> *Mike, stop it!*

MIKE stops, takes a deep breath, and somehow gets hold of himself. Outside the WIND GUSTS, and we hear the FAINT SOUND OF CRASHING WAVES.

> MIKE
> (he's breathing hard)
>
> Take off your boots.

> LINOGE
>
> I'll have to let go of the bars to do that. They lace up.

MIKE kneels. He grabs the shotgun. He props the stock against the floor and plants the barrels dead center in the seat of LINOGE'S jeans.

> MIKE
>
> If you move, sir, you'll never have to worry about constipation again.

HATCH looks more and more scared. This is a side of MIKE he's never seen (and could have done without). MIKE, meanwhile, unties LINOGE'S boots and loosens the laces. Then he stands up, takes the shotgun, and stands back.

> MIKE
>
> Kick them off.

LINOGE kicks them off. MIKE nods to HATCH, who bends down (keeping a skittery eye on LINOGE as he does) and picks them up. HATCH feels inside them, then shakes them.

> HATCH
>
> Nothing.

> MIKE
>
> Toss them over by the desk.

HATCH does.

> MIKE
>
> Step into the cell, Mr. Linoge. Move slowly and keep your hands where I can see them.

LINOGE opens the door of the cell and swings it back and forth a time or two before going in. The door SQUEAKS, and doesn't hang quite true when it's all the way open. LINOGE touches a couple of the home welds with the ball of one finger, and smiles.

> MIKE
>
> You think it won't hold you? It'll hold you.

Yet MIKE doesn't look entirely sure, and HATCH looks even more doubtful. LINOGE steps in, crosses the cell, and sits down facing the door. He draws his legs up so that the heels of his stocking feet (white athletic socks) are on the edge of the cot and he is looking at us from between his bent knees. We will see him in this same posture for some little time, now. His hands dangle limply. He wears a trace of a smile. If we saw a guy looking at us this way, we'd probably run. It's that caged-tiger look—very still and watchful, but full of pent-up violence.

MIKE closes the cell door, and HATCH uses a key from the ring to lock it. With that done, he shakes the door. It's locked, but he and MIKE share an unhappy glance, just the same. That door is as rattly the last tooth in an old man's jaw. The cell is for the likes of SONNY BRAUTIGAN, who has a nasty habit of getting drunk and breaking the windows in his ex-wife's house with stones . . . not for a stranger with no ID who beat an old widow to death.

MIKE crosses to the loading dock door, looks at the dead bolt, then tries the knob. The door opens easily, letting in a FRIGID GASP OF WIND and a SWIRL OF SNOW. HATCH'S mouth drops open.

> HATCH
> Mike, I swear it wouldn't budge.

MIKE closes the door. As he finishes doing that, ROBBIE BEALS comes in. He crosses to the desk and reaches for one of the gloves.

> MIKE
> Don't touch that!

> ROBBIE
> (draws his hand back)
> Does he have any ID on him?

> MIKE
> I want you out of here.

ROBBIE picks up the joke sign and shakes it at MIKE.

> ROBBIE
> I want to tell you something, Anderson: your sense of humor
> is entirely—

HATCH, who actually put that sign around the dummy's neck, looks embarrassed. Neither of the other men notice. MIKE snatches the damned thing out of ROBBIE'S hand and dumps it in the wastebasket.

> MIKE
> I don't have the time or the patience for this. Get out or I'll
> throw you out.

ROBBIE looks at him and sees that MIKE absolutely means it. ROBBIE backs toward the door.

> ROBBIE
> Come town meeting, there's maybe going to be a change in
> law enforcement on Little Tall.

MIKE

Town meeting's in March. This is February. Now get the hell
out.

ROBBIE leaves. MIKE and HATCH hold their positions for a moment,
and then MIKE lets out his breath in a long WHOOSH. HATCH looks
relieved.

MIKE

I think I handled that pretty well, don't you?

HATCH

Like a diplomat.

MIKE takes another long, steadying breath. He opens the sandwich
bags. As he and HATCH finish talking, he puts the bloody gloves in two
bags, and the cap in a third.

MIKE

I have to go out and—

HATCH

You're going to leave me alone with him?

MIKE

Try to raise the state police barracks in Machias. And stay
away from him.

HATCH

I should say you can count on that.

138    INTERIOR: THE REAR OF THE MARKET, BY THE MEAT COUNTER.

Perhaps two dozen TOWNSFOLK have clogged the aisles, looking
hopefully and fearfully toward the constable's office door. To one side,
glowering like a banked furnace, is ROBBIE. ROBBIE has now been
joined by the other two members of his family . . . wife SANDRA and
the charming DON, from day care. In the forefront of the TOWNS-
FOLK is MOLLY, with RALPHIE in her arms. When the door opens
and she sees MIKE, she hurries forward. MIKE puts a reassuring arm
around her.

RALPHIE
You didn't hurt him, Daddy, did you?

MIKE
No, honey, just put him safe.

RALPHIE
In the jail? Did you put him in the jail? What did he do?

MIKE
Not now, Ralph.

He kisses the fairy saddle on RALPHIE'S nose and turns to the gathered people.

MIKE
Peter! Peter Godsoe!

People look around, MURMURING. After a moment or two, PETER GODSOE shoulders forward, looking embarrassed and blustery (also a little frightened).

PETER GODSOE
Mike, about what that fellow said—that's the biggest crock of—

MIKE
Uh-huh. Go on back there with Hatch. We're gonna watch this guy, and it's gonna be by the buddy system.

PETER GODSOE
(immensely relieved)
Okay. You bet.

He goes through the door to the constable's office. MIKE, his arm still around MOLLY, faces his neighbors.

MIKE
I feel like I have to have to close the store, folks.
(murmurs of reaction)
You're welcome to take what you've got; I trust you to settle up when the storm's over. Right now, I've got a prisoner to deal with.

A worried-looking middle-aged woman, DELLA BISSONETTE, pushes forward.

DELLA

Did that man really kill poor old Martha?

More murmurs this time—FRIGHTENED, UNBELIEVING. MOLLY is looking at her husband tensely. She also looks as if she wishes she could strike RALPHIE temporarily deaf.

MIKE

In time you'll have the whole story, but not now. Please, Della—all of you—help me do my job. Grab your stuff and go home before the storm gets any worse. I want a few of you men to stick around a minute or two longer. Kirk Freeman . . . Jack Carver . . . Sonny Brautigan . . . Billy Soames . . . Johnny Harriman . . . Robbie . . . that'll do for a start.

The men move forward as the others turn and start to go. ROBBIE looks typically puffed up with self-importance. BILLY has a wad of paper towels pressed to his nose.

139    INTERIOR: THE CONSTABLE'S OFFICE.

HATCH is at the desk, trying to use the radio. PETER looks at the cell, with nervous fascination. LINOGE, sitting on the bunk, looks back from between his spread knees and cocked feet.

HATCH

Machias, this is Alton Hatcher on Little Tall. We have a police emergency here. Do you read, Machias? Come on back, if you read.

Lets go of the button. There's nothing but STATIC.

HATCH

Machias, this is Alton Hatcher on channel 19. If you read—

PETER GODSOE

They don't. You've lost your good antenna off your roof.

HATCH sighs. He knows it, too. He turns down the SOUND, muting the STATIC.

### PETER GODSOE
Try the phone.

HATCH gives him a startled look, then picks up the phone. He listens, pushes a few buttons at random, then hangs up.

### PETER GODSOE
No, huh? Well, it was a long shot.

PETER looks back toward LINOGE, who is staring at him. HATCH, meanwhile, is looking at PETER with some fascination.

### HATCH
You don't really have a load of Panama Red out there behind your lobster traps, do you?

PETER looks at him . . . and says nothing.

140   INTERIOR: THE REAR OF THE MARKET, FEATURING MOLLY, RALPHIE, MIKE.

The townspeople are on the move (except for the little group of men MIKE has singled out), draining toward the front of the market and the outside world. There's a STEADY JINGLING from the bell over the door as folks leave.

### MOLLY
You going to be all right?

### MIKE
Coss.

### MOLLY
When will you be home?

### MIKE
When I can. Take the truck—you won't get three hundred yards in the car. I've never seen it come down s'hard 'n' fast.

I'll use the Island Services truck, or get someone to drop me off when this is squared away. I have to go back to Martha's house long enough to secure it.

There are a thousand questions she'd like to ask, but really can't. Little pitchers have big ears. She kisses him on the corner of the mouth and turns to go.

141   INTERIOR: BY THE CASH REGISTER, WITH CAT AND TESS MARCHANT.

CAT is still SOBBING. TESS holds her and rocks her, but we can see she (TESS) is pretty blown away by what LINOGE said. MOLLY gives TESS a questioning look as she carries RALPHIE toward the door. TESS nods, as if to say she's go it under control. MOLLY nods back and goes on out.

142   EXTERIOR: IN FRONT OF THE MARKET.

MOLLY carries RALPHIE carefully down the steps in what has become a BLINDING SNOWSTORM. She walks toward THE CAMERA, having to brace against the wind with every step . . . and this baby is just getting warmed up.

> RALPHIE
> (shouting to be heard)
> The island won't blow away, will it?

> MOLLY
> No, honey, of course not.

But MOLLY doesn't look so sure.

143   EXTERIOR: THE CENTER OF TOWN, HIGH ANGLE.

The snow is coming down furiously. There are a few vehicles moving on Main and Atlantic, but they won't be moving much longer. Little Tall Island is effectively cut off from the outside world. The WIND SHRIEKS; the SNOW SHEETS; and we:

FADE TO BLACK. THIS ENDS ACT 5.

# Act 6

144  EXTERIOR: THE TOWN, A HIGH ANGLE—LATE AFTERNOON.

This is the same shot we went out on, but it's later, now—there isn't much daylight left. The WIND SHRIEKS.

145  EXTERIOR: THE WOODED AREA SOUTH OF TOWN—LATE AFTERNOON.

We're looking down at the SURGING OCEAN through a power-line cut. There's a CRACKING SOUND and a HUGE OLD PINE topples on the lines. They go down in a SHOWER OF SPARKS.

146  EXTERIOR: MAIN STREET—LATE AFTERNOON.

In a reprise of the first scene, all the lights, including the blinker at the intersection, GO OUT.

147  INTERIOR: THE CONSTABLE'S OFFICE, WITH HATCH AND PETER.

The LIGHTS GO OUT.

                    HATCH
     Aw, damn!

PETER makes no response. He's looking at:

148  INTERIOR: THE JAIL CELL, FROM PETER'S POINT OF VIEW.

LINOGE is just a dark hump . . . except for his eyes. They GLOW with a TROUBLED RED LIGHT . . . like wolf's eyes.

149  INTERIOR: RESUME HATCH AND PETER.

HATCH is rummaging in the desk drawer. As he pulls out a flashlight, PETER seizes his arm.

                    PETER GODSOE
     Look at him!

HATCH, startled, wheels to look at LINOGE. The prisoner is still sitting just as before, but there's no WEIRD LIGHT shining out of his eyes. HATCH turns on the flashlight and hits LINOGE in the face with the beam. LINOGE looks back calmly.

>                     HATCH
>                    (to PETER)
> What?

>                  PETER GODSOE
> I . . . nothing.

He looks back toward LINOGE, perplexed and a little afraid.

>                     HATCH
> Maybe you've been smokin' too much of what you're selling.

>                  PETER GODSOE
>              (mixed shame and anger)
> Shut up, Hatch. Don't talk about what you don't understand.

150    INTERIOR: THE MARKET'S COUNTER, WITH MIKE AND TESS MAR-
CHANT.

Looks like they're the only two left, now, and with the lights out, the market is very dim—the front windows are big, but the light coming through them has started to fail. MIKE comes behind the counter and opens a UTILITY BOX built into the wall. Inside are circuit breakers and one larger switch. He flicks this one.

151    EXTERIOR: BEHIND THE MARKET—LATE DAY.

There's a little shed marked GENERATOR to the left of the loading dock. An ENGINE STARTS UP inside it, and blue smoke, immediately ripped away by the WIND, starts to chug from the exhaust stack.

152    INTERIOR: THE CONSTABLE'S OFFICE.

The lights come back on. HATCH SIGHS WITH RELIEF.

>                     HATCH
> Hey . . . Pete.

He wants to apologize, and he wants PETER to help him with it a little, but PETER'S not in the mood. He walks away and looks at the bulletin board on the wall.

> HATCH
>
> I was out of line.

> PETER
>
> Yeah, way out.

PETER turns and gives LINOGE a look. LINOGE looks back at him, SMILING FAINTLY.

> PETER
>
> What are *you* looking at?

LINOGE doesn't reply, just goes on looking at PETER with that FAINT SMILE. PETER turns back to the bulletin board, troubled. HATCH looks at PETER, wishing he could take back his smart-ass comment.

153    EXTERIOR: THE STORE'S PORCH, WITH MIKE AND TESS.

TESS is wearing a parka, gloves, and a pair of high gum-rubber boots. Still, the WIND rocks her on her feet, and MIKE has to steady her before going to the display window on one side of the door. Here, on either side of the window at the bottom, there are crank handles. MIKE grabs one, and TESS makes her way to the other. They crank as they talk (SHOUTING to be heard over the wind) and lower the slatted wooden STORM SHUTTER over the glass.

> MIKE
>
> Will you be all right? Because I can give you a lift—

> TESS
>
> It's the wrong direction! And I'm only six houses down . . . as you well know. Don't baby me!

He nods and gives her a smile. They move to the window on the other side of the door and lower the other storm shutter.

> TESS

Mike? Do you have any idea why he came here, or why he'd want to kill Martha?

> MIKE

No. Go on home, Tess. Make yourself a fire. I'll lock up.

They finish with the shutter and move to the steps. TESS winces and tightens her hood as another gust slams into them.

> TESS

You mind him careful. We don't want him out and prowling around with this—
> (lifts her chin into the blizzard)
—going on.

> MIKE

Don't worry.

She looks at him a moment longer and is reasonably comforted by what she sees. She nods and clumps down the snow-laden steps, holding tight to the railing as she goes. With her back to him, MIKE allows his face to show how worried he really is. Then he heads back inside and shuts the door. He turns the OPEN sign to CLOSED and pulls down the shade.

154    INTERIOR: THE CONSTABLE'S OFFICE.

MIKE comes in, still stamping the snow off his boots, and looks around. HATCH has found a second flashlight and has set out some candles, as well. PETER is still studying the litter of notices on the bulletin board. MIKE goes over to the bulletin board, taking a paper from his back pocket.

> MIKE

Everything okay back here?

> HATCH

Reasonably okay, but I can't raise the state police in Machias. I can't raise anybody.

MIKE

Doesn't really surprise me.

He thumbtacks the scribbled duty roster to the bulletin board, where PETER immediately begins studying it. MIKE walks over to the desk and opens a bottom drawer.

MIKE
(to HATCH)

You and Peter until eight, Kirk Freeman and Jack Carver from eight till midnight, Robbie Beals and Sonny Brautigan from midnight until four, Billy Soames and Johnny Harriman from four until eight tomorrow morning. After that, we'll figure some more.

MIKE finds a small attaché case and a Polaroid camera. He takes them, shuts the drawer, and looks at the two men for comments. He gets only an awkward silence.

MIKE

You guys all right with this?

HATCH
(too hearty)

Fine.

PETER

Yeah, fine.

MIKE looks at them more closely and gets an idea of which way the wind is blowing. He opens the case—we catch a glimpse of various items that might come in handy if you're a small-town police officer (big flashlight, bandages, first aid kit, etc.). He puts the Polaroid inside.

MIKE

Stay alert. Both of you. Understand?

No reply. HATCH is embarrassed, PETER is sulky. MIKE looks back at LINOGE, who looks at him with that faint smile.

MIKE

Later on we're going to have that talk you wanted, sir.

He closes the case and starts for the door. A HUGE GUST OF WIND hits the building, making it CREAK. Out back, something falls over with a CRASH. HATCH winces.

> HATCH
> What do we do with him if Robbie and Ursula decide to blow the town whistle and bring everybody in? We can't very well sit him in a corner of the town hall basement with a blanket and a cup of chowder.

> MIKE
> I don't know. Stay right here with him, I guess.

> PETER
> And blow away if he blows away?

> MIKE
> You want to go home, Pete?

> PETER
> No.

MIKE nods and leaves.

155   EXTERIOR: MARTHA CLARENDON'S HOUSE—DUSK.

The Island Services vehicle comes out of the growing gloom, crunching through drifts and driving over fallen limbs in the street. It stops by MARTHA'S gate. MIKE gets out, carrying the little case, and goes up the walk. The storm is worse than ever; the GUSTS OF WIND push MIKE around. He struggles up the snow-laden porch steps.

156   EXTERIOR: THE PORCH, WITH MIKE—DUSK.

He opens his case, takes out the flashlight and the cased Polaroid. He hangs the camera around his neck on its strap. The WIND MOANS. Branches CLACK against the porch. MIKE looks around, a little nervous, then returns his attention to the case. He takes out a roll of white adhesive tape and a Sharpie-type pen. Holding the flashlight (now turned on) between his chest and his arm, MIKE tears off a strip of the tape and puts it on MARTHA'S door. He uncaps the pen, thinks, then prints: "CRIME SCENE DO NOT ENTER MICHAEL ANDERSON

CONSTABLE." Then he puts the roll of tape on his arm like a bracelet and opens the door.

He picks up MARTHA'S walker, holding the grips in his gloved hands, and sets it in the hall. Then he closes his case, picks it up, and steps inside himself.

157   INTERIOR: THE HALLWAY—DARK.

MIKE puts his flashlight, turned on, in his coat pocket. The beam SHINES UPWARD at the ceiling. MIKE himself is little more than a MOVING SHAPE in the dark as he readies the Polaroid and raises it to his face.

FLASH! and we see:

158   INTERIOR: MARTHA CLARENDON.

Her battered, bloody face. Just for a moment. Then it FADES. This picture and those that follow have the stark quality of crime-scene photos . . . of evidence . . . which is just what they will be in a court-room someday. Or so MIKE hopes.

159   INTERIOR: THE HALLWAY—DARK.

MIKE turns, putting the first photo in his coat pocket, then triggers the Polaroid again.

FLASH! and we see:

160    INTERIOR: PICTURES ON THE HALLWAY WALL.

Boats at sea. The town dock in 1920. Old Fords chugging up Atlantic Street Hill in 1928. Girls having a picnic by the lighthouse. The pictures are stippled with BLOOD. Between them, on the wallpaper, are THICKER SPRAYS OF BLOOD. FADES.

161    INTERIOR: THE HALLWAY—DARK.

The shape that is MIKE ANDERSON bends a little.

FLASH! and we see:

163    INTERIOR: THE HALLWAY—DARK.

MIKE moves up the hall toward the living room.

164    INTERIOR: THE LIVING ROOM—DARK.

It's pretty spooky in here, with the furniture just dim shapes and the WIND HOWLING outside. BRANCHES TAP and TREES GROAN.

MIKE moves forward, the flashlight beam still spraying up from his coat pocket. He inadvertently KICKS SOMETHING. A DARK SHAPE rolls across the floor, hits a leg of MARTHA'S chair, and ricochets out of frame. MIKE follows after, takes the flashlight out of his pocket, and shines it into the lens of THE CAMERA—he's looking at the object he kicked, although we can't see it from where we are. He replaces the flashlight in his pocket, raises the Polaroid, and bends forward.

FLASH! and:

165    INTERIOR: DAVEY'S BASKETBALL.

Splotched and stained with blood. Looks like some weird planet. FADES.

166    INTERIOR: THE LIVING ROOM, WITH MIKE—DARK.

He rips off a piece of the tape, prints "EVIDENCE" on it, and sticks it to the basketball. Then he walks around the chair and aims the Polaroid at the TV.

FLASH! and:

167    INTERIOR: THE TELEVISION.

The picture tube totally smashed. The electronic guts of the thing visible inside the ragged hole. It's like a gouged-out eye. FADES.

168    INTERIOR: THE LIVING ROOM, WITH MIKE—DARK.

He's frowning, puzzled, thinking about the TV. He and Hatch *heard* the damned thing. They really did. He moves carefully toward it, then turns and raises the POLAROID.

FLASH! and:

169    INTERIOR: MARTHA'S CHAIR.

Stark and bloodstained, as creepy as an instrument of torture. The cookie plate and bloodstained teacup are still on the table beside it.

170    INTERIOR: RESUME MIKE.

He wants a second one of this. He raises the Polaroid, then stops. He looks up at:

171    INTERIOR: ABOVE THE DOOR BETWEEN THE LIVING ROOM AND THE HALL.

There's something up there, written on the wallpaper above the arch. We can see it, but it's too dark to read.

172    INTERIOR: RESUME MIKE.

He points the Polaroid up, aims, and—

FLASH!

173    INTERIOR: ABOVE THE DOOR BETWEEN THE LIVING ROOM AND THE HALL.

It's a message printed in MARTHA CLARENDON'S blood: "GIVE ME WHAT I WANT AND I'LL GO AWAY." Above it is a drawing—

We may or may not recognize it. FADES.

174   INTERIOR: RESUME MIKE.

He's shaken, and badly. Still, he's determined to do his job. He raises the Polaroid for that second shot of the chair.

FLASH!

175   INTERIOR: MARTHA'S CHAIR.

This time LINOGE'S cane lies across the arms of the chair, the bloodstained wolf's head snarling into the flash. If we didn't understand the significance of the drawing on the wall, we do now.

176   INTERIOR: RESUME MIKE.

The camera drops out of his hands; if not for the strap, it would fall to the floor. He is understandably freaked. The cane wasn't there before. The WIND GUSTS—the strongest one yet. Behind MIKE, the window facing the street EXPLODES INWARD. SNOW SWIRLS into the room, twisting in ghostly cyclones. The sheers billow like ghostly arms.

MIKE is startled (hopefully we will be, too) but recovers quickly. He pulls the drapes across the broken window. They BILLOW OUT, but he quickly moves a table into place to anchor them. Then he turns back to MARTHA'S chair . . . and that unexpected cane. He bends over it, then raises the Polaroid.

FLASH! and:

177   INTERIOR: THE WOLF'S HEAD CANE, CLOSE-UP.

It stares at us with its bloody teeth and eyes like a ghost wolf in a stroke of lightning, then FADES.

178   INTERIOR: RESUME MIKE.

He remains where he is for a moment, trying to get himself back together. Then he pockets the last picture, tears off another strip of white tape, and tags the cane. On it he prints "EVIDENCE" and "POSS. MURDER WEAPON."

179   INTERIOR: MARTHA'S DINING ROOM—DARK.

MIKE comes in, removes the pine-cone-and-candle centerpiece from the table, then removes the white linen tablecloth.

180   INTERIOR: THE HALL, WITH MIKE.

He comes out of the dining room and approaches the shape of MARTHA'S body. As he does, he notices something on the wall by the door. He trains the beam of his flashlight on it. It is a key rack, in the shape of a key. MIKE runs the light along it, and finds the set of keys he's looking for. He takes them off their peg.

181   INTERIOR: THE KEYS ON MIKE'S PALM, INSERT.

The tag on one reads "FRONT DOOR" in MARTHA'S spidery old-lady's writing.

182   INTERIOR: RESUME HALL, WITH MIKE.

He pockets the keys and sets his case and camera aside on the stairs for the moment.

                              MIKE
        I'm so sorry, old girl.

He billows the tablecloth over MARTHA, then takes up his gear again. He opens the door to the porch just enough to slip through and goes out into the SHRIEKING STORM. Night has fallen.

183   EXTERIOR: ON THE PORCH, WITH MIKE—NIGHT

He uses MARTHA'S key to lock the door. Tries it to make sure it's locked. Then he goes down the steps and begins floundering back down the walk to the Island Services vehicle.

184   EXTERIOR: A HOUSE ON UPPER MAIN STREET—NIGHT.

We can barely see it through the sheeting snow.

185   INTERIOR: THE CARVER KITCHEN, WITH JACK, ANGELA, AND BUSTER.

No generator here. The kitchen is lit with two Coleman gas lanterns, and there are big shadows in all the corners. The little family is eating cold cuts and drinking soda. Each time the wind GUSTS and the house CREAKS, ANGELA looks around nervously. JACK is a lobsterman and less worried about weather (what's to worry about when you're on dry-back land, for gorry's sake?). He's playing airplane with BUSTER. The plane is a bologna sandwich; BUSTER'S open mouth is the hangar. JACK keeps approaching (making the appropriate airplane noises as he does), then pulling away. BUSTER is laughing heartily. Daddy is *such* a comedian.

There's a RENDING, SPLINTERING CRASH from outside. ANGELA grabs JACK'S arm.

                    ANGELA
    What was that?


                    JACK CARVER
    Tree. Robichaux's backyard, from the sound. Hope it didn't
    hit their porch.

He starts playing airplane again, this time landing the sandwich in BUSTER'S mouth. BUSTER chomps off a bite and chews with gusto.

                    ANGELA
    Jack, do you *have* to go back to the store?

                    JACK
    Ayuh.

                    BUSTER
    Daddy's gonna guard the bad guy! Make sure he doesn't get
    away. In a PLAYYNE!

                    JACK
    That's right, big guy.

JACK dive-bombs another bite into BUSTER'S mouth and ruffles his hair, then looks seriously at ANGELA.

                    JACK
    This is a bad situation, honey. Everybody's got to do his part.
    Besides, I'll be with Kirk. It's the buddy system.

                              BUSTER
Don Beals is *my* buddy! He knows how to be a monkey!

                               JACK
Ayuh. Trick he learned from his dad, most likely.

ANGIE laughs and covers her mouth. JACK smiles at her. BUSTER
starts making monkey sounds and scratching at his pits. Typical five-
year-old dinner behavior. The parents treat him with absentminded
love.

                               JACK
If you hear the whistle, take Buster and go. Hell, go before
then, if you get nervous—bundle up and take the snowmobile.

                             ANGELA
Are you sure?

                               JACK
Ayuh. Fact is, the earlier you go, the better bed you and
Buster are apt to have. People headed that way already. I
seen the lights.
              (lifts his chin toward the window)
You be here or there when my watch is over—don't matter.
I'll find you.

He smiles at her. She smiles back, reassured. The WIND SCREAMS.
They listen, smiles fading. FAINT, we hear the SOUND OF POUNDING
WAVES.

                               JACK
Town hall basement's probably gonna be the safest place on
the island for the next forty-eight hours. There's going to be
one helluva storm surge tonight, tell you that.

                             ANGELA
Why did that man have to come today, of all days?

                              BUSTER
What did the bad man do, Mommy?

Here we are again—little pitchers and their big ears. ANGELA leans over and kisses him.

                              ANGELA
Stole the moon and brought the wind. How about another sandwich, big boy?

                              BUSTER
Yeah! And Daddy can fly it!

186    EXTERIOR: GODSOE FISH & LOBSTER—DARK.

The waves are crashing higher than ever.

187    EXTERIOR: THE LIGHTHOUSE—DARK.

Now just a vague shape in the storm, illuminating a WILDERNESS OF SNOW each time the light comes around.

188    EXTERIOR: MAIN AND ATLANTIC INTERSECTION—DARK.

The WIND tears the darkened blinker loose, and it goes flying to the end of its cord, like a yo-yo to the end of its string, before finally thumping down into the snowy street.

189    INTERIOR: THE CONSTABLE'S OFFICE JAIL CELL, WITH LINOGE—DARK.

LINOGE is sitting as before, with his feet up and his hungry face framed by his slightly spread knees. He's intent, focused, still wearing the shadow of a smile.

190    INTERIOR: ANGLE ON THE CONSTABLE'S OFFICE, WITH HATCH AND PETER.

HATCH has got a PowerBook open; its glow shines on his rapt face. He's running a crossword puzzle program and is deep into it. He doesn't notice PETER, who is sitting below the bulletin board and staring back at LINOGE, slack-faced and wide-eyed. PETER is hypnotized.

191    INTERIOR: LINOGE, CLOSE-UP.

His smile widens. His EYES DARKEN TO BLACK, and that red starts to roll into them again.

192    INTERIOR: RESUME HATCH AND PETER.

Without removing his gaze from LINOGE'S, PETER reaches behind him and pulls an old Department of Fisheries red-tide notice from the board. He turns it over. He has a ballpoint in his flap pocket. He now clicks the tip and puts pen to paper. He never looks down at what he's doing, though; his gaze never leaves LINOGE.

> HATCH
> (not looking up)
> Say, Pete—what do you s'pose this one is? "Yodeler's perch." Three letters.

193    INTERIOR: LINOGE, CLOSE-UP.

Smiling, he mouths a word that looks like a gulp.

194    INTERIOR: RESUME HATCH AND PETER.

> PETER
> Alp.

> HATCH
> Coss it is.
> (types it into the grid)
> This is a great program. I'll let you try later, if you want.

> PETER
> Sure.

He sounds okay, but never takes his eyes from LINOGE. His pen never stops moving, either. Never even slows.

195    INTERIOR: THE BACK OF THE FISHERIES FLYER.

Written there over and over again in jagged capital letters is this: "GIVE ME GIVE ME GIVE ME GIVE ME WHAT I WANT GIVE ME WHAT I WANT GIVE ME WHAT I WANT." Drawn around the words, like bizarre illuminations on a monk's manuscript, is the same shape we saw over MARTHA'S living room door. Canes.

196    INTERIOR: LINOGE, CLOSE-UP.

Grinning. Black, beastlike eyes full of ROILING RED. We can just see the tips of his fanglike teeth.

197   EXTERIOR: THE WOODS ON THE LITTLE TALL HEADLAND—NIGHT.

The WIND SHRIEKS. The trees bend in the BLIZZARD, their branches CLATTERING.

198   EXTERIOR: LITTLE TALL, A HIGH SHOT—NIGHT.

The buildings are already snow-covered; the two streets are snow-choked. There are only a few lights. This is a town cut off from the entire outside world. We HOLD ON THIS, then:

FADE TO BLACK. THIS ENDS ACT 6.

# Act 7

EXTERIOR: THE TOWN HALL—NIGHT.

JACK CARVER was right—the islanders without woodstoves for heat, or those who live in the path of a possible storm surge at high tide, are already coming in for shelter. Some arrive in four-wheel drives, some come on snowmobiles or in Sno-Cats. Some are on snowshoes and skis. Even with the HOWL OF THE WIND, we can hear the BULL-THROATED ROAR OF THE TOWN HALL GENNIE.

Approaching along the sidewalk are JONAS STANHOPE and his wife, JOANNA. They aren't kids, but they're healthy, even athletic-looking—like the actors in the Ensure commercials. They are on snowshoes, and each has a pull line. Behind them is a chair secured to a child's sled, making it into a kind of one-person sleigh. Sitting in the chair, bundled up in robes and an ENORMOUS FUR HAT, is CORA STANHOPE, JONAS'S mother. She's about eighty and looks as regal as Queen Victoria on her throne.

> JONAS
>
> You okay, Mom?

> CORA
>
> Fine as the flowers in May.

> JONAS
>
> What about you, Jo?

> JOANNA
> (rather grim)
>
> I'll make it.

They turn into the parking lot beside the town hall. This lot is rapidly filling up with a variety of snow-friendly vehicles. Pairs of skis and snowshoes have been left upright in the snowbank in front of the building. The building itself is—courtesy of its big generator—lit up like an ocean liner on a stormy sea, an island of safety and relative

115

comfort on a wild night. Of course, the *Titanic* probably looked the same way before it hit the iceberg.

Folks walk toward the steps, talking and chatting with nervous excitement. We've built up a relatively large cast of characters, and here we get some payoff, recognizing old friends from the cluster at MARTHA'S house and the shoppers at the market.

We spy JILL and ANDY ROBICHAUX getting out of a four-wheel drive. As JILL undoes the straps holding five-year-old HARRY in his car seat (HARRY'S one of MOLLY'S day-care kids), ANDY slogs gamely over to the STANHOPE family.

> ANDY
>
> How you doing, Stanhopes? Some wild night, huh?

> JONAS
>
> It sure is. We're fine, Andy.

But JOANNA, while far from death's door, is also a long way from fine. She's PANTING HARD and uses the break to bend over and clutch the legs of her snowpants.

> ANDY
>
> Let me spell you there, Joanna—

> CORA
> (Her Imperial Majesty)
> Joanna is fine, Mr. Robichaux. Just needs to get her breath. Don't you, Joanna?

JOANNA gives her elderly mother-in-law a smile that says, "Thanks, right, and, oh, how I'd like to stuff a parking meter up your scrawny old butt." ANDY sees it.

> ANDY
>
> Jilly could use some help with the baby, Jo. Would you? I got this. Really.

> JOANNA
> (very grateful)
> You bet.

ANDY grabs JOANNA'S half of the harness. As JOANNA goes to JILL (CORA gives her daughter-in-law a look as icy as the storm, one that says "Quitter" loud and clear), DAVEY HOPEWELL, his PARENTS, and MRS. KINGSBURY pile out of a big old Suburban.

                         JONAS
            Well, Andy, what do you say? Ready?

                         ANDY
                (cheerily, God love him)
         Mush!

They resume pulling the old lady toward the town hall. CORA rides with her blade-thin New England nose regally lifted. JILL and JOANNA walk along behind, CHATTING; HARRY, so bundled up he looks like the Sta-Puft Marshmallow Man, trudges next to his mom, holding her hand.

200    INTERIOR: THE TOWN OFFICE—NIGHT.

URSULA, TESS MARCHANT, and TAVIA GODSOE are checking people in by handing them clipboards and getting them to sign the names of family members who plan to spend the night in the lower level of the town hall. Behind the WOMEN are FOUR MEN, looking important but not doing much. There's ROBBIE BEALS, the town manager, plus the three town selectmen: GEORGE KIRBY, BURT SOAMES, and HENRY BRIGHT. HENRY is the husband of CARLA BRIGHT, and is currently holding his son, another day-care pupil, in his arms. FRANK is fast asleep.

Again, we see faces that we know coming in; an island is a small community. There are no kids older than day-care age; the big kids all got stranded on the mainland side of the reach.

                         URSULA
                  (plenty harried)
         Sign in, everybody! We have to know who's here, so please
         sign in before you go downstairs!

She casts an impatient look at the men, who are basically standing around and gossiping.

201   INTERIOR: ANGLE ON ROBBIE AND THE SELECTMEN.

#### BURT SOAMES
So what'd he say?

#### ROBBIE
What *could* he say? Hell, everybody north of Casco Bay knows Peter Godsoe wholesales nine pounds of pot for every pound of lobster.

He casts an eye on URSULA and TAVIA—the latter is rummaging in a supply cupboard for pillows, work ROBBIE wouldn't do unless you stuck a gun in his ear.

#### ROBBIE
I don't blame him—hell, ain't he got a houseful of women to support?

BURT SOAMES CHORTLES. GEORGE KIRBY and HENRY BRIGHT exchange a more doubtful look. They're not completely comfortable with the meanness of the gossip.

#### GEORGE KIRBY
Question is, Robbie, how'd that fella *know?*

ROBBIE rolls his eyes, as if to say, "What a dope."

#### ROBBIE
They're likely in business together. Why would a fella kill a harmless old lady like Martha Clarendon in the first place, 'less he was stoned? Tell me that, George Kirby!

#### HENRY BRIGHT
That doesn't explain how he could know Cat Withers 'us up in Derry for n'abortion.

#### WOMAN'S VOICE
Ursula! Are there more blankets?

#### URSULA
Robbie Beals! Henry Bright! You boys think you could go downstairs and bring some more blankets out of that back

storeroom? Or aren't you far enough along with your poli-
tickin' yet?

ROBBIE and HENRY walk over, ROBBIE with a contemptuous grin,
HENRY looking ashamed that he hasn't been more help already.

> ROBBIE
> What's the matter, Ursula—that time of the month, dear?

She gives him a look of utter contempt and brushes hair back from her
face.

> TESS
> Don't you think it's about time to blow the whistle and bring
> 'em in, Robbie?

> ROBBIE
> Looks like enough of 'em are coming in on their own. As for
> the rest, they'll ride it out just fine. All this is a bunch of
> foolishness, far's I'm concerned. Do you think our grand-
> mothers and grandfathers all got together in the town hall
> when it stormed, like a bunch of cave people scared of
> lightning?

> URSULA
> No—they used the Methodist church. I've got a picture I
> could show you. Storm of '27. I can point out your granddad
> in it, if you want. He looks like he's stirring a pot of soup.
> Nice to know there was at least one fellow in your family
> knew how to pitch in.

ROBBIE looks ready to come back on her, but before he can:

> HENRY BRIGHT
> Come on, Robbie.

HENRY, still holding his sleeping child, heads downstairs. GEORGE
KIRBY follows. ROBBIE'S effectively shut up. GEORGE is easily
twenty years older than he is, and if he's not above getting blankets,
ROBBIE will at least have to go along and *look* busy.

URSULA, TAVIA, and TESS look at each other and kind of roll their eyes as the men leave. Meanwhile, people continue to come in by twos and threes, and the storm continues to ROAR outside.

> URSULA
>
> Sign in before you go downstairs, folks! Please! There's room for everybody, but we have to know who we have!

MOLLY ANDERSON comes in, brushing snow from her hair and holding RALPHIE by the hand.

> MOLLY
>
> Ursula, have you seen Mike?

> URSULA
>
> No, but I'll be able to catch his car radio if he calls in, I think.
> (points at the CB)
> It's not good for much else tonight. Take off your coat, pitch in.

> MOLLY
>
> How's it going?

> URSULA
>
> Oh, we're having a ball. Hi, Ralphie.

> RALPHIE
>
> Hi.

MOLLY kneels on the wet floor and begins the job of peeling RALPHIE out of his snowsuit. People continue to come in as she does so. Outside, the SNOW SWIRLS and the WIND HOWLS.

202   EXTERIOR: THE VOLUNTEER FIRE DEPARTMENT—NIGHT.

The pumper we saw being washed at the top of the show has long since been put away, but now the fire station's side door opens and FERD ANDREWS struggles out, pulling up the hood of his coat. He looks downhill at:

203   EXTERIOR: GODSOE FISH & LOBSTER—NIGHT.

The tide is almost high. The mainland has disappeared in a curtain of gray and black. The reach is running with waves so big they're nightmarish. These slosh rhythmically over the end of the dock, pelting the long shed with spray.

204   INTERIOR: GODSOE FISH & LOBSTER—NIGHT.

We're in a long, high storage area stacked with lobster traps, crates, and fishing gear. One entire wall is hung with slickers, waterproofs, high boots. The SOUND OF THE STORM is MUTED, but only a little. SPRAY PELTS THE WINDOWS.

THE CAMERA MOVES down an aisle of traps, then past a LONG TANK full of lobsters. THE CAMERA SWINGS around the end of the tank, and a few RATS scutter out of sight. Here, in a dusty little passage between the tank and the wall, is stored a LONG OBJECT covered with blankets.

THE WIND SHRIEKS. THE BUILDING CREAKS. A huge SPLASH OF SPRAY hits one of the windows and SHATTERS IT. Wind, water, and snow SWIRL IN. The wind strips the blanket back from the end of the long object, and we see STACKED BALES OF POT, all neatly wrapped in sheets of plastic.

The traps hung overhead CLACK BACK AND FORTH. SOUND of another window BREAKING.

205   EXTERIOR: THE LITTLE TALL MARKET.

We can hear the FAINT CHUG OF THE GENERATOR, and a few lights shine bravely. The only vehicles still parked in front are MOLLY'S little car and a snow-caked pickup with GODSOE FISH & LOBSTER on the side.

206   INTERIOR: CROSSWORD PUZZLE ON POWERBOOK SCREEN, CLOSE-UP.

It's mostly filled in. HATCH adds a word.

207   INTERIOR: THE CONSTABLE'S OFFICE NIGHT.

HATCH stretches, then stands. In the cell, LINOGE sits as before, back to the wall and looking out from between his knees.

HATCH
Got to use the can. You want a coffee or a cold drink, Pete?

PETE doesn't respond at first. The sheet of paper he pulled from the bulletin board is in his lap, but turned over so the print side, with its red-tide warning, is faceup. PETER'S eyes are wide and blank.

> HATCH

Peter—Earth to Peter.

HATCH waves a hand in front of PETER'S face. PETER blinks, and awareness—or a semblance of it—seeps back into his eyes. He looks up at HATCH.

> PETER

What?

> HATCH

Just asked if you wanted a soda or a coffee.

> PETER

No. Thanks, though.

> HATCH
> (starts toward the door, then turns)

You all right?

> PETER
> (after a beat)

Yeah. Spent all day battening down for the storm, and now I guess I'm almost asleep with my eyes open. Sorry.

> HATCH

Well, hang in there. Jack Carver and Kirk Freeman should be along in twenty minutes or so.

HATCH grabs a magazine to read in the can and leaves.

208    INTERIOR: LINOGE, CLOSE-UP.

His eyes DARKEN. He looks at PETER. His lips move soundlessly.

209 INTERIOR: PETER, CLOSE-UP.

He's totally blank again. Hypnotized. Suddenly THE SHADOW OF LINOGE'S CANE appears on his face. PETER looks up at:

210 INTERIOR: AN OVERHEAD BEAM, FROM PETER'S POINT OF VIEW.

The cane is hooked over it. The bloody WOLF'S HEAD SNARLS.

211 INTERIOR: THE CONSTABLE'S OFFICE—NIGHT.

PETER gets up and slowly crosses the room, the notice he was writing on trailing from one hand. He walks directly beneath the cane. LINOGE sits on the cell's cot, watching him, only his weird eyes moving. PETER stops at a wall-mounted cabinet and opens it. There are all sorts of tools inside. There's also a COIL OF ROPE. He takes it.

212 EXTERIOR: GODSOE FISH & LOBSTER—NIGHT.

A GIGANTIC WAVE rolls out of the reach, smashes the end of the town dock, and chews off the end of Peter Godsoe's building. We can hear the SNAP OF WOOD even above the storm.

213 EXTERIOR: FERD ANDREWS, BY THE FIRE DEPARTMENT SIDE DOOR.

FERD ANDREWS
Oh . . . my . . . *God!* (raises his voice) Lloyd! Lloyd, you gotta see this!

214   INTERIOR: THE FIRE STATION GARAGE, WITH LLOYD WISHMAN—
NIGHT.

The two island pumpers are apple green. The passenger window of one
is partly open. Hanging from it is the bloody wolf's head of LINOGE'S
cane. Standing nearby, looking as blank as PETER GODSOE, is
LLOYD. In one hand he has a small can of red paint. In the other is a
brush. He's working with the care of a Manet or van Gogh.

> FERD ANDREWS (voice-over)
> *Lloyd! It's gonna take Godsoe's! It's gonna take the whole*
> *dock!*

LLOYD WISHMAN pays no attention. Goes on painting.

215   INTERIOR: THE CONSTABLE'S OFFICE, A HIGH ANGLE.

The cane no longer hangs over the beam, but a coil of rope is flung up
and over the place where it was. In the background, LINOGE sits in his
cell, face predatory, eyes ROLLING WITH RED AND BLACK.

216   EXTERIOR: GODSOE'S FISH & LOBSTER—NIGHT.

Another HUGE WAVE smashes into the town dock, tearing a lot more
of it away and capsizing a small boat someone foolishly left tied there.
It also takes another huge bite out of the warehouse.

217   INTERIOR: GODSOE'S FISH & LOBSTER—NIGHT.

We can see right outside through a RAGGED HOLE in the end of the
building: the amputated dock and the heaving waves of the reach. Now
another of these big ones ROLLS TOWARD THE CAMERA, inundating
what's left of the dock and SMASHING INTO THE WAREHOUSE.
Lobster traps are lifted and sucked away. The lobster tank is overturned, and lobsters are freed by the dozens, a sudden and unexpected
commutation of their death sentence. And, as the big wave retreats,
BALES OF POT also float out of the hole at the end of the building.

218   EXTERIOR: OUTSIDE THE FIRE DEPARTMENT, WITH FERD ANDREWS.

> FERD ANDREWS
> (shouting)
> You better come, Lloyd, if you want to see sumpin' you ain't
> never gonna see again! She's a-goin'! She's a-goin'!

219    INTERIOR: THE FIRE STATION, WITH LLOYD WISHMAN.

LLOYD is also a-goin', as it happens. As he finishes painting, THE CAMERA MOVES around, showing us what is written in big red capitals up the side of the green pumper. Overlaying the gold letters that read LITTLE TALL ISLAND V.F.D. is this message: "GIVE ME WHAT I WANT AND I'LL GO AWAY."

FERD ANDREWS (voice-over)
*Git out here, Lloyd! The whole shebang's goin' into the drink!*

Taking no notice, LLOYD sets the paint can down on the running board of the pumper and puts the brush neatly across the top. As he does these things, we see that the cane that was hanging from the partly open window is gone . . . or maybe it was never there in the first place. Maybe it was just in LLOYD WISHMAN'S mind.

LLOYD moves to the side of the pumper and opens one of the tool storage compartments. He takes out a fire axe.

220    INTERIOR: THE CONSTABLE'S OFFICE—NIGHT.

PETER GODSOE, eyes blank, is standing on a chair. The end of the rope he threw over the beam has been fashioned into a noose, and the noose is around his neck. Pinned to his shirt is his "homework": the sheet with "GIVE ME WHAT I WANT" written all over it, plus the cane drawings. Written in extra-big letters at the top, like a title, is "GIVE ME WHAT I WANT AND I'LL GO AWAY."

221    INTERIOR: LINOGE, CLOSE-UP.

Lips moving. Chanting silently. Eyes BIG BLACK HOLES shot through with RED FIRE.

222    INTERIOR: THE FIRE STATION—NIGHT.

LLOYD stands with the keen blade of the axe pointing at the center of his face. He's gripping the handle far up on the shaft, the kind of grip you want if you're going to chop kindling out back of the house . . . or your own face in two.

223   INTERIOR: LINOGE, CLOSE-UP.

Lips moving faster now. Weird eyes wider. Hands clenched into fists in front of him.

224   EXTERIOR: THE OCEAN SIDE OF THE FIRE STATION, WITH FERD.

His face is filled with awe and terror. His mouth hangs open.

### FERD ANDREWS
My sainted hat!

225   EXTERIOR: THE TOWN DOCK, WITH WHAT REMAINS OF GODSOE'S.

Bearing down on it through the HOWLING SNOW is a huge wave—almost a tidal wave.

226   INTERIOR: THE CONSTABLE'S OFFICE, WITH PETER'S FEET.

They kick away the chair with a CLATTER, then begin to JITTER.

227   EXTERIOR: THE ONCOMING WAVE—NIGHT.

It dwarfs the dock and the warehouse.

228   INTERIOR: THE MARKET, WITH HATCH.

He stops pouring his coffee and turns toward the constable's office door, reacting to the CLATTER OF THE CHAIR.

### HATCH
Peter?

229   INTERIOR: THE AXE, CLOSE-UP.

It swings out of the frame, and we hear an unpleasant SOUND—it's like someone slapping mud with the flat of his hand. *CHUMP!*

230   INTERIOR: GODSOE FISH & LOBSTER—NIGHT.

We're looking out at the reach . . . but suddenly the view is blotted out by the ONCOMING WAVE. There's nothing to be seen through the broken-off stump of the warehouse but SURGING GRAY WATER. It SMASHES INTO GODSOE'S, and suddenly THE CAMERA IS UNDERWATER. A SMASHED TRAP, a BALE OF POT, and a LOBSTER with its claws still pegged go floating past in gusts of bubbles.

231   EXTERIOR: THE TOWN DOCK—NIGHT.

What remains is inundated and torn completely away. The retreating wave carries off a tangle of boats, ropes, cleats, rubber boat-bumpers, and Godsoe's shingled roof. Maybe we see part of the sign—GODSOE FISH & LOBSTER—before it all disappears into the BELLOWING BLIZZARD.

232   INTERIOR: THE TOWN HALL, WITH URSULA, TAVIA, TESS, ETC.

All the bustle is momentarily silent. The CRACKLE AND HISS of the CB is very loud. Everyone has turned toward the door.

                    RALPHIE
      Mommy, what's wrong?

                    MOLLY
      Nothing, hon.

                    JONAS
      What in God's name was it?

                    CORA
      The town dock, setting off to sea.

ROBBIE comes up the stairs, followed by GEORGE, HENRY BRIGHT, and BURT SOAMES. ROBBIE'S bluster and swagger are gone.

                    ROBBIE
      Ursula. Blow the whistle.

233   EXTERIOR: OUTSIDE THE FIRE DEPARTMENT, WITH FERD—NIGHT.

He's as excited and dismayed as a man who has just seen Satan peering at him from around a tree trunk. He turns and runs back to the door of the firehouse.

234   INTERIOR: THE CONSTABLE'S OFFICE, FEATURING THE DOOR.

HATCH comes through the door, Styrofoam cup of joe in one hand.

                    HATCH
      Pete? You okay? I heard—

His face fills with startled horror. His eyes go upward, presumably to the face of the man who has hung himself from the beam. The coffee drops from his hand, hits the floor, splashes his boots.

235   INTERIOR: THE FIREHOUSE, WITH FERD.

### FERD ANDREWS
Lloyd! Where the hell are you? Did you go to sleep, or wh—

He starts around the rear of the closest pumper, then stops. There's a pair of boots sticking out.

### FERD
Lloyd? *Lloyd . . . ?*

Slowly, not really wanting to, he goes the rest of the way around, to where he can see his partner. For a moment he's silent, so shocked he is unable to vocalize. Then FERD screams like a woman.

236   INTERIOR: HATCH, CLOSE-UP.

His face is frozen in an expression of utter horror.

237   INTERIOR: THE SIDE OF THE PUMPER.

"GIVE ME WHAT I WANT AND I'LL GO AWAY" painted in bloodred capital letters.

238   INTERIOR: THE SIGN AROUND PETER GODSOE'S NECK.

"GIVE ME WHAT I WANT, GIVE ME WHAT I WANT, GIVE ME WHAT I WANT AND I'LL GO AWAY." Plus those creepy little dancing canes.

239   INTERIOR: THE SCREEN OF HATCH'S POWERBOOK, CLOSE-UP.

The answers he filled in are gone. Now, filling the crossword grid, are the words "GIVE ME WHAT I WANT AND I'LL GO AWAY." Across, down, interlocking at every point. And in the center of every black square is a little white cane-icon.

240   INTERIOR: LINOGE, EXTREME CLOSE-UP.

Grinning. The sharp tips of his teeth showing.

SLOW DISSOLVE TO:

241   EXTERIOR: THE CENTER OF TOWN, HIGH ANGLE—NIGHT.

It's mostly dark, except for the town hall. And now the storm emergency signal begins to blow: two shorts, one long, a pause, and then once again. Take shelter.

The image of LINOGE LINGERS, superimposed over the snowy town and perhaps suggesting there will be no shelter for the inhabitants of Little Tall Island . . . not tonight, perhaps not ever again. At last LINOGE'S image FADES OUT . . . and we do the same.

THIS ENDS PART ONE.

# PART 2

# The Storm of the Century

## Act 1

[We begin with a MONTAGE OF SCENES from PART ONE. This ends with the final image: LINOGE'S predatory tiger's face superimposed upon the intersection at the center of town.]

1    EXTERIOR: THE CENTER OF TOWN—NIGHT.

The blizzard is rising toward a state of total fury, with snow falling so fast and hard that the buildings look like ghosts. Drifts are already beginning to pile up against the storefronts on Main Street.

As LINOGE'S image fades, we hear a SOUND, LOW at first, then UP TO FULL: THE TOWN WHISTLE, blowing the EMERGENCY SIGNAL over and over again: two shorts and one long.

On Main Street, we can see a STRING OF MOVING LIGHTS and hear the SOUND OF ENGINES as folks comply.

2    EXTERIOR: MAIN STREET SIDEWALK, WITH FERD ANDREWS—NIGHT.

He comes pelting along toward the town hall through the snow,
sometimes slipping and falling, then picking himself up again. He
makes no attempt to go around the building drifts, but bulls his way
straight through. He approaches a group of five or six men who are
skiing toward the town hall. One of them is BILL TOOMEY.

BILL TOOMEY
    Say, Ferd—where's the fire?

Because of Ferd's job (it says LITTLE TALL V.F.D. right across the back of
his parka), this breaks BILL'S friends right up—it doesn't take much to
amuse island people, let me tell you, and these fellows have probably
been having a little storm refreshment.

FERD takes no notice, just picks himself up again and continues
running toward the town hall.

3    EXTERIOR: MIKE ANDERSON'S STORE—NIGHT.

Battened down for the storm. The porch has already drifted in. The
storm shutters RATTLE on their tracks. PETER GODSOE'S pickup
truck and MOLLY'S little car are now little more than snow-covered
humps, but in the case of the truck, it's no big deal; PETER'S driving
days are over.

4    INTERIOR: THE CONSTABLE'S OFFICE—NIGHT.

HATCH is as we left him at the end of Part One, staring up at PETER'S
dangling legs. Nearby is the overturned chair PETER stood on while he
was putting the noose around his neck.

5    INTERIOR: THE SIGN AROUND PETER'S NECK, CLOSE-UP.

"GIVE ME WHAT I WANT" written all over it, helter-skelter, along
with the dancing canes. And, at the top, like a title, is the complete
thought in capital letters so big they almost scream: "GIVE ME WHAT
I WANT AND I'LL GO AWAY."

6    INTERIOR: RESUME CONSTABLE'S OFFICE.

HATCH looks from the dangling legs to LINOGE, sitting there in the
cell, his stocking feet cocked up on the cot's edge, his faintly smiling

face peering out from between his spread knees. LINOGE'S eyes have gone back to normal, but he projects a terrible quality of hunger and predation, just the same. He's locked up, yes, but it's such a ridiculous sham of a cell, with its wood floor and home-welded bars. HATCH is getting the idea that *he* is the one in trouble, locked up with this tiger in human form. We can take it a step further: the whole town is in trouble.

Between the dangling body and the silent, staring LINOGE, HATCH starts to lose it.

> HATCH
> What are you lookin' at?
> (no reply from LINOGE)
> Did you make him do it, somehow? Make him write that around his neck and then hang himself? Did you?

Nothing from LINOGE. He only sits there, looking at HATCH. HATCH has had enough and heads for the door. He tries to do it at a walk, but can't hold on to himself well enough to keep that pace. He begins to hurry . . . then simply BOLTS. He grabs the knob, turns it, yanks the door open . . . and there is a SHAPE out there by the meat counter. It GRABS HATCH. HATCH shrieks.

7    INTERIOR: TOWN HALL BASEMENT, FEATURING PIPPA HATCHER, CLOSE-UP.

In one hand PIPPA holds a tail (actually a rolled-up hankie) with a pin sticking out of it. She walks slowly toward a piece of paper that has been taped up to the wall. On the paper, MOLLY ANDERSON has drawn a smiling donkey. Gathered around PIPPA, calling "Warmer!" and "Colder!" are all but one of MOLLY'S day-care pupils: RALPHIE, DON BEALS, HARRY ROBICHAUX, HEIDI ST. PIERRE, BUSTER CARVER, and SALLY GODSOE (who has become fatherless but fortunately doesn't know it yet). FRANK BRIGHT is sleeping on a cot nearby.

Behind the children, we see CAT WITHERS, MELINDA HATCHER, and LINDA ST. PIERRE making beds. Standing nearby, holding piles of blankets, are GEORGE KIRBY, HENRY BRIGHT, and ROBBIE BEALS. ROBBIE doesn't look happy about it.

CARLA BRIGHT comes up to MOLLY, who is monitoring the festivities.

                    CARLA
Evening sessions now?

                    MOLLY
It's sort of fun. But . . .

PIPPA manages to plant the tail somewhere in the region of the donkey's ass.

                    MOLLY
                  (continues)
. . . when they all finally fall asleep, I intend to track down
the nearest alcoholic beverage and make it disappear.

                    CARLA
I'll pour.

                  DON BEALS
I wanna be next!

                    MOLLY
                  (to CARLA)
Done deal.

She takes the blindfold off PIPPA and starts putting it on DON.

8    INTERIOR: THE TOWN HALL, UPSTAIRS—NIGHT.

FERD ANDREWS bursts in, wild-eyed and covered with snow from top
to tail.

                    FERD
                (top of his lungs)
   *Lloyd Wishman's dead!*

All bustle and activity stops. Forty or fifty faces turn to FERD. Central
to this group is URSULA GODSOE, with her clipboard.

9   INTERIOR: THE TOWN HALL BASEMENT.

The KIDS are still having a good time, shouting "Warmer!" and "Colder!" to DON BEALS as he tries to pin the tail on the donkey, but all the ADULTS have turned toward the SOUND of that SHOUT. ROBBIE BEALS drops his pile of blankets and heads up the stairs.

10   INTERIOR: THE CONSTABLE'S OFFICE—NIGHT.

HATCH grapples with the SHAPE, hysterical with fear, until—

                    MIKE
    Stop it, Hatch! Whoa! Whoa!

HATCH stops it and looks up at MIKE, his terror becoming relief. He hugs MIKE tightly—does everything but rain kisses on MIKE'S face.

                    MIKE
    What's the—

Then, without the distraction of being grappled by his rather over-weight second-in-command, MIKE sees what the trouble is. His face fills with wonder. He walks slowly past HATCH to the dangling body. He looks at it . . . then looks at LINOGE. LINOGE smiles back at him.

11   INTERIOR: THE TOWN HALL, FEATURES FERD—NIGHT.

                    FERD
    Lloyd Wishman's killed himself! Chopped his face in two
    with a axe! Oh, God, it's awful! Blood everywhere!

ROBBIE comes upstairs. His wife, SANDRA (a plain little thing), is there, and she grabs ineffectually at his shoulder, probably wanting some comfort. He yanks her hand off him without so much as a look (pretty much the way he treats her even in ordinary circumstances) and goes to FERD.

                    FERD
                  (babbling)
    I ain't never seen nothin' like it! Knocked his own brains
    right out! And he wrote on the side of the new pumper, didn't
    make no sense—

ROBBIE
(grabs him, shakes him)
Get hold of yourself, Ferd! Get a damn grip!

FERD quits babbling. It's so quiet now you could hear a pin drop—except, of course, for the CEASELESS WHOOP OF THE STORM OUTSIDE. FERD'S eyes are filling with tears.

FERD
Why would Lloyd chop his head in two, Robbie? He was going to get married, come spring.

12    INTERIOR: THE CONSTABLE'S OFFICE—NIGHT.

HATCH
(also babbling)
I just went out to use the can and get a fresh coffee—he was fine then. But *he* kept lookin' at him . . . like a snake lookin' at a bird . . . he . . . he . . .

MIKE looks at LINOGE. LINOGE looks back.

MIKE
What did you do to him?

No reply. MIKE turns to HATCH.

MIKE
Help me get him down.

HATCH
Mike . . . I don't know's I can.

MIKE
You can.

HATCH gives him a pleading look.

LINOGE
(very pleasant)
Let me out and *I'll* help, Michael Anderson.

MIKE looks at him, then back at HATCH, who is pale and sweaty. But HATCH takes a deep breath and nods.

HATCH

Okay . . .

13   EXTERIOR: BEHIND THE STORE—NIGHT.

A snowmobile pulls up next to the loading dock, and two men, bundled up in heavy nylon snowsuits, clamber off. They have rifles strapped over their shoulders. It's KIRK FREEMAN and JACK CARVER, the next watch. They go up the steps.

14   INTERIOR: THE CONSTABLE'S OFFICE.

MIKE and HATCH have just finished putting a blanket over PETER— we can see GODSOE'S fisherman's boots poking out—when a HAMMERING on the back door begins. HATCH gasps and lunges for the desk, where the pistol sits beside the makeshift sign, which the men took off the suicide's chest. MIKE grabs HATCH'S arm.

MIKE

Relax.

He goes to the door and opens it. KIRK and JACK come in with snow swirling around them, stamping their feet.

KIRK FREEMAN
Right on time, by God, storm or no st—
(sees the blanket-covered corpse)
What—! Mike, who's that?

JACK CARVER
(sick to his stomach)
Peter Godsoe. I reckinize the boots.

JACK turns to look at LINOGE. KIRK follows his gaze. These men are new to the situation, but still understand instinctively that LINOGE has been a part of what has happened—they feel his power.

In the corner, the CB RADIO CRACKLES.

URSULA (radio voice)
. . . ike . . . come in, Mike An . . . have a bad sit . . . town hall . . . Lloyd Wish . . . gency . . . emergency . . .

That last word, at least, comes through clearly. MIKE and HATCH exchange a startled, worried look—what now? MIKE goes to the shelf where the CB sits and snatches up the microphone.

MIKE
Ursula, say again! Say again, please . . . and go slow! The roof antenna's snapped off and I'm barely picking you up. What is your emergency?

He lets go of the button. There is a tense pause. HATCH reaches past him and TURNS UP THE VOLUME. SOUND OF STATIC, then:

URSULA (radio voice)
. . . oyd . . . shman . . . Ferd   says . . . Robbie   Beals . . . Henry Bright . . . have . . . can . . . hear me?

MIKE looks frustrated, then has an idea.

MIKE
(to HATCH)
Go out front and get her on the Island Services CB. Come back as soon's you know what her trouble is.

HATCH
Right.

He starts away, then looks back doubtfully.

                              HATCH
     You'll be okay?

                              MIKE
     He's locked up, isn't he?

HATCH looks more doubtful than ever, but he leaves.

                        KIRK FREEMAN
     Mike, do you have any idea what's going on here?

MIKE holds up a hand, as if to say, "Not now." He reaches into his coat
pocket and brings out the Polaroids he took at MARTHA CLAREN-
DON'S house. He shuffles through them until he finds the one from
over the door. He lays this down in the corner of the paper he and
HATCH took from around PETER GODSOE'S neck. They are
identical—even the drawing of the cane over MARTHA'S living room
door looks the same as the ones dancing on the sheet of paper.

                        JACK CARVER
     What in God's name is happening?

MIKE starts to straighten up, then sees something else.

15   INTERIOR: THE OPEN POWERBOOK, FROM MIKE'S POINT OF VIEW.

The entire grid of HATCH'S crossword has been filled in with varia-
tions of "GIVE ME WHAT I WANT AND I'LL GO AWAY," plus the little
cane-icons in the black squares.

16   INTERIOR: RESUME CONSTABLE'S OFFICE.

                              MIKE
     I'll be damned if I know.

17   INTERIOR: THE TOWN OFFICE, WITH URSULA—NIGHT.

She's working the CB microphone for all it's worth. Behind her,
looking anxious, are a number of men and women, SANDRA BEALS
and CARLA BRIGHT among them.

> URSULA

Mike, are you there?

MOLLY, also understandably worried, works her way through the knot of onlookers.

> MOLLY

Can't you get him?

> URSULA

The wind's knocked the damned antennas down! Over here . . . over there . . . all over the island, most likely.

> HATCH (staticky radio voice)

Ursula, do you read me? Come on back.

> URSULA

I'm here! I read you! You gettin' me, Alton Hatcher?

> HATCH (radio voice)

You're breaking up some, but it's better than it was. What's your problem?

> URSULA

Ferd Andrews says Lloyd Wishman has killed himself over at the firehouse—

> HATCH (radio voice)

*What?*

> URSULA

—only it doesn't sound like any suicide I ever heard of . . . Ferd says Lloyd cut his own head open with an axe. And now Robbie Beals and Henry Bright have gone over there. To investigate, Robbie said!

> HATCH (staticky radio voice)

And you let 'em go?

CARLA takes the mike from URSULA.

> CARLA
>
> There was no way to stop Robbie. He practically shanghaied my husband. And there could be somebody there! Where's Mike? I want to talk to Mike!

18   INTERIOR: THE ISLAND SERVICES VEHICLE, WITH HATCH.

He sits behind the wheel, holding the mike and thinking this over. Events are spinning out of control here, and HATCH knows it. At last he raises the mike to his lips again.

> HATCH
>
> I'm calling from the truck—Mike's inside. With the man who . . . you know, the prisoner.

> CARLA (very staticky voice)
>
> You have to send him down there!

> HATCH
>
> Well . . . we got us a little bit of a situation right here, you see, and . . .

19   INTERIOR: THE TOWN OFFICE—NIGHT.

MOLLY grabs the microphone from CARLA.

> MOLLY
>
> Is Mike all right, Hatch? You come on back and tell me.

20   INTERIOR: THE ISLAND SERVICES VEHICLE, WITH HATCH.

Poor guy actually looks relieved. Here, finally, is a question for which he can provide a satisfactory answer.

> MOLLY
>
> He's fine, Moll. That's a big 10-4. Listen, I have to go. I'll pass on the message. This is Island Services.

He lowers the mike, looking simultaneously perplexed and relieved, then racks it. He opens the door and gets out into the HOWLING STORM. MIKE has parked the vehicle next to GODSOE'S truck. Now, as HATCH looks up, he sees LINOGE'S ghastly, grinning face peering out at him from the snow-caked driver's side window of the pickup truck. LINOGE'S eyes are DEAD BLACK.

HATCH GASPS and staggers backward. He looks at the window of the truck again. Nothing there. Must have been his imagination. He starts toward the porch steps, then turns and looks back, like "it" trying to catch one of the other children moving in a game of Red Light. Sees nothing. Goes on.

21    INTERIOR: LINOGE, CLOSE-UP.

Grinning. He knows perfectly well what HATCH saw in GODSOE'S truck.

22    EXTERIOR: THE FIRE STATION—NIGHT.

The side door is open—FERD didn't bother to close it when he fled the sight of his partner's corpse—and the emergency lights inside the garage are throwing their glow out onto the snow.

A HEADLIGHT appears; the WASPY WHINE of a Sno-Cat accompanies it. The Sno-Cat pulls up. ROBBIE gets out from one side (the driver's side, naturally) and HENRY BRIGHT from the other.

> HENRY

I don't know about this, Robbie—

> ROBBIE

You think we can wait for Anderson? On a night like this? Someone's got to take charge, and we happen to be the ones on the scene. Now come on!

ROBBIE strides in through the open side door, and after a moment, HENRY BRIGHT follows.

23    INTERIOR: THE FIREHOUSE GARAGE.

ROBBIE is standing to one side of the nearest pumper. His hood is pushed back, and he has once again lost most of his pompous authority. In one hand he holds his little gun, and now he waggles the barrel at the floor. HENRY looks, and the two men exchange an uneasy glance. FERD left BLOODY TRACKS when he fled.

ROBBIE and HENRY are both reluctant now, but as ROBBIE pointed out, they're on the scene. They walk around the back of the pumper.

24    INTERIOR: ROBBIE AND HENRY.

As they come around the pumper, their eyes widen and their faces KNOT WITH REVULSION. HENRY claps both hands over his mouth, but that isn't going to keep it in. He bends out of the frame, and we hear the SOUND OF VOMITING. (Sort of like the SOUND OF MUSIC, only louder.)

ROBBIE looks at:

25    INTERIOR: THE BLOODY AXE, FROM ROBBIE'S POINT OF VIEW.

It lies on the floor, beside one of LLOYD WISHMAN'S boots. THE CAMERA TRAVELS UP the side of the pumper to the words printed there in paint as red as blood: "GIVE ME WHAT I WANT AND I'LL GO AWAY."

26    INTERIOR: ROBBIE BEALS, CLOSE-UP.

Wide-eyed. Beginning to pass fear and perplexity and into the land where panic dwells and really bad decisions are made.

27  EXTERIOR: ANGLE ON ATLANTIC STREET—NIGHT.

The **STORM IS HOWLING**. We hear a LOUD, RENDING CRACK, and a tree branch falls into the street, crushing the snow-covered roof of a parked car. Conditions are still getting worse.

28  INTERIOR: THE CONSTABLE'S OFFICE.

JACK CARVER and KIRK FREEMAN are looking at LINOGE, fascinated. MIKE is still standing by the desk, looking at the weird crossword puzzle on the PowerBook. He's still got the Polaroids in his hand. When JACK takes a step toward the cell, MIKE speaks without looking up.

> ### MIKE
> Don't go over there.

JACK stops moving at once, looking guilty. HATCH comes in through the market, shedding snow at every step.

> ### HATCH
> Ursula says Lloyd Wishman's dead over at the firehouse.

> ### KIRK FREEMAN
> Dead! What about Ferd?

HATCH

Ferd's the one who found him. He says it's suicide. I think
Ursula's afraid it might be murder. Mike . . . Robbie Beals
took Henry Bright over there. To investigate, I guess.

JACK CARVER claps his hand to his face. MIKE, however, hardly
reacts. He's holding on to his cool, and thinking furiously.

MIKE

Streets still passable? What do you think?

HATCH

In a four-wheel drive? Yeah. Probably until midnight. After
that—

HATCH shrugs, indicating "Who knows."

MIKE

You take Kirk and go on over to the fire station. Find Robbie
and Henry. Keep your eyes open and be careful. Lock the
place up, then bring them back here.
(long look at LINOGE)
We can keep an eye on our new pal while you do that. Can't
we, Jack?

JACK

I dunno as that's such a good idea—

MIKE

Maybe not, but right now it's the *only* idea. I'm sorry, but it
is.

None of them look really happy, but MIKE is the boss. HATCH and
KIRK FREEMAN head out, zipping up their coats. JACK has gone back
to looking at LINOGE.

When the door is closed, MIKE starts shuffling through the Polaroids
again. Suddenly he stops, looking at:

29    INTERIOR: THE POLAROID OF MARTHA'S CHAIR, CLOSE-UP.

Bloody and spooky as an old electric chair, but empty. MIKE'S HANDS
shuffle to the next photo of the chair. In this one, the chair is *also*
empty.

30   INTERIOR: MIKE, CLOSE-UP.

Surprised and puzzled. Remembering.

31   INTERIOR: MARTHA'S LIVING ROOM, WITH MIKE *(flashback)*.

He has just pulled the drapes across the broken window and anchored them with the table. He turns back to MARTHA'S chair, raises the Polaroid, and TRIGGERS IT.

32   INTERIOR: THE WOLF'S HEAD CANE, CLOSE-UP *(flashback)*.

It stares at us with its bloody teeth and eyes like a ghost wolf in a stroke of lightning, then FADES.

33   INTERIOR: RESUME CONSTABLE'S OFFICE, FEATURES MIKE.

He's got three two pictures of MARTHA'S chair, side by side.

MIKE

It's gone.

JACK

What's gone?

MIKE doesn't answer. He shuffles a fourth photo out of the stack. This is the one featuring the message written in MARTHA'S blood, and the rudimentary drawing of the cane. MIKE looks slowly up at LINOGE.

34   INTERIOR: LINOGE.

He cocks his head and puts his forefinger beneath his chin, like a girl being coy. He smiles a little.

35   INTERIOR: RESUME CONSTABLE'S OFFICE.

MIKE walks toward the cell. As he goes, he hooks a chair to sit in, but his eyes never leave LINOGE'S face. He's still got the Polaroids.

JACK<br>(nervous)

Thought you said to stay away.

MIKE

If he grabs me, why don't you shoot him? Gun's there on the desk.

JACK glances that way, but makes no move for the pistol. The poor guy looks more nervous than ever.

36    EXTERIOR: THE ISLAND DOCKS—NIGHT.

They have been pretty well erased by the **POUNDING OCEAN.**

37    EXTERIOR: THE HEADLAND LIGHTHOUSE—NIGHT.

It stands straight and white in the **SHEETING SNOW,** its big light going round and round. **WAVES CRASH HIGH** around it.

38    INTERIOR: LIGHTHOUSE CONTROL ROOM—NIGHT.

It's completely automated, and empty. Lights **BLINK** and **FLASH.** The **SOUND OF THE WIND** outside is very strong, and the anemometer is flickering between fifty and sixty-three MPH. We can hear the place **CREAKING** and **GROANING.** Wave-spume splatters the windows and beads up on the glass.

39    EXTERIOR: THE LIGHTHOUSE—NIGHT.

A big wave—a monster like the one that destroyed **PETER GODSOE'S** warehouse—strikes the headland and all but inundates the light-house.

40    INTERIOR: LIGHTHOUSE CONTROL ROOM—NIGHT.

Several windows shatter, and water **SPRAYS ACROSS THE EQUIP-MENT.** The wave withdraws and everything continues working . . . so far, at least.

41    EXTERIOR: THE SIDE OF THE FIREHOUSE—NIGHT.

**ROBBIE BEALS** and **HENRY BRIGHT** come out, shoulders hunched against the storm. They're not the men they were when they went in . . . **ROBBIE** is especially shaken. He takes out a huge ring of keys (**ROBBIE** has keys to almost everything on the island, town manager's perogative) and begins to fumble through them, meaning to lock the door. HENRY puts a tentative hand on his arm. Once again, both men SHOUT to be heard above the HOWL OF THE STORM.

> ### HENRY
> Shouldn't we at least check upstairs? See if anyone else—

> ### ROBBIE
> That's the constable's job.

He sees the look HENRY'S giving him, the one that says, "You sure changed *your* tune," but he won't back down; it would take a lot more man than HENRY BRIGHT to get ROBBIE upstairs after what they just saw downstairs. He finds the right key and turns it in the lock, securing the firehouse.

> ### ROBBIE
> We ascertained that the victim is dead, and we have secured the scene. That's enough. Now come on. I want to get back to the—

> ### HENRY
> (pedantic, fussy)
> We never really made sure he was dead, you know . . . never took his pulse, or anything . . .

> ### ROBBIE
> His brains were all over the running board of Pumper Number Two, why in God's name would we have to take his pulse?

> ### HENRY
> But there might be someone else upstairs. Jake Civiello . . . Duane Pulsifer, maybe . . .

> ### ROBBIE
> The only two names written on the duty board were "Ferd Andrews" and "Lloyd Wishman." Anyone else in there would likely turn out to be a friend of that Linoge, and I don't want to meet any of his friends, if it's all the same to you. Now come on!

He grabs HENRY by the coat and practically drags him back to the Sno-Cat. ROBBIE fires it up, guns it impatiently as he waits for HENRY to clamber in, then turns it in a circle and heads back for the street.

As he does, the Island Services four-wheel drive comes trudging out of the storm. ROBBIE corrects his course, meaning to go around, but HATCH sees his intention and cuts him off neatly.

42   EXTERIOR: FEATURES SNO-CAT AND ISLAND SERVICES VEHICLE— NIGHT.

HATCH gets out of his vehicle, flashlight in hand. ROBBIE opens the canvas-sided door of the Sno-Cat and leans out. He has recognized HATCH and has regained his previous hectoring authority. Once again, EVERYONE SHOUTS to be heard over the SOUND OF THE WIND.

> ROBBIE
> Get out of my way, Hatcher! If you want to talk, follow us back to the town hall!

> HATCH
> Mike sent me! He wants you over at the constable's! Henry, you too!

> ROBBIE
> I'm afraid that's impossible. We have wives and children waiting at the town hall. If Mike Anderson wants either of us to stand a watch later, that's fine. But for the time being—

> HENRY
> Lloyd Wishman's dead . . . and there's something written on the side of one of the fire trucks. If it's a suicide note, it's the weirdest one I ever heard of.

KIRK comes around to the front of the Island Services truck, holding his hat down with both hands.

> KIRK
> Come on, let's get going! This ain't no place for a discussion!

> ROBBIE
> (annoyed)
>
> I agree. We can have our discussion back at the town hall, where it's still warm.

He starts to close the door of the Sno-Cat. HATCH grabs it.

> HATCH
>
> Peter Godsoe's dead, too. Hung himself. (pause) He also left a weird suicide note.

ROBBIE and HENRY are dumbfounded.

> HATCH
>
> Mike asked me to come get you, Robbie Beals, and that's what I'm doing. You come on and follow me back to the store. I don't want to hear any more sass about it.

> HENRY
> (to ROBBIE)
>
> We better do it.

> KIRK
>
> Coss you better do it! Hurry up!

> HENRY
>
> Peter Godsoe . . . my God in heaven, why?

ROBBIE is being driven in a direction he doesn't want to go, and he hates it. He grins without humor at HATCH, who stands pudgy and determined behind his flashlight.

> ROBBIE
>
> You're the one who keeps putting that department store dummy on the porch of the store. Do you think I don't know that?

> HATCH
>
> We can talk about it later on, if you want. Right now the only thing matters is that we've got bad trouble tonight . . . and not just the storm. I can't make you pitch in and help if you don't want to, but I can make sure that when this is over, people know you were asked . . . and you said no.

> HENRY

I'll come, Hatch.

> KIRK

Good boy!

HENRY opens the door on his side preparatory to getting out and joining HATCH and KIRK. ROBBIE grabs him by the jacket and hauls him back into his seat.

> ROBBIE

All right . . . but I'll remember this.

> HATCH

You do that. Did you lock the place up?

> ROBBIE
> (contemptuously)

Of course. Do you think I'm stupid?

HATCH won't touch that one with a ten-foot pole . . . although he probably could if he wasn't set on being as diplomatic as possible. He only nods and starts slogging back toward the Island Services vehicle, his flashlight cutting arcs through the falling snow. HENRY opens his door again to call after him.

> HENRY

Can you raise the town hall on the CB? Tell Carla and Sandy we're okay?

HATCH gives him a thumbs-up and climbs into the truck. He revs the engine, then pulls slowly around so he's headed back toward the market, all four wheels whirring and spuming up snow. The Sno-Cat, with ROBBIE at the controls, follows.

43  INTERIOR: THE CAB OF THE ISLAND SERVICES VEHICLE, WITH HATCH.

> HATCH
> (on the radio)

Ursula? Are you there, Ursula? Come on back?

44    INTERIOR: THE TOWN OFFICE.

There's a good-sized crowd, very anxious, grouped around URSULA. Among them is FERD ANDREWS, now out of his coat, sipping a hot drink and wearing a blanket. Also prominent are MOLLY, CARLA, and SANDY, who now has DON with her, for comfort.

> HATCH (staticky radio voice)
> . . . sala? . . . Come on . . . ack . . .

URSULA ignores the voice for a moment, holding the mike against her shoulder and looking uneasily at the crowd, which is hemming her in even more closely now, eager to hear any fresh news. These are her neighbors, sure, but . . .

MOLLY sees the incipient agoraphobic reaction and turns to the crowd.

> MOLLY
> Come on, folks, give Ursula some room. Back off . . . If we hear anything, you'll know.

> TESS MARCHANT
> (joining in)
> Move back! Move back! If you don't have anything else to do, go on downstairs and watch the storm on the Weather Network!

> UPTON BELL
> Can't! The cable's out!

But they move back and give URSULA some room. She flashes MOLLY and TESS a look of thanks, then raises the microphone and pushes the transmit button.

> URSULA
> You're weak, but I've got you, Hatch. Talk slow and loud, come on back.

45    INTERIOR: THE ISLAND SERVICES VEHICLE, WITH HATCH.

HATCH
Robbie and Henry are fine. Thought you'd want to know that, come back.

46   INTERIOR: THE TOWN HALL, FEATURING URSULA.

SANDRA BEALS and CARLA BRIGHT both register relief. DON, never one to rest for long when there are toys to be destroyed and peers to humiliate, tears free of his mother and hurtles back downstairs.

DON BEALS
My dad's okay! He's the town manager! He can pass a football nine miles! Last year he sold a billion-billion dollars of insurance! Who wants to play monkey?

URSULA
Is Lloyd Wishman really dead, Hatch?

47   INTERIOR: THE ISLAND SERVICES VEHICLE, WITH HATCH.

He hesitates and exchanges a glance with KIRK FREEMAN. No help there. HATCH knows he must be careful; deciding what information to give out and what to sit on is really MIKE'S job. He checks the rearview, just to make sure the Sno-Cat's still behind him. It is.

HATCH
Uh . . . I don't know all the details yet, Urse. Just tell Sandy and Carla their boys'll be a while longer. Mike wants 'em over to the store for a little bit.

URSULA (very staticky voice)
Why . . . ore? Is that . . . ocked up? Molly wants . . . know . . .

HATCH
Can't hear you very well, Urse—you're breakin' up. I'll try you again in a little while. This is Island Services, 10-60 by.

He hangs up the mike with an expression of guilty relief, sees KIRK looking at him, and gives KIRK a little shrug.

HATCH
Hell, *I* don't know what to tell 'em! Let Mike do that part— it's what they pay him for.

KIRK

Yeah—grocery money, with a few bucks left over for lottery
tickets.

48   INTERIOR: MIKE AND LINOGE, IN THE CONSTABLE'S OFFICE—NIGHT.

MIKE is sitting in the chair he dragged over. LINOGE is sitting on his
bunk with his back to the wall and his knees apart. They look at each
other through the bars. In the background, by the desk, JACK CARVER
stands watching them.

MIKE

Where's your cane?
(no response from LINOGE)
You had a cane—I know you did—where is it?
(no response from LINOGE)
Sir, how did you get to Little Tall Island?
(no response)

MIKE holds up the Polaroid that shows the message over MARTHA'S
living room door.

MIKE

"Give me what I want and I'll go away." Did you write that?
You did, didn't you?
(no response)
Just what is it you want, sir?

No response . . . but the prisoner's eyes gleam. The tips of his teeth
show in that creepy little smile. MIKE gives him time, but there is no
more.

MIKE

Andre Linoge. I take it you're French. There are a lot of
people of French descent on the island. We've got St.
Pierres . . . Robichauxes . . . Bissonettes . . .
(no response)
What happened to Peter Godsoe? Did you have something to
do with that?
(no response)
How did you happen to know he was running pot out of his
warehouse? Always assuming that he was?

LINOGE

I know a lot, Constable. I know, for instance, that when you were at the University of Maine, and in danger of losing your scholarship over a D in chemistry during your sophomore year, you cheated on the midterm exam. Not even your wife knows that, does she?

MIKE is rocked. He doesn't want LINOGE to see it, but he can't help it.

MIKE

I don't know where you get your information, but you're wrong on that one. I was going to—I had a crib sheet, Mr. Linoge, and every intention of using it—but I threw it away at the last minute.

LINOGE

I'm sure that over the years, you've convinced yourself that's the truth . . . but right now we both know better. You ought to tell Ralphie sometime. It would make a nice bedtime story, I think. "How Daddy Got Through College."
(shifts his attention to JACK)
You never cheated on an exam in college, did you? Never *went* to college, and nobody bothers you for pulling *D*'s in high school.

JACK is staring, wide-eyed.

                         LINOGE
They still put you in jail for assault, though . . . if you get
caught. You were lucky last year, weren't you? You and
Lucien Fournier and Alex Haber. Lucky boys.

                         JACK
Shut up!

                         LINOGE
That fella just rubbed you guys the wrong way, didn't he? Had
kind of a lisp . . . and that blond hair, curly like a girl's
hair . . . not to mention the way he walked . . . Still, three
against one . . . and pool cues . . . well . . . hardly sporting—

LINOGE makes a *tsk-tsk* sound. JACK takes a step toward the desk, and
his fists CLENCH.

                         JACK
I'm warning you, mister!

                         LINOGE
                      (smiling)
The kid lost an eye—how about that, huh? You could go and
see for yourself. He lives in Lewiston. He wears a paisley eye-
patch his sister made him. He can't cry out of that eye—the
tear duct is toast. He lies in bed late at night and listens to the
cars on Lisbon Street and the live bands from the bottle
clubs, the ones that can play anything as long as it's "Louie
Louie" or "Hang On Sloopy," and he prays to St. Andrew to
bring back the sight in his left eye. He can't drive anymore;
he lost his depth perception. That happens when you lose an
eye. He can't even read for long, because it gives him
headaches. Still, he had that swishy way of walking . . . and
that lisp . . . and you guys kind of liked the way his hair
looked, all around his face like it was, although you'd never
say that to each other, would you? Kind of turned you on.
Kind of wondered what it would feel like to run your hands
through it—

JACK grabs the gun off the desk and points it at the cell.

JACK
Shut up or I'll shut you up! I swear!

MIKE
Jack, put that down!

LINOGE never moves, but his face has taken on a kind of DARK GLOW. No special contact lenses or special-effects tricks here; it's all in his face—goading . . . hateful . . . powerful.

LINOGE
There's another bedtime story for a stormy night. I can see you in bed with your arm around your little boy's shoulders. "Buster, Daddy wants to tell you how he put the nasty queer man's eye out with the end of a pool cue, 'cause—"

JACK pulls the trigger of the pistol. MIKE falls off the chair he's been sitting in. He utters a CRY OF PAIN. LINOGE never budges from his place on the bunk, but now MIKE is on the floor, face down.

FADE TO BLACK. THIS ENDS ACT 1.

# Act 2

49 EXTERIOR: THE ISLAND MARKET—NIGHT.

The storm is HOWLING, the snow falling so thick and fast the store looks like a ghost.

SOUND: A RENDING, SPLINTERING CRACK. A tree falls, missing GODSOE'S truck but mashing the front end of MOLLY'S little car and pulverizing one end of the porch rail.

> JACK (voice-over)
> Mike! Mike, are you all right?

50 INTERIOR: THE CONSTABLE'S OFFICE.

MIKE is getting to his knees. His right hand is clapped to his left biceps, and a little blood is trickling through his fingers. JACK is overwhelmed with remorse and terror at what he's done . . . or almost done. He drops the gun back on the desk and rushes forward. MIKE, meanwhile, is getting to his feet.

> JACK
> (babbling)
> Mike, I'm sorry . . . I didn't mean . . . are you all r—

MIKE pushes him violently backward.

> MIKE
> Keep a safe distance from him—didn't I tell you that?

But that's not why MIKE pushed him; MIKE pushed him for being an asshole, and JACK knows it. He stands between the cell and the desk, his mouth quivering and his eyes wet. MIKE takes his hand away from his arm to examine the damage. His shirt is torn, and blood is oozing out of the rip.

158

SOUND: ENGINES. The four-wheel drive and the Sno-Cat, approaching.

> MIKE
> Barely clipped the skin. Lucky.
> (relief from JACK)
> But six inches to the left, I'm dead and he's laughing.

MIKE turns and looks at the cell. One of the bars has a scar of fresh, gleaming metal. MIKE reaches out and touches this with the tip of one finger, his expression wondering.

> MIKE
> Where—

> LINOGE
> Here.

He holds out one hand, curled into a fist. Like a man in a dream, MIKE puts his arm through the bars, his hand open and palm up.

> JACK
> *Mike, no!*

MIKE pays no attention. LINOGE'S curled hand hovers over his palm, then opens. Something small and black drops. MIKE withdraws his hand. JACK comes forward a step or two. MIKE tweezes the tiny object between his fingers and holds it up so they can both see it. It's the slug from the bullet JACK fired.

SOUND OF ENGINES IS LOUDER.

> MIKE
> (to LINOGE)
> You caught this? You did, didn't you?

LINOGE only looks at him, smiling, saying nothing.

51   EXTERIOR: THE MARKET—NIGHT.

The Island Services four-wheel drive pulls into the parking area, and the Sno-Cat pulls in next to it. The four men get out and look at the downed tree that's mashed the car and the porch.

> HATCH
> Will his insurance cover that, Robbie?

> ROBBIE
> (don't bother me with trivialities)
> Come on. Let's get out of this.

They start up the porch steps.

52   INTERIOR: THE CONSTABLE'S OFFICE.

MIKE'S shirtsleeve is rolled up, showing a shallow gash across his biceps. There's an open first-aid kit on the desk beside the handgun. JACK puts a folded-over gauze pad on the wound, then anchors it with a Band-Aid.

> JACK
> Mike, I'm really sorry.

MIKE takes a deep breath, holds it, lets it out, and stops being mad. It takes an effort, but he manages.

The market's main door opens. The bell above it TINKLES; there's the CLOMP OF BOOTS and the MURMUR OF APPROACHING VOICES.

> MIKE
> That's Hatch!

> JACK
> About the stuff that guy said . . .

JACK turns a hateful, bewildered look on LINOGE, who looks back at him calmly. MIKE holds up a hand to quiet JACK. The door opens. HATCH comes in, followed by HENRY BRIGHT and KIRK FREE-MAN. Last of all is ROBBIE BEALS, looking both truculent and scared. Not a good combination.

> ROBBIE
> All right, what's going on here?

MIKE

Robbie, I wish I knew.

53    EXTERIOR: THE INTERSECTION OF MAIN AND ATLANTIC—NIGHT.

The storm HOWLS. The drifts are deeper than ever now.

54    EXTERIOR: THE STORE WINDOW OF THE ISLAND DRUGSTORE—NIGHT.

There's a mural showing winter scenes: folks sledding, skiing, and skating. Hanging in front of it on threads are bottles of vitamins. KEEP YOUR WINTER RESISTANCE UP WITH NU-U GLOW VITAMINS! the legend at the top of the mural says. Standing by the wall to the left is a pendulum clock reading 8:30.

SOUND: Another of those RENDING, SPLINTERING crashes. A HUGE BRANCH crashes through the show window, SHATTERING IT and pulling down the mural. Snow goes flying into the drugstore.

55    EXTERIOR: THE TOWN HALL—NIGHT.

We can barely see it for the thickly falling snow.

56    INTERIOR: A CORNER OF THE TOWN HALL BASEMENT.

This is kid country. PIPPA HATCHER, HARRY ROBICHAUX, HEIDI ST. PIERRE, and FRANK BRIGHT are already asleep. MOLLY is sitting on the side of RALPHIE'S bed. RALPHIE is pretty sleepy.

Outside, THE WIND GUSTS NOISILY. The building, although brick, CREAKS. MOLLY looks up.

RALPHIE

We won't blow away, will we? Like the house of straw and the house of twigs?

MOLLY

No, because the town hall's made of bricks, just like the third little pig's house. The storm can huff and puff all night long, and we'll still be safe.

RALPHIE
(sleepy)

Is Daddy safe?

MOLLY

Yes. Safe as can be.

She kisses the fairy-saddle birthmark on the bridge of his nose.

RALPHIE

He won't let the bad man get out and hurt us, will he?

MOLLY

Nope. I promise.

DON BEALS
(angry, yelling voice)
Put me down! Stop it! Leave me alone!

MOLLY turns toward:

57    INTERIOR: THE STAIRS TO THE BASEMENT—NIGHT.

SANDRA BEALS is trudging down them, carrying a kicking, squealing DON in her arms. The expression on her face suggests that she is used to such tantrums . . . *too* used to them, perhaps.

As she reaches the foot of the stairs, MOLLY comes hurrying to help, and DON finally succeeds in squirming free of his mother's grasp. He's tired and furious, exhibiting the sort of behavior that causes young marrieds to resolve never to have children.

MOLLY

Need some help?

SANDRA BEALS
(with a tired smile)
No . . . he's just a little scratchy . . .

DON BEALS

My *daddy* puts me to bed, not you!

SANDRA

Donnie, honey . . .

He kicks her. It's a child's kick, delivered by a sneaker, but it hurts.

                              DON
                          (spits it)
    My *daddy!* Not you!

For a moment we see real loathing for this child on MOLLY'S face. She
reaches out—DON cringes away from her a little, eyes narrowing—

                            SANDRA
    Molly, no!

—but MOLLY only turns him around and gives him a swat on the
fanny.

                             MOLLY
                      (pleasant as pie)
    Go upstairs. Wait for your daddy.

DON BEALS, charming to the end, BLOWS A RASPBERRY at
MOLLY, showering her with droplets of spittle. Then he scampers
upstairs. The two women watch him go, SANDRA embarrassed over
her son's behavior, MOLLY pulling herself back together. We should
see that, good mom and day-care teacher or no, it at least crossed her
mind to slap the little snothead's face for him, instead of swatting him
lightly on the butt.

                            SANDRA
    I'm sorry, Moll. I thought he might be ready. He's . . . he's
    used to having his dad tuck him in at night.

                             MOLLY
    Better let him stay up—I think Buster's still running around
    up there, too. They'll play tag for a while and then fall asleep
    in a corner somewhere.

During this, they walk back into the kiddie area, lowering their voices
as they go.

                            SANDRA
    As long as he didn't disturb anyone . . .

                             MOLLY
    Nah, they're out like lights.

And that includes RALPHIE. MOLLY pulls the blanket up to his chin and kisses the corner of his mouth. SANDRA looks at this enviously.

> SANDRA
> I worry about Donnie sometimes. I love him, but I worry about him, too.

> MOLLY
> They go through stages, Sandy. Don may have his . . . his unlovely moments now, but in the end he'll be fine.

She's dubious, though, hoping what she says is true but not really believing it. Outside, the WIND SCREAMS. The two women look up uneasily . . . and SANDRA gives in to a sudden urge to confide.

> SANDRA
> I'm leaving Robbie in the spring. I'm taking Donnie and going back to my folks' on Deer Isle. I didn't think I'd made up my mind for sure, but . . . I guess I have.

MOLLY looks at her with a combination of sympathy and confusion. Doesn't know how to respond.

58   INTERIOR: THE TOWN HALL KITCHEN—NIGHT.

This is a pretty well equipped place—a lot of bean suppers and holiday meals have been prepared here. Now a number of WOMEN are bustling around, making ready for tomorrow's storm center breakfast. One of them is MRS. KINGSBURY; another is JOANNA STANHOPE. JOANNA'S mother-in-law sits by the door like a queen, overseeing the proceedings. CAT WITHERS comes into the room, dressed for outdoors.

> MRS. KINGSBURY
> Going to help Billy?

> CAT
> Yes, ma'am.

> MRS. KINGSBURY
> See if there's any oatmeal on the very back shelf. And tell Billy to remember the juice.

CORA

Oh, I imagine he don't have any problem in the juice department. Does he?

CORA, who has no idea of what happened when LINOGE was brought through the store, and consequently has no idea of the trouble that's now between CAT and BILLY, gives a nasty old woman's chuckle. CAT is not amused. She crosses to the back door. Her face—what we can see of it between her pulled-up scarf and pulled-down hat—is care-worn and unhappy. Yet she's determined to talk to BILLY and to save the relationship if she can.

59    EXTERIOR: THE REAR OF THE TOWN HALL—NIGHT.

Here is a snow-covered, drifted-in walk leading to a small brick annex—the supply shed. The shed door is open, and the faint light of a Coleman lantern drifts out into the blowing snow, showing us a wide, flat track, which is already drifting over.

THE CAMERA moves into this shed, and we see BILLY SOAMES, also bundled up, putting supplies onto the toboggan he has pulled out here. Mostly they're the concentrates URSULA spoke of—pour water over the powder and then gag it down—but there are also cartons filled with packages of cereal, a basket of apples, and several bags of potatoes.

CAT (voice-over)

Billy?

He turns.

60    INTERIOR: THE SUPPLY SHED—NIGHT.

CAT is standing in the doorway. BILLY looks back at her. Their breath SMOKES in the uncertain light of the gas lantern. There is a vast gulf of distrust between them now.

CAT

Can I talk to you?

BILLY

I guess. Why not?

CAT

Billy, I—

BILLY

Is it true, what he said? Let's talk about that. Did you go up
Derry and have an abortion?

She says nothing. It's answer enough.

BILLY

I guess that's all the talk we need, isn't it? I guess that says it
all.

He deliberately turns away from her and starts rummaging on the
shelves again. CAT reacts to this with frustrated anger and enters the
shed, stepping over the half-loaded toboggan to get to him.

CAT

Don't you want to know why?

BILLY

Not particularly. It was ours—at least I guess it was—and
it's dead. Guess that's all I need to know.

CAT is angrier than ever. She's forgetting she came out here to save the
village, not destroy it. Given his attitude, that's maybe not surprising.

CAT

You asked me one; I'll ask you one. What about Jenna
Freeman?

There's a challenging tone in her voice. BILLY'S hands freeze on the
cans he's been sorting. These are cafeteria-sized cans of apple juice.
Each label reads "McCALL'S BRAND" above a picture of a ripe apple.
Below the apple are the words "GRADE A FANCY." BILLY turns to
CAT, chin pugnaciously forward.

BILLY

Why do you ask, if you already know?

CAT

Maybe to get that Little Minister look off your face. Yeah, I knew. The biggest tramp on the coast, and you chasing her like she was on fire and you wanted to put her out.

> BILLY

It wasn't like that.

> CAT

Then what *was* it like? Tell me.

No answer from BILLY. He's got his back to the shelves now; he's facing her, but he won't meet her eyes.

> CAT

I don't understand it—I never told you no. Never once did I tell you no. And *still* . . . Billy, how many times a day do you itch?

> BILLY

What has that got to do with our baby? The one I had to hear about from a stranger, and in front of half the town?

> CAT

I knew who you were running with, don't you get that? How was I supposed to trust you to do the right thing? *How was I supposed to trust you at all?*

BILLY doesn't reply. His jaw is set. If there is truth in what she's saying, he's not seeing it. *Won't* see it, likely.

> CAT

Do you know what it's like to find out you're pregnant one week, and that your boyfriend is spending his afternoons with the town pump the next?

She's now right in his face, shouting up at him.

> BILLY
> (shouting back)

That baby was half mine! You went up to Derry and murdered it, and it was half mine!

> CAT
> (jeering)
> Yeah, sure. Now that it's gone, it's half yours.

61   INTERIOR: THE CONSTABLE'S OFFICE, FEATURING LINOGE—NIGHT.

The five men—MIKE, HATCH, KIRK, JACK, and ROBBIE—are gathered around the desk, while MIKE tries to reach the Machias state police on the radio. HATCH is watching MIKE, but the rest can't keep their eyes off LINOGE.

Suddenly the prisoner sits up, his eyes widening. JACK elbows MIKE to get his attention. MIKE turns to look. As he does, LINOGE extends one hand with the forefinger pointed down. He revolves it once in the air.

62   INTERIOR: SUPPLY SHED, WITH CAT AND BILLY—NIGHT.

BILLY turns back to the shelf, so his back is to her. This move exactly mimes the turning gesture LINOGE made with his finger.

> BILLY
> What's that supposed to mean?

> CAT
> That I'm not stupid. If I'd come to you when you were still chasing after Jenna, I know what you would have thought— "Little bitch got herself pregnant just to make sure I wouldn't get away."

> BILLY
> You did a whole lot of my thinking for me, didn't you?

> CAT
> You ought to thank me! You sure haven't been doing much for yourself!

> BILLY
> And what about the baby? The one you murdered? How much thinking did you do about the baby?
> (no reply from CAT)
> Get out of here. I can't stand listening to you.

CAT

Dear God. You're unfaithful, and that's bad, but you're a coward, and that's worse—too chicken to own up to the part of this that belongs to you. I thought maybe I could save us, but there's nothing to save. You're only a stupid kid, after all.

She turns to go. BILLY'S face cramps with rage. He stands facing the shelves, and now he sees:

63    INTERIOR: THE CANS OF JUICE, FROM BILLY'S POINT OF VIEW.

"McCALL'S BRAND" at the top has been replaced by "McCANE'S BRAND." The ripe apple on the labels has been replaced by a black cane with a silver wolf's head. And instead of "GRADE A FANCY," each can reads "GRADE A BITCHY."

64    INTERIOR: THE CONSTABLE'S OFFICE, FEATURES LINOGE.

LINOGE puts out his hand and MIMES GRIPPING AN OBJECT.

KIRK

What's he doing?

MIKE shakes his head. He doesn't know.

65    INTERIOR: THE STORAGE SHED, WITH BILLY AND CAT.

He takes one of the cans off the shelf, gripping it like a club as CAT, headed for the door, steps over the half-loaded toboggan behind him.

66    INTERIOR: THE CONSTABLE'S OFFICE, FEATURES LINOGE.

MIKE

What's up, sir? Mind telling me?

LINOGE takes no notice. He's totally absorbed. He makes the twirling gesture with his forefinger again, then scissors his fingers in the air to mime WALKING.

67    INTERIOR: THE SHED, WITH BILLY AND CAT.

She's at the door, back to him, when BILLY turns with the big can of apple juice. He steps toward her—

68   INTERIOR: THE CONSTABLE'S OFFICE.

MIKE walks toward the cell as LINOGE gets to his feet and raises his arm above his head. His hand is cupped, as if holding an object that only he can see.

69   INTERIOR: THE SHED, WITH BILLY AND CAT.

As CAT steps out into the storm, BILLY raises the can over his head.

70   INTERIOR: THE CELL, WITH LINOGE.

He raises his other hand, now MIMING A TWO-HANDED GRIP.

71   EXTERIOR: OUTSIDE THE SUPPLY SHED, WITH CAT—NIGHT.

She stands just outside the door on the rapidly disappearing toboggan track. She wipes the tears from her cheeks with her gloved palms, then readjusts her scarf.

It gives BILLY plenty of time. He appears behind her in the doorway with the can raised over his head in both hands, his face twisted into a hateful grimace.

72   INTERIOR: THE CELL, WITH LINOGE.

MIKE stands outside the bars, looking at his prisoner with perplexity and fear. The other men huddle behind him. LINOGE ignores them all and BRINGS HIS HANDS DOWN.

73   EXTERIOR: THE SUPPLY SHED, WITH BILLY AND CAT.

BILLY almost does it. We see the heavy can of apple juice actually start an arc of descent that would mime the one described by LINOGE'S hands, and then it stops. The expression of BLIND RAGE on BILLY'S face breaks up into one of bewilderment and horror—my God, he's almost caved her skull in!

CAT neither knows nor intuits any of this. She begins trudging back toward the town hall with her head lowered and the ends of her scarf blowing in the gale.

74   INTERIOR: THE CELL, WITH LINOGE.

He's still bent over, his linked hands swinging by his knees, the picture of a man who has just delivered a hard blow with a heavy object. But he knows he's failed. His face is BEADED WITH SWEAT, and his eyes are hot with fury.

LINOGE
She's right. You *are* a coward.

MIKE
What in the hell are you—

LINOGE
(roaring)
*Shut up!*

On the table, one of the Coleman gas lamps BLOWS APART, glass spraying. The men by the desk CRINGE.

LINOGE wheels around, looking wild and distracted—more like a tiger in a cage than ever—and then throws himself facedown on the cot, with his arms wrapped around his head. He's MUTTERING. MIKE leans as close as the cell bars will allow, listening.

LINOGE
The back step . . . the back step . . . by the back step . . .

75   EXTERIOR: THE BACK STEPS OF THE TOWN HALL—NIGHT.

We're looking through the snow-filled panes into the kitchen, where CORA still sits, observing the bustle of JOANNA and MRS. KINGS-BURY. They have now been joined by CARLA ST. PIERRE and ROBERTA COIGN—these two are loading the dishwasher. It all looks cozy and pleasant, especially given the HOWLING WIND and DRIV-ING SNOW just outside.

THE CAMERA PANS DOWN. Beside the snow-covered stoop is a milk storage box. And leaning against the milk box, buried to half its length in a snowdrift, is LINOGE'S CANE. The wolf's head glares.

CAT'S GLOVED HAND comes down and touches the silver head. One finger runs over the wolf's snarling muzzle.

76    EXTERIOR: CAT, CLOSE-UP—NIGHT.

Wide-eyed. Fascinated.

77    INTERIOR: THE CELL, WITH LINOGE—NIGHT.

Still facedown on his bunk, arms wrapped around his head, MUTTER-ING RAPIDLY. CHANTING. MIKE doesn't know what's going on, but he knows it's bad news.

> MIKE
>
> Stop it, Linoge!

LINOGE pays no attention. If anything, the RAPID MUMBLE of his words SPEEDS UP.

78    EXTERIOR: THE BACK STOOP OF THE TOWN HALL—NIGHT.

CAT is gone, but we can see her tracks—where she turned around and headed back to the supply shed again.

The cane is gone, too. Blowing snow is rapidly softening the edges of the hole where its barrel was shoved into the snowbank.

79    INTERIOR: THE SUPPLY SHED, FEATURING BILLY—NIGHT.

He's squatting to one side of the toboggan, which is now completely loaded. He spreads a piece of tarp over the goods, then begins to secure this with a couple of pieces of elasticized cord.

We can't see the doorway from this angle, but we see the SHADOW SHAPE that falls over him . . . and we also see the SHADOW OF THE CANE when it extends itself from the human shape and begins to rise. The movement attracts BILLY'S eye, as well. He shifts position . . . looks up . . .

80    INTERIOR: CAT WITHERS, FROM BILLY'S POINT OF VIEW—NIGHT.

Transformed into an avenging harpy. Her lips are pulled back from her teeth in a snarl. She is holding the cane by its foot, with the wolf's head protruding.

She SCREAMS and brings the cane down.

81    INTERIOR: LINOGE, FACEDOWN ON THE CELL COT.

SCREAMING TRIUMPHANTLY into the pillow, with his arms still wrapped around his head.

82    INTERIOR: THE CONSTABLE'S OFFICE, WIDER.

MIKE backs away from the cell door, UNNERVED. The other four men are pressed together like sheep in a hailstorm. All of them are TERRIFIED. LINOGE CONTINUES SCREAMING.

83    EXTERIOR: ANGLE ON THE SUPPLY SHED—NIGHT.

From out here, we can't see what's happening, and that's probably good. We can see CAT'S SHADOW, however . . . and the shadow of the cane, rising and falling, rising and falling.

FADE TO BLACK. THIS ENDS ACT 2.

# Act 3

84   EXTERIOR: THE LIGHTHOUSE—NIGHT.

The tide, now on the ebb, sends up explosions of **FOAMY WATER**, but the searchlight continues to swing around. Some of the windows at the top are broken out, but the lighthouse has won out over the storm. For now, anyway.

85   EXTERIOR: THE DISPLAY WINDOW OF THE ISLAND DRUGSTORE—NIGHT.

The aisles of the store are filling up with snow, and it's started to coat the glass over the face of the pendulum clock, but we can still read the time: 8:47.

86   INTERIOR: A CORNER OF THE TOWN HALL BASEMENT, WITH MOLLY.

She's in a wing chair in one corner, with a pair of Walkman earphones on. They're on crooked and slipping down further all the time. We can hear **THE FAINT SOUND OF CLASSICAL MUSIC. MOLLY** is fast asleep.

Hands reach into the frame and take off the headphones. When this happens, MOLLY opens her eyes. There's a girl of about seventeen standing beside her. ANNIE smiles, a bit embarrassed, and holds out the headphones.

                    ANNIE HUSTON
Want 'em back? They were, like, slipping off.


                    MOLLY
No, thanks, Annie. With those things I always end up asleep
and listening to Schubert on my fillings.

She gets up, stretches, then puts the Walkman on the seat of the chair. The part of the downstairs that serves as an activity area has been curtained off from the sleeping area, which we can see through the gap

174

in the makeshift draw curtains. The KIDS are all sleeping, now, and a few adults have turned in, as well.

There's a TV against one wall of the activity area. About forty people are gathered around it, some sitting on the floor, some in folding wooden Bingo chairs, some standing at the back. The TV is broadcasting a FUZZY PICTURE that shows the weatherman from WVII, the Bangor ABC affiliate. Standing beside the TV and turning the rabbit ears this way and that, hoping for a better picture (pretty much a lost cause, I'm afraid) is LUCIEN FOURNIER, a good-looking man of about thirty in a reindeer sweater. He's one of JACK CARVER'S gay-bashing buddies.

> WEATHER GUY
>
> At this time the storm is continuing to build, with the greatest concentrations of snow in the coastal and central areas. We here at Channel Seven find the numbers almost impossible to believe, but Machias is already reporting a fresh foot and a half . . . this is without the drift factor, remember, and zero visibility. No traffic is on the roads. (laughs) Hey, what roads, right? Conditions in Bangor are nearly as bad, with power outages reported all up and down the grid. Brewer is entirely dark, and in Southwest Harbor, a church steeple has reportedly blown over. It's bad out there, and we haven't seen the peak of the storm yet. This is one you'll be telling your grandchildren about . . . and they probably won't believe you. Every now and then I have to look out the newsroom window to believe it myself.

Standing near the back of the crowd, peering around the other standees, is URSULA GODSOE. MOLLY taps her on the shoulder, and URSULA turns to her, unsmiling.

> MOLLY
> (nods toward the TV)
> What're they saying?

> URSULA
> Howl and blast followed by blast and howl. Such condition to continue through tomorrow and into tomorrow night, when things are finally supposed to start quieting down.

Power's out from Kittery to Millinocket. Coastal communities are cut off. Us island guys . . . forget it.

She looks really dreadful. MOLLY sees it; she reacts with sympathy and some curiosity, as well.

> MOLLY
>
> What's wrong?

> URSULA
>
> I don't know. I've just got a feeling. A really bad one.

> MOLLY
>
> Well, who wouldn't? Martha Clarendon murdered . . . Lloyd Wishman kills himself . . . the Storm of the Century right over our heads . . . who wouldn't?

> URSULA
>
> I think it's more than that.

87    EXTERIOR: ANGLE ON THE SUPPLY SHED—NIGHT.

For a moment or two the doorway is empty, and then CAT steps slowly into it and stops. Her eyes are wide and blank. On the strip of visible skin between the top of her scarf and the bottom of her hat, we can see SMALL STIPPLES OF BLOOD on her cheeks. They look almost like freckles. In one hand she still holds the cane. The wolf's head is once more CAKED WITH BLOOD.

THE CAMERA BEGINS TO MOVE IN as some comprehension of what she's done flickers in CAT'S eyes. She looks down at the cane and drops it.

88    EXTERIOR: THE CANE, FROM CAT'S POINT OF VIEW.

It lies just outside the doorway in the snow, leering up at her. The silver wolf's eyes are full of blood.

89    EXTERIOR: RESUME CAT, IN THE SUPPLY SHED DOORWAY—NIGHT.

She raises her gloved hands to her cheeks. Then, perhaps feeling something, she takes them away and looks at them. Her face is still blank, drugged-looking . . . she's in a state of shock.

90    INTERIOR: THE BASEMENT, FEATURES MOLLY AND URSULA.

URSULA looks around to see if they're being overheard. They're not, but she leads MOLLY toward a relatively deserted area near the foot of the stairs anyway, just to be safe. MOLLY looks at her, concerned and worried. Outside, the WIND HOWLS BIG. The women, on the other hand, are very small.

> URSULA
> When I get these feelings, I trust them. Over the years, I've *learned* to trust them. I . . . Molly, I think something's happened to Peter.

> MOLLY
> (instant concern)
> Why? Has anyone come back from the store? Has Mike—

> URSULA
> No one's come in from that end of town since eight o'clock, but Mike's okay.

She sees MOLLY isn't convinced, and smiles a little bitterly.

> URSULA
> Nothing psychic about that part of it—I've picked up a couple of broken transmissions on the radio. Once it was Hatch; once I'm pretty sure it was Mike.

> MOLLY
> Saying what? Talking to who?

> URSULA
> With the antennas blown down, it's impossible to tell, base unit to base unit; it's just voices. I imagine they're still trying to raise the staties in Machias.

> MOLLY
> So you haven't heard anything about Peter, and you can't know—

> URSULA

No . . . but somehow I do. If I can get Lucien Fournier to stop fiddling with that TV and take me down to the constable's on his snow machine, can you mind things here? Unless the roof falls in, all it amounts to is saying everything's fine, breakfast's at seven, and we still need folks on the serving crew and to do cleanup after. Work's mostly done for tonight, thank God. People've already started going to bed.

> MOLLY

I'll come with you. Tavia can handle things here. I want to see Mike.

> URSULA

No. Not with Ralphie here and a maybe dangerous prisoner down there.

> MOLLY

You've got a kid to think about, too. Sally's here.

> URSULA

It's *Sally's* Dad I'm worried about, not Ralphie's. As for Tavia Godsoe . . . I'd never say this to her face because I love her, but she's got old maid's disease—she worships her brother. If she gets the idea anything happened to Peter . . .

> MOLLY

All right. But you tell Mike I want him to set a guard—however many men he needs, none of 'em's doing anything else tonight, anyway—and get back here. Tell him his wife wants to see him.

> URSULA

I'll give him the message.

She leaves MOLLY and makes her way through the crowd around the TV, aiming for LUCIEN.

91   EXTERIOR: ANGLE ON THE SUPPLY SHED—NIGHT.

CAT is still looking at her hands, but now a kind of comprehension is starting to dawn in her eyes. She looks from the bloody cane to her bloody gloves . . . back to the cane . . . back to the gloves . . . up into the storm. Then she opens her mouth as wide as it can go, and SHRIEKS.

92    INTERIOR: THE TOWN HALL KITCHEN—NIGHT.

JOANNA, who is washing pots in the sink and happens to be closest to the back door, looks up, frowning. The others continue on with their work.

> JOANNA
>
> Did you hear something?

> CORA
>
> Just the wind.

> JOANNA
>
> It sounded like a scream.

> CORA
> (exaggerated patience)
> That's how the wind *sounds* tonight, deah.

JOANNA, who is just about fed up with her mother-in-law, looks at MRS. KINGSBURY.

> JOANNA
>
> Did that girl from the market come back in? She didn't, did she?

> MRS. KINGSBURY
> No, not this way—

> CORA
> I imagine they had things to discuss, Joanna.

A sly look. Accompanying it, probably the dirtiest gesture we can get away with on network TV (or maybe it's too dirty): the old lady makes a loose fist, then taps the forefinger of her other hand around the edge of the hole, smiling as she does so.

JOANNA looks at this with distaste, then grabs a parka from the coat tree in the corner. It's too big, but she zips it up.

### CORA

My mother always said, "Peep not at a keyhole, lest ye be vexed."

### JOANNA

It sounded like a *scream*.

### CORA

I find that ridiculous.

### JOANNA

Shut up. *Mother.*

CORA is stunned. MRS. KINGSBURY is surprised, but also pleased— clearly restraining an impulse to yell, "You go, girl!" JOANNA, who knows a good exit line when she says one, flips up the fur-lined hood of the parka and slips out the back door into the HOWLING DARK.

93   INTERIOR: RESUME TOWN HALL BASEMENT, WITH MOLLY.

She watches URSULA speak to LUCIEN, who stops twiddling the rabbit ears and listens intently. On the snowy TV screen, we see a map of Maine. Most has been colored in red, with the words "SNOW EMERGENCY" displayed in big white letters. Also "3 TO 5 !!!FEET!!! + DRIFTING, BLOWING SNOW." During this:

### WEATHER GUY

If you are in an outlying area, you are advised to stay where you are even if you have lost power and have no heat. Tonight shelter is your prime necessity. If you are in a sheltered place, do not leave it. Keep warm, bundle up, share your food, and share your strength. If there was ever a night for good neighbors, this is it. There is a state of snow emergency in central and coastal Maine tonight—repeat, there is a state of snow emergency on the coast and in the central regions of the state.

JOHNNY HARRIMAN and JONAS STANHOPE come downstairs, bearing big trays of cake and cookies. Behind them comes ANNIE HUSTON, with her arms wrapped around the shiny steel belly of an industrial-sized coffee urn. MOLLY, still very worried, stands aside to let them pass. She's intently watching URSULA'S conversation with LUCIEN.

> JOHNNY
> Everything all right, Molly Anderson?

> MOLLY
> Fine. Just fine.

> JONAS STANHOPE
> This is gonna be one to tell your grandchildren about.

> MOLLY
> It already is.

94    EXTERIOR: BETWEEN THE BACK OF THE TOWN HALL AND THE SHED—NIGHT.

Here comes JOANNA, struggling along. The parka she grabbed flaps around her like a sail, and the hood keeps flying back. At last, however, she approaches the supply shed. The door is still open, but CAT is no longer standing in it.

Still, JOANNA stops perhaps six feet outside the door. Something is wrong here, and like URSULA, she feels it.

> JOANNA
> Katrina? Cat?

Nothing. She comes forward another two steps, into the hard, flickery light thrown by the gas lamp. She looks down at:

95    EXTERIOR: THE SNOW OUTSIDE THE DOOR, FROM JOANNA'S POINT OF VIEW—NIGHT.

Most of the evidence has either been blown away or covered over by the SHRIEKING WIND, but there is still some PINKISH STAIN where CAT dropped LINOGE'S cane, although the cane itself is gone. And, beyond it, is a BRIGHTER STAIN on the shed's doorsill, where CAT stood.

96   EXTERIOR: RESUME JOANNA—NIGHT.

JOANNA

Cat . . . ?

She would like to go back now—it's scary out here in the blizzard—but she's come too far. She steps very slowly toward the shed door, holding the parka's hood pinched shut at the base of her throat like an old woman's shawl.

97   INTERIOR: THE SHED DOORWAY, LOOKING OUT—NIGHT.

JOANNA comes to the doorway and stands, eyes slowly widening with horror.

98   INTERIOR: THE SUPPLY SHED, FROM JOANNA'S POINT OF VIEW—NIGHT.

There's blood everywhere—on the industrial-sized boxes of cereal and powdered milk, the bags of rice and flour and sugar, the large plastic bottles labeled COLA, ORANGE DRINK, and FRUIT PUNCH. There's blood SIZZLING on the side of the lantern, blood on the wall calendar, and BLOODY GLOVEPRINTS on the bare boards and beams (this is a pretty utilitarian place). There's blood on the goods BILLY piled onto the toboggan, too. We can see this stuff because the tarp is gone.

99   INTERIOR: RESUME JOANNA, IN THE SHED DOORWAY.

Looks at:

100   INTERIOR: A CORNER OF THE SUPPLY SHED, FROM JOANNA'S POINT OF VIEW.

Here's the tarp. It's been used to cover BILLY'S body, but his feet stick out.

THE CAMERA PANS across the back of the shed. Here, in the other corner, CAT WITHERS is crouched in a fetal position, her knees drawn up to her chest and the fingers of one hand crammed into her mouth. She looks up at JOANNA—THE CAMERA—with wide, dazed eyes.

101   INTERIOR: RESUME JOANNA, IN THE SHED DOORWAY.

JOANNA

Cat . . . what happened?

102    INTERIOR: RESUME CAT, CROUCHED IN THE CORNER.

CAT

I covered him up. He wouldn't want people to see him the way he is now, so I covered him up. (pause) I covered him up because I loved him.

103    INTERIOR: RESUME JOANNA, IN THE SHED DOORWAY.

Utter horror.

104    INTERIOR: RESUME CAT, CROUCHED IN THE CORNER.

CAT

I think it was the cane with the wolf's head that made me do it. I wouldn't touch it, if I were you.
(looks around)
So much blood. I loved him, and now look. I went and I killed him.

Slowly, she puts her fingers back into her mouth.

105    INTERIOR: RESUME JOANNA, IN THE SHED DOORWAY.

JOANNA

Oh, Cat. Oh, my God.

She turns and blunders away into the dark, headed back in the direction of the town hall.

106    INTERIOR: RESUME CAT, CROUCHED IN THE CORNER.

She's huddled, looking around with big eyes. Then she begins to sing in a lilting little-girl's voice. The words are muffled by her fingers, but we can make them out:

CAT
(sings)

"I'm a little teapot, short and stout. . . . Here is my handle, here is my spout. You can pick me up and pour me out. . . . I'm a little teapot, short and stout."

107    EXTERIOR: JOANNA—NIGHT.

She's struggling back toward the town hall. The hood of the parka has been flipped back by the wind once more, but this time she makes no effort to pull it back up. She stops, seeing:

108    EXTERIOR: THE TOWN HALL PARKING LOT, FROM JOANNA'S POINT OF VIEW—NIGHT.

Two figures are fighting their way through the snow toward a rank of snowmobiles near the side of the building.

109    EXTERIOR: RESUME JOANNA—NIGHT.

JOANNA
*Hey! Help! Help!*

110    EXTERIOR: RESUME PARKING LOT—NIGHT.

The two figures keep on moving. They haven't heard JOANNA over the HOWL OF THE WIND.

111    EXTERIOR: RESUME JOANNA—NIGHT.

She changes course, heading for the parking lot instead of the kitchen door, and tries to run. She throws one terrified glance back over her shoulder at the open door of the supply shed.

112    EXTERIOR: THE PARKING LOT, WITH URSULA AND LUCIEN.

They reach one of the snowmobiles. LUCIEN gets on the front.

URSULA
(shouts to be heard)
Don't you dump me in a snowbank, Lucien Fournier!

LUCIEN
No, ma'am.

URSULA studies him for a moment, as if to make sure he is telling the truth, then gets on the snowmobile. LUCIEN turns the key. The headlight and the rudimentary dashboard lights come on. He pushes the starter. The ENGINE CRANKS but does not immediately start.

URSULA
What's wrong?

> LUCIEN

Nothing, she's just bein' grumpy.

He yanks the choke and prepares to start again.

> JOANNA
> (faint voice)

*Hey! Help! HELP!*

URSULA puts her hand over LUCIEN's before he can punch the starter, and now they both hear. They turn toward:

113   EXTERIOR: JOANNA, FROM URSULA AND LUCIEN'S POINT OF VIEW—NIGHT.

She comes struggling and floundering through the drifts, reaching the parking lot, waving one hand like a drowning woman. She is snow-covered (has taken at least one tumble, I'd guess) and GASPING FOR BREATH.

114   EXTERIOR: AN ANGLE ON THE PARKING LOT—NIGHT.

LUCIEN gets off the snowmobile and makes his way to JOANNA. He's just in time to catch her before she can fall again. He helps her back toward the snowmobile and URSULA joins them, very concerned.

> URSULA

Jo, what's wrong?

> JOANNA

Billy . . . dead . . . back there!
> (points)

Katrina Withers killed him.

> URSULA

*Cat?*

> JOANNA

She's sitting in the corner . . . I think she tried to tell me she hit him with a cane . . . but there's so much blood . . . When I left, I think she was *singing* . . .

Shocked and bewildered reactions from URSULA and LUCIEN. UR-
SULA recovers a little more quickly.


                          URSULA
Are you really saying Cat Withers killed Billy Soames?
                  (JOANNA nods violently)
Are you sure? Jo, are you sure he's dead?


                          JOANNA
                         (nodding)
She covered him with a tarp, but I'm sure . . . so much
blood . . .


                          LUCIEN
We better go back and look.


                          JOANNA
                         (terror)
I'm not going back there! I'm not going anywhere near there!
She's in the corner . . . if you'd seen her . . . the look on her
face . . .


                          URSULA
Lucien, can I drive this thing?


                          LUCIEN
If you take it slow, sure, I guess. But—


                          URSULA
I'll take it slow, believe me. Jo and I are going to drive
downstreet and talk to Mike Anderson. Aren't we, Jo?


JOANNA nods with pitiful eagerness and climbs on the back of
LUCIEN'S snow machine. She'll agree to go anywhere before she
agrees to go back to the supply shed.


                          URSULA
                       (to LUCIEN)
Get a couple of guys, go out to the supply shed, and see
what's what, okay? But don't broadcast it . . . and play it
smart.

LUCIEN

What's going on here, Ursula?

She goes to the snowmobile, gets on the front, and thumbs the starter button. Now that the engine's been choked, it starts easily. She guns the throttle, then settles her gloved hands on the handgrips.

URSULA

I have no clue.

She drops the snowmobile in gear and drives away in a spume of snow, with JOANNA clinging to her. LUCIEN stands and watches them go, a picture of bewilderment.

115   EXTERIOR: THE ISLAND MARKET—NIGHT.

It's now little more than a drifted-in shape in the blizzard. The few lights seem feeble and forlorn.

116   EXTERIOR: THE LOADING DOCK BEHIND THE STORE—NIGHT.

The snowmobile on which JACK CARVER and KIRK FREEMAN arrived is almost buried in snow. On the loading dock itself, we see a shape that is PETER GODSOE. His body has been wrapped in a blanket and then secured with rope. He looks like a corpse that's ready for burial at sea.

117   INTERIOR: LINOGE, CLOSE.

His face is wolfish, intent. The eyes are bright and interested.

THE CAMERA DRAWS SLOWLY BACK through the bars. As our view of LINOGE widens, we see he has resumed his favorite position—back to the wall, heels on the edge of the cot, peering through his slightly spread knees.

118   INTERIOR: THE CONSTABLE'S OFFICE, ANGLE ON THE DESK.

Here are MIKE, HATCH, ROBBIE, HENRY BRIGHT, KIRK FREEMAN, and JACK CARVER. The latter five look at LINOGE with a mixture of distrust and fear. MIKE is looking at him with perplexity.

                          KIRK
I never seen anyone throw a fit like that in my life.


                          HENRY
                        (to MIKE)
No ID of any kind?


                          MIKE
No ID, no wallet, no money, no keys. No clothing tags, either,
not even on his blue jeans. He's just . . . here. And that's not
all.
                        (to ROBBIE)
Did he tell you anything? When you went into Martha's
house, Robbie, did he tell you anything he had no business
knowing?


ROBBIE is immediately nervous. He does not, as they say, want to go
there. But:


                      LINOGE (voice)
You were with a whore in Boston when your mother died in
Machias.


                          MIKE
Robbie?


119   INTERIOR: MARTHA CLARENDON'S LIVING ROOM *(flashback)*.

LINOGE PEEPS ROGUISHLY around one wing of MARTHA'S chair,
his face streaked with MARTHA'S blood.


                          LINOGE
She's waiting for you in hell. And she's turned cannibal. Hell
is repetition, Robbie. Isn't it? Born in sin, come on in . . .
CATCH!


DAVEY HOPEWELL'S bloodstained basketball FLIES AT THE
CAMERA.


120   INTERIOR: RESUME CONSTABLE'S OFFICE—NIGHT.

ROBBIE flinches as if the basketball were flying at his head; that's how
strong the memory is.

MIKE

He did, didn't he?

ROBBIE

He . . . said something about my mother. You don't need to know.

His eyes turn mistrustfully to LINOGE, who sits watching. LINOGE shouldn't be able to hear what they're saying—their voices are low-pitched, and they're most of the way across the room—but ROBBIE thinks (almost *knows*) that he can. He knows something else, as well. LINOGE could tell the others what he told ROBBIE: that ROBBIE was rolling around with a prostitute when his mother died.

HATCH

I don't think he's human.

He looks at MIKE almost pleadingly, as if asking him to contradict this. But MIKE doesn't.

MIKE

Neither do I. I don't know what he is.

JACK

God help us all.

121    INTERIOR: LINOGE, CLOSE-UP.

Watching them with wide-eyed intensity while the STORM HOWLS outside.

FADE TO BLACK. THIS ENDS ACT 3.

# Act 4

122   EXTERIOR: THE TOWN STORE—NIGHT.

We are looking up Main Street toward the center of town. A headlight appears, and we hear the WASP WHINE of an approaching snowmobile. It's URSULA, with JOANNA hanging on for dear life.

123   INTERIOR: THE DOORWAY OF THE SUPPLY SHED—NIGHT.

> CAT (voice)
> "I'm a little teapot, short and stout. . . . Here is my handle, here is my spout. . . ."

LUCIEN FOURNIER stands in the doorway. Behind him are UPTON BELL, JOHNNY HARRIMAN, old GEORGE KIRBY, and SONNY BRAUTIGAN. All of the men wear similar expressions of SHOCKED HORROR.

124   INTERIOR: CAT, IN THE CORNER OF THE SUPPLY SHED—NIGHT.

She's rocking back and forth, fingers in her mouth, blood-spattered face blank.

> CAT
> "You can pick me up and pour me out. . . . I'm a little teapot, short and stout."

125   INTERIOR: RESUME THE MEN IN THE DOORWAY.

> LUCIEN
> (with an effort)
> Come on. Help me get her inside.

126   INTERIOR: THE CONSTABLE'S OFFICE, WITH MIKE AND THE OTHERS.

> KIRK
> That fit he threw . . . what was *that* about?

MIKE shakes his head. Doesn't know. Turns to ROBBIE.

190

MIKE
Did he have a cane when you saw him?

ROBBIE
You bet. It had a big silver wolf's head on top. It was bloody. I
had an idea that was what he used to . . . to . . .

SOUND: The snowmobile. LIGHT FLASHES across the barred window high up in the cell. URSULA is driving down the alley to the back.
MIKE returns his attention to LINOGE. As always, he addresses
LINOGE with the calm of a police officer, although we can tell this is
getting harder and harder to maintain.

MIKE
Where's your cane, sir? Where is it now?
(no response)
What is it you want?

LINOGE still won't say. JACK CARVER and KIRK FREEMAN move
toward the back door to see who's coming. HATCH has done an
admirable job of handling himself, but he's getting more and more
scared all the time, and we can see it. Now he turns to MIKE.

HATCH
We didn't take him out of Martha's . . . did we? He *let*
himself be taken. Maybe he *wanted* to be taken.

ROBBIE
We could kill him.

HATCH is shocked, wide-eyed. MIKE looks less surprised.

ROBBIE
Nobody would have to know. Island business is island
business, always has been and always will be. Like whatever
Dolores Claiborne did to her husband during the eclipse. Or
Peter and his marijuana.

MIKE
*We'd* know.

ROBBIE

I'm just saying we could . . . and maybe we should. Tell me the idea hasn't already crossed your mind, Michael Anderson.

127   EXTERIOR: BEHIND THE STORE—NIGHT.

LUCIEN'S snowmobile pulls up beside the half-buried one JACK and KIRK came on. URSULA gets off and helps JOANNA off. Above them, the door between the constable's office and the loading dock is open. JACK CARVER stands in the light.

JACK

Who's there?

URSULA

Ursula Godsoe and Joanna Stanhope. We have to talk to Mike. Something's happened at the . . .

She's climbing the steps to the loading dock, and now she sees the WRAPPED SHAPE that has been put out here where it's cold. JACK and KIRK exchange a dismayed "Ah, shit" look. JACK reaches forward, attempting to take her arm and help her in before she gets too good a look.

JACK

Ursula, I wouldn't look at that, if I were you . . .

She pulls free and sinks to her knees beside the wrapped corpse of her husband.

KIRK

(back over his shoulder)

Mike! You better come here!

URSULA pays no mind. PETER'S green rubber boots are still sticking out, boots she knows well and may have patched herself. She touches one of them and begins CRYING SOUNDLESSLY. JOANNA stands behind her in the BLOWING, SWIRLING SNOW, not knowing what to do.

MIKE appears in the doorway, with HATCH behind him. MIKE understands the situation at once, and speaks with great gentleness.

> MIKE
> Ursula. I'm sorry.

She takes no notice, only kneels in the snow, holding the patched boot and crying. MIKE bends, gets his arm around her shoulders, and helps her to her feet.

> MIKE
> Come on in, Urse. Come on in where there's light and it's warm.

He leads her in past JACK and KIRK. JOANNA follows, with one quick, shying look down at the bundle with the boots sticking out of it. JACK and KIRK follow, and KIRK closes the door behind him against the night and the storm.

128    EXTERIOR: THE TOWN HALL—NIGHT.

Wrapped in thick clouds of BLOWING SNOW.

129    INTERIOR: THE TOWN HALL KITCHEN, WITH CAT WITHERS.

She sits on a stool, wrapped in a blanket, her eyes staring emptily. MELINDA HATCHER leans into the frame. She's got a damp cloth and begins to wipe the SPATTERS OF BLOOD from CAT'S face. She does this gently and kindly.

> SONNY BRAUTIGAN
> I don't know as you're supposed to do that, Mrs. Hatcher. It's evidence, or somethin'.

During this, THE CAMERA PULLS BACK, and we see a crowd of lookie-loos lined up against the kitchen walls and crowding in through the door. Next to SONNY—an aspiring Archie Bunker with a big belly and a sour disposition—is his friend UPTON BELL. We also may see LUCIEN FOURNIER and the others from the shed, plus JONAS STANHOPE and young ANNIE HUSTON. MELINDA looks at SONNY for a moment in wordless contempt, then goes on cleaning the eerily silent CAT'S FACE.

MRS. KINGSBURY is at the stove, ladling broth into a coffee mug. Now she crosses with it to where CAT sits.

MRS. KINGSBURY
Katrina, have a little broth. It'll warm you up.

UPTON BELL
Ought to spike it with rat poison, Missus Kingsbury . . .
*that'd* warm her up, all right.

There's a little RUMBLE OF AGREEMENT . . . and SONNY laughs
out loud at his friend UPTON'S sophisticated wit. MELDINDA gives
them both a smoking look.

MRS. KINGSBURY
Upton Bell, you shut up your ignorant mouth!

SONNY
(sticking up for his pal)
You're treatin' her like she saved his damn life instead of
sneakin' up behind him and bashin' his brains out!

Another RUMBLE OF AGREEMENT. MOLLY ANDERSON pushes
through the crowd. She looks at SONNY with a withering contempt he
can't stand up to, then at UPTON, then at the others.

MOLLY
Get out of here, all of you! This isn't a sideshow!

They shift around a little, but don't really move.

MOLLY
(a little more reasonable)
Come on—you've known this girl all your lives. Whatever
she did, she deserves a chance to breathe a little.

JONAS STANHOPE
Come on, folks. Let's go. They've got it in hand.

JONAS is some sort of professional man—a lawyer, perhaps—and has
enough moral weight to get them moving. SONNY and UPTON resist
the tide for a moment.

JONAS STANHOPE
Come on, Sonny . . . Upton. There's nothing here you can do.

SONNY
Can take her down to the constable's and throw her murder-
in' ass in jail!

UPTON BELL
(what a great idea)
Yeah!

JONAS STANHOPE
I think they've already got a guy in there . . . and she doesn't
exactly look like she's going to break loose, now does she?

He gestures to the girl, who is (pardon the pun) just about CATatonic.
She has totally ignored the whole thing, may not even know it's
happening. SONNY sees what STANHOPE means, and shuffles out,
UPTON after him.

MOLLY
Thank you, Mr. Stanhope.

MRS. KINGSBURY, meanwhile, sets the cup of broth aside—it's a lost
cause—and looks at CAT with tired perplexity.

JONAS STANHOPE
(to MOLLY)
Not a problem. Where's my mom, have you seen her?

MOLLY
I think she's getting ready for bed.

JONAS STANHOPE
Good. Good.

He leans back against the wall, his face and body language saying,
"Good God, what a day."

130    INTERIOR: THE TOWN MEETING HALL—NIGHT.

The benches and the speaker's podium are empty, but a few people in
nightwear are going up and down the side aisle. The only woman is old

CORA STANHOPE, Little Tall's self-appointed queen. She has an overnight bag in one hand.

An older gent named ORVILLE BOUCHER passes her going the other way. He's wearing a bathrobe, slippers, white socks. In one hand he's got his plastic toothbrush case.

> ORVILLE
> Say, there, Cora! Just like camp, ain't it? Someone oughtta
> put a bedsheet up on the wall and show cartoons!

CORA sniffs, raises her nose slightly into the air, and passes by without a word . . . although she cannot help a horrified glance at ORV'S white and hairy old-man's shins, a generous portion of which are on view above the tops of his socks and below the hem of his robe.

131   EXTERIOR: REAR OF THE TOWN HALL—NIGHT.

There's a small brick structure in the foreground, and the ENGINE ROAR identifies it as the generator shed. All at once the STEADY ROAR FALTERS; the engine COUGHS.

132   INTERIOR: RESUME TOWN MEETING HALL SIDE AISLE, WITH ORV AND CORA.

The lights FLICKER ON AND OFF; we see the two old folks looking up (any others that have been using the town hall's bathroom facilities, as well) through intervening shutters of darkness.

> ORV
> Relax, Cora, it's just the gennie clearing her throat.

133   EXTERIOR: THE GENERATOR SHED—NIGHT.

Settles down to a STEADY ROAR again.

134   INTERIOR: RESUME MEETING HALL SIDE AISLE, WITH ORV AND CORA.

> ORV
> See? Bright as you could ever want!

He just wants to be friendly, but she acts like he's trying to lure her onto one of those hard New England benches so he can do the dirty boogie with her. She hurries on without a word, nose higher than ever. At the end of the aisle are two doors marked with male and female icons. CORA pushes open the one with the woman on it and goes inside. ORV watches her, more bemused than offended.

ORV
(strictly to himself)
Cora, friendly as ever, ayuh.

He heads back to the stairs leading to the area below.

135   INTERIOR: THE CONSTABLE'S OFFICE—NIGHT.

HATCH comes in from the market area, holding a tray carefully in front of him. Loaded on it are nine Styrofoam cups of coffee. He sets it down on MIKE'S desk, looking nervously at URSULA, who is sitting in MIKE'S chair with her hood back and her coat unzipped. She still looks stunned. At first, when MIKE offers her one of the cups, she doesn't seem to see it.

MIKE
Go on, Urse. It'll warm you up.

URSULA
I don't think I'll ever be warm again.

But she takes two of the cups and hands one to JOANNA, who is standing behind her. MIKE takes another. ROBBIE hands cups to JACK and KIRK; HATCH gives one to HENRY. When all have been passed out, there's one cup left. HATCH looks toward LINOGE.

HATCH
Oh, what the hell. Want a cup?

No reply from LINOGE, who sits in his usual posture, watching.

ROBBIE
(with an edge)
Don't they drink coffee on your planet, mister?

MIKE
(to JOANNA)

Tell me again.

JOANNA

I've told you half a dozen times already.

MIKE

This'll be the last. Promise.

JOANNA

She said, "I think it was the cane with the wolf's head that
made me do it. I wouldn't touch it, if I were you."

MIKE

But you didn't see a cane. With or without a wolf's head.

JOANNA

No. Mike, what are we going to do?

MIKE

Wait out the storm. It's all we can do.

URSULA

Molly wants to see you. She told me to tell you that. Said for
you to set a guard and get back to her. Said you could have as
many men as you need; none of 'em are doing much tonight,
anyway.

MIKE

That's for sure. (pause) Hatch, step out here with me. Want
to talk to you a minute.

They start toward the door leading into the store. MIKE hesitates and
looks back at URSULA.

MIKE

You going to be all right?

URSULA

Yes.

MIKE and HATCH go out. URSULA realizes LINOGE is looking at her.

> ### URSULA
> What are you looking at?

LINOGE goes on looking. And smiling slightly. Then:

> ### LINOGE
> (sings)
> "I'm a little teapot, short and stout. . . ."

136  INTERIOR: THE TOWN HALL LADIES' ROOM—NIGHT.

ANGELA CARVER, in a soft and pretty nightgown, is at one of the basins, brushing her teeth. From one of the CLOSED STALLS behind her, we hear THE RUSTLE OF CLOTH and the SNAP OF HEAVY ELASTIC as CORA changes into her own nightwear.

> ### CORA
> (sings from the stall)
> ". . . Here is my handle, here is my spout!"

ANGELA looks in that direction, puzzled at first and then deciding to smile. She gives her teeth a final rinse, picks up her overnight bag, and leaves. As she does, CORA comes out of the stall she changed in, wearing woolly pink all the way down to the tips of her toes . . . and a nightcap on her head. Yes! She puts her own overnight bag on one of the sinks, unzips it, and brings out a tube of cream.

> ### CORA
> You can pick me up and pour me out . . .

137  INTERIOR: THE CONSTABLE'S OFFICE.

The four men and two women watch LINOGE in surprise and perplexity. He MIMES CREAMING HIS FACE.

> ### LINOGE
> (sings)
> "I'm a little teapot, short and stout!"

> ### HENRY BRIGHT
> He's totally crazy. Got to be.

138   INTERIOR: BY THE MEAT COUNTER OF THE STORE, WITH MIKE AND HATCH.

It's shadowy and spooky here, with just the fluorescents in the meat counter for illumination.

> MIKE
>
> I'm going to leave you in charge here for a little while.

> HATCH
>
> Oh, Mike, I wish you wouldn't do that . . .

> MIKE
>
> Just for a while. I want to take those women back to the town hall in the four-wheel drive while it'll still move. Make sure Molly's all right—and let her see that I am. Give Ralphie a kiss. Then I'm going to pack every man who looks halfway useful into the truck and come back here. We'll guard him in groups of three or four until the storm's over. In *fives,* if that's what it takes to feel comfortable.

> HATCH
>
> I won't feel comfortable until he's in Derry County Jail.

> MIKE
>
> I know what you mean.

> HATCH
>
> Cat Withers . . . I can't believe it, Mike. Cat wouldn't hurt Billy.

> MIKE
>
> I know that, too.

> HATCH
>
> Who's holding who prisoner here? Can you say for sure?

MIKE considers this question very, very carefully, then shakes his head.

> HATCH
>
> This is a mess.

MIKE
Yeah. You going to be okay with Robbie?

HATCH
I'll have to be . . . won't I? Say hi to Melinda for me, if she's
still up. Tell her I'm okay. And give Pippa a little kiss.

MIKE
I will.

HATCH
How long do you think you'll be gone?

MIKE
Forty-five minutes, an hour at most. And I'll be back with a
truckload of wide-bodies. Meantime, you have Jack, Henry,
Robbie, Kirk Freeman . . .

HATCH
Do you really think any of us'll make a difference, if that guy
starts to rock and roll?

MIKE
Do *you* really think the town hall's any safer? Or any place on
the island?

HATCH
Considering Cat and Billy . . . no.

MIKE goes back into the constable's office. HATCH follows.

139   INTERIOR: LINOGE, CLOSE-UP.

Rubbing invisible cream into his cheeks, humming "I'm a Little
Teapot."

140   INTERIOR: CORA, IN THE TOWN HALL BATHROOM.

Rubbing real cream into her cheeks—she's making a night mask for
herself—and humming "I'm a Little Teapot." She seems really happy
for the first time since being dragged to the town hall by her son and
daughter-in-law. Reflected in the mirror is the ladies' room, now
empty.

All at once THE LIGHTS GO OUT as the gennie stutters again.

> CORA (voice in the dark)
>
> Oh, *drat!*

The lights come back on. CORA looks relieved and begins creaming her face again. All at once she stops. LINOGE'S cane leans against the tiled wall beneath the hand dryer. It wasn't there before, but it is now, reflected in the mirror. There's no blood on it. The silver head GLEAMS ENTICINGLY.

CORA looks at it, then turns and walks toward it.

141   INTERIOR: LINOGE, CLOSE-UP.

> LINOGE
>
> Like Dad's!

142   INTERIOR: THE CONSTABLE'S OFFICE.

The men are clustered near MIKE'S desk. URSULA is seated; JOANNA stands beside her. None of those in the office notice MIKE and HATCH'S return. They are fascinated by LINOGE'S new dumb show.

> JOANNA
>
> What's he doing?

URSULA shakes her head. The men are equally puzzled.

143   INTERIOR: THE TOWN HALL LADIES' ROOM, WITH CORA.

> CORA
> (picks up the cane)
>
> Like Dad's!

144   INTERIOR: RESUME CONSTABLE'S OFFICE.

MIKE and the others watch LINOGE. He ignores them, concentrating on his business with CORA. He grips two invisible objects, one in each hand, and turns them. He pushes something else down with his thumb, as you would a small plunger. Then he MIMES RUMMAGING IN SOMETHING and finding a small object, which he holds up gripped between the thumb and first two fingers of his left hand.

145   INTERIOR: RESUME TOWN HALL LADIES' ROOM, WITH CORA.

She has laid "Dad's cane" across two of the sinks and returned to the one where she was when she saw the cane. She grips a faucet handle in each hand and turns them, starting the water. She pushes the stopper down with her thumb and the basin begins to fill. While it does, she rummages in her overnight bag and finds a lipstick. She holds it up between the thumb and first two fingers of her left hand.

146   INTERIOR: RESUME CONSTABLE'S OFFICE.

LINOGE leans back against the wall behind the cot, with the air of a man who has accomplished some difficult and tiring task. He looks at the octet across the room and smiles at them a little.

> LINOGE
> Go on, Mike, go on—we'll be fine. Give that little guy of yours a big old smackeroo for me. Tell him his pal from the market says hi.

MIKE'S face knots. He'd like to smash LINOGE'S face.

> HATCH
> How do you know so much? What the hell do you want?

LINOGE places his forearms on his knees and says nothing.

> MIKE
> Hatch, why don't a pair of you spend the time until I get back in here with him—the others can hang in the market. You can adjust the mirror out there so you can see in here.

> HATCH
> You don't want him to be able to get at all of us at the same time. Do you?

> MIKE
> Well . . . it's a plan.

He turns to the women before HATCH can reply.

MIKE

Ladies? Let's take a ride back to the town hall.

URSULA hands him a key on a key ring.

URSULA

This goes to Lucien Fournier's snowmobile, out back. Thought you might need it. Mike?

MIKE hands the key to HATCH, then turns back to her.

URSULA

Peter will be all right out there, won't he?

MIKE

Yes. And when this is over, we'll see to him proper . . . the way we always do. Come on.

URSULA gets to her feet and zips up her coat.

147   INTERIOR: TOWN HALL AISLE—NIGHT.

JILL ROBICHAUX heads down the aisle in her robe, carrying her own overnight bag. Outside, the WIND HOWLS.

148   INTERIOR: THE LADIES' ROOM, ANGLE ON THE DOOR—NIGHT.

It opens, and JILL comes in. For a moment her face remains calm, the face of a woman embarked on her regular getting-ready-for-bed ritual. Then it FILLS WITH HORROR. She drops her little bag and claps her hands to her mouth to stifle a scream. She stands where she is a moment longer, frozen by whatever it is she sees. Then she WHEELS AND RUNS.

149   INTERIOR: THE SLEEPING AREA OF THE TOWN HALL BASEMENT—NIGHT.

The lights have been turned low. In kid country, all of MOLLY'S daycare pupils are fast asleep; even the loathsome DON BEALS has given up. Probably half the beds meant for the adults are occupied, mostly by OLDER RESIDENTS.

MOLLY ANDERSON holds aside one of the makeshift draw curtains (perhaps they're only blankets hung up on clotheslines for this occasion) so that ANDY ROBICHAUX can step through. ANDY has got CAT in his arms. He carries her toward one of the cots. Following ANDY comes MOLLY and MRS. KINGSBURY.

When they reach a cot fairly deep in the room and away from most of the other sleepers, MOLLY strips back the blanket and top sheet. ANDY puts CAT down, and MOLLY pulls the bedclothes back up over her. They SPEAK LOW, so as not to disturb the other sleepers.

ANDY ROBICHAUX
Whoo! She's really out!

MOLLY gives MRS. KINGSBURY a questioning look.

MRS. KINGSBURY
They're very light sleeping pills . . . any lighter, Doc Grissom said, and I could buy them right over the counter. I think it's just shock. Whatever she's done, or whatever's been done to her, she's away from it now. That's probably best.

MRS. KINGSBURY bends, and, perhaps surprising herself, puts a kiss on the sleeping girl's cheek.

MRS. KINGSBURY
Sleep well, dear.

ANDY
Do you think someone ought to sit with her? Like a guard?

MOLLY and MRS. KINGSBURY exchange a bewildered glance that sums up just how out of control this has become. Put a guard on inoffensive little CAT WITHERS? It's nuts.

MOLLY
She doesn't need guarding, Andy.

ANDY
But—

MOLLY
Come on.

She turns to go. MRS. KINGSBURY follows. ANDY lingers by the cot for a moment, not so sure. Then he follows.

150   INTERIOR: THE BASEMENT "LIVING ROOM" AREA OF THE TOWN HALL.

MOLLY, ANDY, and MRS. KINGSBURY come out through the draw curtains. To their left, forty or fifty people, many now in their pj's or nightgowns, are watching the fuzzy TV. To their right are the stairs. Coming down them are SANDRA BEALS, MELINDA HATCHER, and JILL ROBICHAUX. SANDRA is terrified; MELINDA is frightened and grim; JILL is on the verge of hysterics but holding it in . . . at least until she sees her husband. She throws herself into his arms, CRYING.

> ANDY
> Jill? Honey? What's wrong?

A few of the TV watchers look around to see what's up. MOLLY looks at MELINDA'S pale face and knows something else has gone wrong . . . but this is no time to stir up the others, who are finally settling down for the night.

> MOLLY
> Come on. Upstairs. Whatever it is, we'll talk about it there.

They go up, ANDY with his arm around his wife's waist.

151   EXTERIOR: THE INTERSECTION OF MAIN AND ATLANTIC—NIGHT.

The Island Services vehicle comes along, trudging through the snow. It's making progress, but it's also crashing through drifts that are nearly hood high. It won't be making many more trips through *this* blizzard.

152   INTERIOR: THE ISLAND SERVICES VEHICLE, WITH MIKE, URSULA, JOANNA.

> JOANNA
> I'm so scared.

> MIKE
> So am I.

153   INTERIOR: OUTSIDE THE TOWN HALL LADIES' ROOM.

Standing back from the door, arms around each other, are ANDY and
JILL ROBICHAUX. Closest to the bathroom are MELINDA HATCHER
and MOLLY. SANDRA BEALS stands between the two pairs.

                    SANDRA
    I'm sorry . . . I can't. I can't take any more.

She brushes past JILL and ANDY and hurries back down the aisle.

154   INTERIOR: THE TOWN OFFICE—NIGHT.

SANDRA, weeping now, hurries into this area, meaning to go downstairs. Before she can, the front doors open and MIKE comes in,
covered with snow and stamping more snow off his boots. He is
followed by URSULA and JOANNA. SANDRA stops and gives the new
arrivals a wild, startled glance.

                    MIKE
    Sandra, what is it? What's wrong?

155   INTERIOR: THE LADIES' ROOM, ANGLE ON THE DOOR.

It opens slowly . . . reluctantly. MOLLY and MELINDA come in together, huddled shoulder to shoulder for comfort. Behind them, we see
ANDY and JILL ROBICHAUX. MOLLY and MELINDA look, faces
filling with horror and wonder.

                    MELINDA
    Oh, my dear God.

156   INTERIOR: THE WASHBASINS, FROM MOLLY AND MELINDA'S POINT OF
VIEW.

Kneeling in front of one of them is CORA STANHOPE. The basin is full
of water, and CORA'S white hair floats on its surface. She has drowned
herself in the basin. Written above it in lipstick, on the line of mirrors,
is the same old song: "GIVE ME WHAT I WANT AND I'LL GO AWAY."
Flanking it at either end, CORA has drawn BLOODY LIPSTICK
CANES. Of the real cane, the one with the wolf's head, there is no sign.

FADE TO BLACK. THIS ENDS ACT 4.

# Act 5

157    EXTERIOR: THE LIGHTHOUSE—NIGHT.

Waves still crash against the headland rocks hard enough to splatter the lighthouse with foam, but the tide is on the ebb, now, and things are better than they were. Temporarily only, however, because:

158    INTERIOR: LIGHTHOUSE CONTROL ROOM—NIGHT.

The lights still BLINK and FLASH, but some of them are now BEADED WITH ICE from the spray, and little drifts of snow are piling up in the corners of the room. The WIND WHISTLES, and the anemometer is still topping sixty MPH.

SOUND: A HIGH-PITCHED COMPUTER BEEP. THE CAMERA MOVES IN on a computer screen that has gone RED. White letters appear on the screen: "NATIONAL WEATHER SERVICE STORM SURGE WARNING FOR ALL OUTER ISLANDS, INCLUDING CRANBERRY, JERROD BLUFF, KANKAMONGUS, BIG TALL, AND LITTLE TALL. HIGH TIDE AT 7:09 AM. MAY PRODUCE SIGNIFICANT FLOODING AND LOWLAND DAMAGE. OUTER ISLAND RESI-

DENTS ARE STRONGLY ADVISED TO MOVE TO INLAND AREAS OF HIGH GROUND."

As if to punctuate this, an especially powerful wave SPLASHES IN through the broken windows and splatters this computer screen with foam.

159    INTERIOR: LOWER ATLANTIC STREET—NIGHT.

Godsoe Fish & Lobster is totally gone, except for the ragged stump of the building. So is the town dock. The waves slap the rocks where the dock was. Splintered pieces of lobster traps float back and forth . . . and a single waterlogged bale of pot BOBS AND SURGES.

160    INTERIOR: THE TOWN OFFICE—NIGHT.

URSULA is comforting SANDRA. MIKE is heading for the meeting hall section of the building, when JOANNA steams past him. He grabs her arm.

MIKE

Slow down, Mrs. Stanhope—easy does it.

The door between the meeting hall and the office area opens. MOLLY and MELINDA HATCHER come through. MOLLY'S distress turns to gladness when she sees MIKE, and she almost hurls herself into his arms. He hugs her hard. JOANNA, meanwhile, doesn't give a shit about "easy does it." She dodges past MELINDA and heads down the aisle that leads to the toilets. URSULA and SANDRA walk to where MIKE and MOLLY are drawing apart a little.

161    INTERIOR: TOWN MEETING HALL—NIGHT.

ANDY and JILL are sitting on a bench about halfway down. ANDY has got an arm around his wife, offering what comfort he can, when JOANNA hurries past toward the ladies' room.

ANDY

Joanna, I wouldn't—

She pays no attention, simply hurries on down the aisle.

162   INTERIOR: LADIES' ROOM, FEATURES THE DOOR.

It opens. JOANNA stands there, eyes widening, mouth dropping open. After a moment, MIKE joins her. He takes one look and then moves her away. As the bathroom door starts to close on its pneumatic hinge:

> MIKE
>
> Moll. Help me.

163   INTERIOR: THE TOWN HALL.

MIKE gently passes the stunned JOANNA to his wife, who walks her up the aisle as far as ANDY and JILL. There JOANNA stumbles and utters a little CRY OF BEWILDERMENT AND GRIEF.

> JILL
>
> Let me.

JILL sits her down and puts an arm around her. JOANNA begins to WEEP.

MOLLY starts back toward the ladies' room. MIKE comes out, his arms wet almost to the elbows. MOLLY looks at him questioningly. MIKE shakes his head and puts his arm around her shoulders. As he leads her past the trio on the bench:

> MIKE
>
> Andy? Can I borrow you a minute?

ANDY looks questioningly at JILL, who nods. She's busy comforting JOANNA.

164   INTERIOR: RESUME TOWN OFFICE AREA.

MIKE, MOLLY, and ANDY come in. URSULA and SANDRA stand nearby, looking the expected question at MIKE.

> MIKE
>
> She's dead, all right. Sandra, can you get me a couple of blankets to wrap her in?

> SANDRA
> (making a big effort)
> Yes. I can do that. Two shakes of a lamb's tail.

MIKE is struggling hard to stay calm and do as many of the right things as he can. There's a sense of him making up the procedure as he goes along, but why not? What kind of procedure is there for a situation like this?

SONNY BRAUTIGAN and UPTON BELL come up the stairs, curious about what's going on now. MIKE spies them.

> MIKE
> Billy Soames—you're sure he's dead?

> SONNY
> Yeah. *Now* what?

> MIKE
> Old Mrs. Stanhope is dead, too. In the ladies' room.

> UPTON BELL
> Holy God! She have a heart attack? Stroke?

> MOLLY
> Suicide.

> MIKE
> Is Billy still out there in the supply shed?

> SONNY
> Yeah. Seemed like the best place. We covered him up. What the *hell*—

SANDRA comes up the stairs with an armload of blankets. Someone else needs covering up now.

> MIKE
> Andy, you and Sonny cover Mrs. Stanhope. Take her out and put her with Billy. Use the back door of the meeting hall. I don't want folks to see a corpse going through, if I can help it.

> SONNY

What about Jonas? Her son? I seen him downstairs, gettin'
ready to turn in—

> MIKE

Let's hope he does. His wife can tell him in the morning.
Upton Bell?

> UPTON

Yessir.

> MIKE

Go downstairs and pick out five or six men from those that
are still up. Guys who can walk through half a mile of deep
snow without having a heart attack, if it comes to that. Don't
tell 'em anything except that I want to see 'em. Okay?

> UPTON

Okay!

Hugely exited, UPTON heads back downstairs.

165   INTERIOR: THE ISLAND MARKET—NIGHT.

HATCH, JACK CARVER, and KIRK FREEMAN are sitting at a card
table they've set up in the canned goods aisle and are playing gin
rummy. HATCH looks up at:

166   INTERIOR: THE SECURITY MIRROR, FROM HATCH'S POINT OF VIEW.

The mirror is now positioned in such a way that HATCH can see into
the constable's office. HENRY is behind MIKE'S desk, leaning back in
the chair, chin down on his chest, arms crossed, dozing. ROBBIE sits
off to one side, watching LINOGE, who is back in his same old
position—heels up, knees apart, head down.

167   INTERIOR: RESUME CARD PLAYERS.

Satisfied, HATCH draws a card, smiles, and spreads them out faceup.

> HATCH

Gin!

KIRK

Aw, boogersnot!

168    INTERIOR: THE CONVEX ANTITHEFT MIRROR, CLOSE-UP.

ROBBIE looks up into the mirror, trying to ascertain if he is being watched. He decides he isn't. Now he reaches over to the corner of the desk, picks up the pistol that's still lying there, and GETS UP.

169    INTERIOR: THE CONSTABLE'S OFFICE.

HENRY is dozing. The men in the market are playing cards. ROBBIE approaches the cell with the gun. LINOGE sits where he is, watching him come. When LINOGE speaks, he does so in the voice of an OLD WOMAN—ROBBIE'S MOTHER.

LINOGE

Where's Robbie? I want to see my Robbie before I go. He said he'd be here. Where are you, Robbie? I don't want to die without someone to hold my hand.

HENRY stirs a bit in his doze, then sinks deeper. ROBBIE reacts with surprise, horror, shame . . . and then his face hardens.

ROBBIE

I think this town's had enough of you.

He raises the gun and points it through the bars.

170    EXTERIOR: THE TOWN HALL—NIGHT.

A side door opens, and a number of MEN come out, ready to augment the crew already at the store. As promised, they're wide-bodies: UPTON, SONNY, JOHNNY HARRIMAN, ALEX HABER, and STAN HOPE-WELL, DAVEY'S father. STAN is a lobsterman we saw briefly in Part One, battening down for the storm on the now nonexistent town dock. They head for the Island Services vehicle, fighting their way through the snow. Two more figures linger in the doorway: MIKE and MOLLY. MOLLY'S wearing a shawl and hugging it to her against the cold.

MOLLY

Is it that man? The one who grabbed Ralphie in the market? It is isn't it?

He doesn't answer.

> MOLLY
> (continues)
> You'll be all right, won't you?

> MIKE
> Ayuh.

> MOLLY
> That man . . . if he *is* a man . . . is never going to see the inside of a courtroom, Michael. I know it. You do, too.
> (beat)
> Maybe you should get rid of him. Make him have an accident.

> MIKE
> Go on inside, before you freeze your tail off.

She kisses him again, a little more lingeringly.

> MOLLY
> Come back to us.

> MIKE
> I will.

She closes the door. MIKE starts down to the truck, walking in the tracks the others have made and bending forward against the RE-LENTLESS WIND.

171   INTERIOR: A SUNLIT BEDROOM—DAY.

This is a beautiful room, full of light. The window is open and the curtains BELL OUT LAZILY toward the bed in a summer breeze. HENRY BRIGHT comes out of the bathroom, wearing only pajama bottoms, with a towel slung around his neck. As he crosses to the window, FRANK BRIGHT, his son, pokes his head around the side of the door.

> FRANK
> Mom says come downstairs and get breakfast, Daddy!

Above FRANK'S head, CARLA'S now appears.

> **CARLA**
> No—Mom says come downstairs and get breakfast *sleepy-head* Daddy!

FRANK puts his hands over his mouth and GIGGLES. HENRY smiles.

> **HENRY**
> I'll be there in a minute.

He goes to the window.

172   EXTERIOR: LITTLE TALL ISLAND, FROM HENRY'S POINT OF VIEW—DAY.

It's beautiful as only a Maine island can be at the height of summer—blue sky over long green meadows that slope down to blue whitecapped water. We can see a few fishing boats out there. GULLS CRY AND SWOOP overhead.

173   INTERIOR: RESUME BEDROOM, WITH HENRY—DAY.

He takes a deep breath, holds it, then lets it out.

> **HENRY**
> Thank God for reality. I had a dream that it was winter . . . there was a storm . . . and this man came to town . . .

> **LINOGE** (voice)
> This *scary* man . . .

Surprised, HENRY turns.

174   INTERIOR: LINOGE, FROM HENRY'S POINT OF VIEW.

Although it's summer in HENRY'S dream, LINOGE is dressed as he was when we first saw him on Atlantic Street, in front of MARTHA CLARENDON'S house: pea coat, watch cap, bright yellow gloves. He GRIMACES INTO THE CAMERA, revealing A MOUTHFUL OF FANGS. His eyes GO BLACK. He thrusts the SILVER HEAD OF HIS CANE at HENRY, and the head COMES ALIVE, snapping and snarling.

175   INTERIOR: THE SUMMER BEDROOM, WITH HENRY.

He steps backward to avoid the silver wolf. His knees hit the bottom of the window, and he tumbles out, SCREAMING.

176   EXTERIOR: HENRY, FALLING.

Only it's not his house he's falling out of, and not the ground of Little Tall Island he's falling toward, hard as that ground might be. He is falling toward a BOILING RED-BLACK PIT OF FIRE. It is a pit of hell; it is also the boiling red and black we've seen in LINOGE'S EYES from time to time.

HENRY falls, SHRIEKING, away from THE CAMERA.

177   INTERIOR: THE CONSTABLE'S OFFICE, FEATURES HENRY.

He twitches in the desk chair, falls out of it, and gives a STRANGLED YELL as he hits the floor. He opens his eyes and looks around, dazed.

178   INTERIOR: THE MARKET, FEATURING THE CARD PLAYERS.

They look up at the sound of HENRY'S YELL and see that ROBBIE is standing by the cell. And—

> KIRK
> Hatch, Robbie's got a gun. I think he's gonna shoot that guy!

HATCH bolts to his feet, knocking over the card table.

> HATCH
> Robbie! Get away from him! Put that down!

179   INTERIOR: THE CONSTABLE'S OFFICE, WITH HENRY.

> HENRY
> Robbie? What—

HENRY gets to his feet. He's soupy, still half-lost in his dream.

180   INTERIOR: THE CELL, WITH ROBBIE AND ROBBIE'S FALSE MOTHER.

She is sitting on the bunk where LINOGE sat (naturally—she *is* LINOGE). She is very old, about eighty, and very thin. She is dressed in

a white hospital johnny; her hair is wild; her face is reproachful.
ROBBIE looks at her, hypnotized.

> FALSE MOTHER
> Robbie, why didn't you come? After all I did for you, all I
> gave up for you—

> HATCH (voice)
> *Robbie, don't!*

> FALSE MOTHER
> Why did you leave me to die with strangers? Why did you
> leave me to die alone?

She holds out her thin, trembling hands to him.

181    INTERIOR: THE MARKET.

HATCH, JACK, and KIRK dash for the open door of the constable's
office.

182    INTERIOR: THE CONSTABLE'S OFFICE.

HENRY, still hardly aware of what's happening, walks toward the cell.
LINOGE is sitting on the bunk, holding out his hands to ROBBIE . . .
and here, from HENRY'S perspective, it really is LINOGE.

LINOGE looks at the door leading into the market. It SLAMS SHUT in
HATCH'S face.

183    INTERIOR: THE MARKET SIDE OF THE DOOR, WITH HATCH, JACK,
KIRK.

HATCH actually strikes the door and BOUNCES OFF. He tries the
handle, but it won't turn. He slams his shoulder against the door, then
turns to the other two.

> HATCH
> Don't just stand there; help me!

184    INTERIOR: RESUME CONSTABLE'S OFFICE.

We hear THUDS as the men outside try to break down the door. The

FALSE MOTHER sits on the cot in her johnny, looking at her wayward son.

>                    FALSE MOTHER
> I waited for you, Robbie, and I'm still waiting for you. Down
> in hell, I'm waiting for you.

>                         ROBBIE
> You stop. Or I'll shoot you.

>                    FALSE MOTHER
> With *that?*

She looks at the gun contemptuously. ROBBIE follows her gaze.

185   INTERIOR: ROBBIE'S HAND, FROM ROBBIE'S POINT OF VIEW, CLOSE-UP.

The gun is gone. He's holding a WRITHING SNAKE. ROBBIE SCREAMS and opens his hand.

186   INTERIOR: THE CONSTABLE'S OFFICE.

We see the rest of this from HENRY BRIGHT'S POINT OF VIEW, which means we see things pretty much as they are. It's the gun ROBBIE drops, not a snake, and it's LINOGE in the cell, now off the bunk and walking toward the bars.

>                         LINOGE
> I'll be waiting for you in hell, Robbie, and when you get
> there, I'll have a spoon. I'm going to use it on your eyes. I'm
> going to eat your eyes, Robbie, over and over again, because
> hell is repetition. Born in sin, come on in.

HENRY bends for the gun. LINOGE looks at it, and it slides all the way across the floor. LINOGE looks back at ROBBIE, looks hard, and ROBBIE suddenly goes FLYING BACKWARD. He strikes the wall, rebounds, and goes to his knees.

>                         HENRY
>                  (horrified whisper)
> What are you?

LINOGE
Your destiny.

He turns and lifts the mattress of the cot. Beneath it is the cane. He takes it and raises it. As he does, a BRILLIANT BLUE LIGHT begins to shine from it.

HENRY backs away, raising an arm to shield his eyes. ROBBIE, who has managed to get up, also shields his eyes. That GLOW becomes BRIGHT, BRIGHTER, BRIGHTEST. The constable's office now SCREAMS WITH LIGHT.

187   INTERIOR: THE MARKET SIDE OF THE DOOR.

LIGHT streams through the keyhole, around the hinges, and through the gap at the foot of the door. The three men step back, afraid.

JACK
What is it? What's happening?

HATCH
I don't know.

188   INTERIOR: THE CONSTABLE'S OFFICE.

HENRY and ROBBIE stand on one side of the room, cringing against that BRILLIANT FLOOD OF LIGHT. In it, we for the first time see LINOGE for what he is: an ancient wizard whose upraised cane is his chief instrument of magic—an evil version of Aaron's staff. It is shedding that BRILLIANT LIGHT in waves.

On the bulletin board, papers come loose and FLOAT in the air. MIKE'S blotter rises from his desk and also FLOATS. The desk drawers open, slowly, one after the other, and the objects inside rise up and begin to circle the desk: pens and paper clips, handcuffs and a forgotten half of ham sandwich. The in/out basket waltzes with HATCH'S PowerBook in midair.

On the far side of the room, the pistol ROBBIE meant to use on LINOGE (what a foolish idea that seems now) rises, turns its muzzle to the wall, and discharges six times.

189    INTERIOR: THE MARKET SIDE OF THE DOOR.

HATCH, KIRK, and JACK react to the shots. HATCH looks around, sees a display of hardware, and grabs a hatchet from it. He turns and begins hacking away at the area around the doorknob. JACK grabs at him.

JACK
Hatch! Maybe you shouldn't—

HATCH shoves him backward and goes on hacking. Maybe he shouldn't, but he's going to do his duty if he can.

190    INTERIOR: THE CONSTABLE'S OFFICE.

The home-welded bars start FALLING AWAY from the cell door one by one, almost like falling leaves. ROBBIE and HENRY watch, numb with terror. The bars fall faster and faster, creating a man-shaped hole. When it's complete, LINOGE steps easily through. He looks at the two COWERING MEN, then turns and raises his cane toward the door leading to the market.

191    INTERIOR: THE MARKET SIDE OF THE DOOR.

HATCH is raising the hatchet for another blow when the door suddenly OPENS ON ITS OWN. BRIGHT BLUISH SILVER LIGHT streams out.

LINOGE (voice)
Hatch.

HATCH steps into that FLOOD OF LIGHT. JACK grabs at him.

JACK
Hatch, no!

HATCH ignores him. He goes into the light, the hatchet slipping from his fingers as he does.

192    EXTERIOR: THE MARKET—NIGHT.

The Island Services four-wheel drive turns into the front parking area. The storm shutters are down over the market's display windows, but we can see BRILLIANT BLUE LIGHT shining through the door.

193    INTERIOR: THE ISLAND SERVICES VEHICLE.

It's crammed with BEEFY GUYS. MIKE is at the wheel.

JOHNNY
(awed)
What in the hell is that?

MIKE doesn't bother answering, but he's out of the truck almost before it has stopped moving. The others follow, but MIKE is first up the steps.

194    INTERIOR: THE CONSTABLE'S OFFICE.

HATCH sleepwalks into that BRILLIANT LIGHT, heedless of the objects floating and swirling in the air. The PowerBook bumps his head. HATCH bats it aside and it floats away like something underwater. He reaches LINOGE, who is almost blindingly bright.

LINOGE is in reality an old man, we see, with ragged white hair falling almost to his shoulders. His cheeks and brow are carved with lines, and his lips are sunken, but it's a strong face, all the same . . . and dominated by the eyes, which SWIRL WITH BLACK AND RED. His ordinary clothes are gone; he is wearing a dark robe that gleams with SHIFTING SILVER PATTERNS. He continues to hold his STAFF UP with one hand (there is still a SILVER WOLF'S HEAD at one end, but now we see the shaft is carved with magical runes and symbols) and grips HATCH'S shoulder with the other . . . only it's not really a hand at all, but a talon full of claws.

LINOGE brings his face down until his brow is almost touching HATCH'S. His lips part, revealing his pointed teeth. During all of this, HATCH stares at him with wide, blank eyes.

> LINOGE
> Give me what I want and I'll go away. Tell them. *Give me what I want . . . and I'll go away.*

He turns, the hem of his robe flaring, and strides toward the door that leads to the loading dock.

195 INTERIOR: THE MARKET, LOOKING TOWARD THE MAIN DOORS— NIGHT.

They burst open, and MIKE runs in, followed by his posse. He moves up the center aisle, jumping the overturned card table, and grabs KIRK FREEMAN.

> MIKE
> What happened? Where's Hatch?

KIRK points numbly into the constable's office. He is beyond words. MIKE plunges through the doorway . . . then stops.

196 INTERIOR: THE CONSTABLE'S OFFICE, FROM MIKE'S POINT OF VIEW.

Looks like a cyclone struck it. Papers and office supplies are strewn everywhere, fluttering in the draft from the open loading-dock door. HATCH'S PowerBook lies shattered on the floor. The jail cell is empty. A litter of bars lies in front of the door, which is still locked but gaping wide, all the same. The hole is vaguely man-shaped.

ROBBIE and HENRY stand against the wall, their arms around each other, like small children who are lost in the dark. HATCH stands in the center of the floor with his back to MIKE and his head lowered.

MIKE approaches cautiously. The other men clog the door to the market, watching with big eyes and solemn faces.

> MIKE
> Hatch? What happened?

HATCH doesn't respond until MIKE actually touches his shoulder.

                    MIKE
    What happened?

HATCH turns. His face has been changed in some fundamental way by his close encounter with LINOGE—stamped by a terror that may never leave him, even if he survives the Storm of the Century.

                    MIKE
                   (reacts)
    Hatch . . . my God . . . what . . . ?

                    HATCH
    We have to give him what he wants. If we do that, he'll go away. He'll leave us alone. If we don't . . .

HATCH looks toward the open loading-dock door, where SNOW is SWIRLING IN. ROBBIE joins them, walking slowly, like an old man.

                    ROBBIE
    Where did he go?

                    HATCH
    Out there. Into the storm.

Now they all look toward the door.

197   EXTERIOR: DOWNTOWN, LOOKING TOWARD THE OCEAN—NIGHT.

The snow is pelting, the drifts are still building, and the sea is still pounding the shore and sending up airbursts of foam. LINOGE is out there someplace, just another part of the storm.

FADE TO BLACK. THIS ENDS ACT 5.

# Act 6

---

198    EXTERIOR: INTERSECTION OF MAIN AND ATLANTIC—NIGHT.

The drifts are deeper than ever, and several show windows have been broken inward. The streets are impassable to even four-wheel drives now; the lampposts are buried halfway to their light globes.

THE CAMERA MOVES BACK TO THE DRUGSTORE, and we see the aisles have become frozen tundra. Frost twinkles on the letters spelling "PRESCRIPTIONS" at the back of the store. Nearer the front there's a sign that reads BEAT OLD MAN WINTER WITH A GENIE HEATER!, but Old Man Winter's got the last laugh this time; the heaters are almost buried in snow.

The pendulum clock is too covered with snow to read, but still working. It begins to STRIKE THE HOUR. One . . . two . . . three . . . four . . .

199    INTERIOR: MARTHA CLARENDON'S FRONT HALL—NIGHT.

We see her body, covered with the tablecloth. And hear another STRIKING CLOCK. Five . . . six . . . seven . . . eight . . .

200    INTERIOR: THE WEE FOLKS DAY-CARE CENTER—NIGHT.

A CUCKOO BIRD MOLLY'S kids must love is running in and out of the clock on the wall, impudent as a tongue. Nine . . . ten . . . eleven . . . twelve. With that last comment, the bird goes back into hiding. The day care itself is spotless but spooky, with its little tables and chairs, its pictures on the walls, the blackboard with "WE SAY PLEASE" and "WE SAY THANK YOU" written on it. There are too many shadows, too much silence.

201    EXTERIOR: THE LOADING DOCK BEHIND THE STORE—NIGHT.

We see PETER GODSOE'S WRAPPED BODY, now just a frozen lump under the tarp . . . but those boots are still sticking out.

202  INTERIOR: THE CONSTABLE'S OFFICE.

It's still littered with paper and office supplies from hell to breakfast, and the fallen bars still lie where they fell, but the place is empty. THE CAMERA MOVES through the door to the market. It is also empty. The overturned table and litter of cards in the canned goods aisle testifies that there was sudden trouble here, but trouble has departed now. The big clock over the checkout counters—a battery job—reads a minute past midnight.

203  INTERIOR: THE SUPPLY SHED BEHIND THE TOWN HALL—NIGHT.

There are two wrapped bodies here—those of BILLY SOAMES and CORA STANHOPE.

204  INTERIOR: THE TOWN HALL KITCHEN—NIGHT.

Neat as a pin—clean counters, swept floor, washed pots heaped high in the drainers. A small army of town ladies with too much time on their hands (no doubt generaled by MRS. KINGSBURY) has put things to rights, and the place is all ready for breakfast—pancakes for two hundred or so. On the wall, the clock reads two past midnight. Like Wee Folks Day-Care, this place feels spooky, with the minimal lighting supplied by the gennie and the WIND SCREAMING outside.

Sitting on stools by the door are JACK CARVER and KIRK FREEMAN. They have HUNTING RIFLES across their laps. Both are close to dozing.

KIRK
How're we supposed to see anything in this?

JACK shakes his head. He doesn't know.

205  INTERIOR: THE TOWN OFFICE—NIGHT.

The CB radio CRACKLES SOFTLY AND MEANINGLESSLY. There's nothing on it but static. At the door, HATCH and ALEX HABER are watching, also armed with hunting rifles. Well . . . HATCH is watching. ALEX is dozing. HATCH looks at him, and we see him debating whether or not to elbow ALEX awake. He decides to have pity.

THE CAMERA SLIPS to URSULA'S desk, where TESS MARCHANT sleeps with her head pillowed on her arms. THE CAMERA STUDIES

HER for a moment, then turns and FLOATS down the stairs. As it does, we hear a FAINT VOICE THROUGH STATIC:

> PREACHER (voice)
> You know, friends, it's hard to be righteous, but it's easy to go along with so-called friends who tell you that sin is all right, that neglect is fine, that no God is watching and you can go ahead and do whatever you think you can get away with, can you say "hallelujah"?

> MUTTERED RESPONSE
> Hallelujah.

There are about ten people left in the TV area. They have gravitated to the few comfortable chairs and a couple of old rummage-sale-quality sofas. All but MIKE are asleep. On the TV, barely visible through the interference, is the slicky-hair PREACHER, looking every bit as trust-worthy as Jimmy Swaggart in the courtyard of a triple-X motel.

> MIKE
> (speaks to the TV)
> Hallelujah, brother. Tell it.

He's in an overstuffed chair a little apart from the rest. He looks very tired and probably won't be awake for much longer. He's already started to nod out. On his hip he's wearing his revolver in a holster.

> PREACHER
> (continues)
> Brethern, tonight I'd like to speak to you especially of the secret sin. And tonight I'd like to remind you, say hellelujah, that sin tastes sweet on the lips but sour on the tongue, and it poisons the belly of the righteous. God bless you, but can you say "amen"?

MIKE cannot, as it happens. His chin has drifted down to his chest, and his eyes have closed.

> PREACHER
> (continues)
> But the secret sin! The selfish heart that says "I need not

share; I can keep it all for myself, and no one'll ever know."
Think of that, brethern! It's easy to say, "Oh, I can keep that
dirty little secret, it's nobody else's business, and it won't hurt
me," and then try to ignore the canker of corruption that
begins growing around it . . . that soul sickness that begins
to grow around it . . .

During this, THE CAMERA PANS some of the sleeping faces—among
them we see SONNY BRAUTIGAN and UPTON BELL, SNORING on
one sofa with their heads together, and on the other, JONAS and
JOANNA STANHOPE with their arms around each other. Then we
FLOAT AWAY AGAIN, toward those makeshift draw curtains. Behind
us, the PREACHER'S VOICE fades. He continues to talk about secrets
and sin and selfishness.

We DRIFT THROUGH the draw curtains. Here, in the sleeping area,
we hear DORMITORY SOUNDS OF REPOSE: COUGHS, WHEEZES,
SOFT SNORES.

We pass DAVEY HOPEWELL, sleeping on his back with a frown on his
face. ROBBIE BEALS, on his side, reaching across to SANDRA. They
are holding hands in their sleep. URSULA GODSOE sleeping with her
daughter, SALLY, and her sister-in-law, TAVIA, close-by, the three of
them drawn as tightly together as they can in the wake of PETER'S
death.

MELINDA HATCHER and PIPPA are sleeping with their cots pushed
together, forehead to forehead, and RALPHIE is cradled in his sleeping
mother's arms.

We drift to the area where the kids were initially put to bed, and quite a
few of them are still there—BUSTER CARVER, HARRY ROBICHAUX,
HEIDI ST. PIERRE, and DON BEALS.

The residents of Little Tall are sleeping. Their rest is uneasy, but they
are sleeping.

206    INTERIOR: ROBBIE BEALS, CLOSE-UP.

He MUTTERS SOMETHING INCOHERENT. His eyeballs move rapidly behind his closed lids. He's dreaming.

207   EXTERIOR: MAIN STREET, LITTLE TALL ISLAND—DAY.

Standing in the street—actually above it, as Main Street is buried under at least four feet of snow—is a TV REPORTER. He is young and conventionally handsome, dressed in a bright purple Thermo-Pak ski suit, matching purple gloves, and wearing skis . . . the only way he could get to his stand-up position, one assumes.

There's four feet of snow in the streets, but that's only the beginning. The stores have been all but buried under MONSTER DRIFTS. Downed power lines disappear into the snow like torn strands of cobweb.

> TV REPORTER
> The so-called Storm of the Century is history in New England now—folks from New Bedford to New Hope are digging out from beneath snowfall amounts that have added not just new entries but new *pages* to the record books.

The REPORTER begins to ski slowly down Main Street, past the drugstore, the hardware store, the Handy Bob Restaurant, the Tie-Up Lounge, the beauty parlor.

> TV REPORTER
> They're digging out everywhere, that is, except here, on Little Tall Island—a little scrap of land off the coast of Maine and home to almost four hundred souls, according to the last census. About half the population sought shelter on the mainland when it became clear that this storm was really going to hit, and hit hard. That number includes most of the island's schoolchildren in grades K through high school. But nearly all the rest . . . two hundred men and women and young children . . . are gone. The exceptions are even more ominous and distressing.

208   EXTERIOR: THE REMAINS OF THE TOWN DOCK—DAY.

Teams of grim-faced EMERGENCY MEDICAL TECHNICIANS are carrying four stretchers down to the POLICE BOAT that has tied up to the stump of the dock. Each stretcher bears a zipped body bag.

> TV REPORTER (voice-over)
> Four corpses have been found so far on Little Tall Island.

Two of them may have been suicides, police sources say, but the other two are almost certainly murder victims, bludgeoned to death by what was probably the same blunt object.

209   EXTERIOR: RESUME MAIN STREET, WITH REPORTER.

Oh-oh. He's still wearing the purple ski suit, still clean-cut and as chipper as a chickadee, but the purple gloves have been replaced by bright yellow ones. If we didn't recognize LINOGE before—and hopefully we didn't—we do now.

> TV REPORTER
> (LINOGE)
> Identities of the dead have been withheld pending notification of next of kin, but all are said to be longtime island residents. And baffled police are asking themselves one question, over and over: *Where are the other residents of Little Tall Island?* Where is Robert Beals, the town manager? Where is Michael Anderson, who owned the island market and served as Little Tall's constable? Where is fourteen-year-old Davey Hopewell, who was at home, recovering from a bout of mononucleosis, when the big one hit? Where are the shopkeepers, the fishermen, the town selectmen? No one knows. There has only been one case like this before, in all of American history.

210   INTERIOR: MOLLY ANDERSON, SLEEPING, CLOSE-UP—NIGHT.

Her eyes move rapidly back and forth beneath her closed lids.

211   INSERT: A DRAWING OF AN EIGHTEENTH-CENTURY VILLAGE.

> WOMAN TV REPORTER (voice-over)
> This is how the village of Roanoke, Virginia, looked in 1587, before everyone disappeared—every man, woman, and child. Their fate has never been discovered. A single possible clue was discovered, a word found carved on a tree—

212   INSERT: A WOODCUT OF AN ELM TREE.

Carved into the bark is the word "CROATON."

> WOMAN TV REPORTER (voice-over)
> —*this* word. "Croaton." The name of a place? A misspelling?

A word written in a language lost over the centuries? No one knows that, either.

213    EXTERIOR: RESUME MAIN STREET, WITH WOMAN TV REPORTER.

She is very pretty in her purple Therma-Pak ski suit; it goes well with her long blonde hair, flushed cheeks . . . and her BRIGHT YELLOW GLOVES. Yes, it's LINOGE again, now speaking in a woman's voice and looking very pretty. This isn't transvestism played for laughs, but a guy who really looks like a young woman and speaks with a woman's voice. This is deadly serious.

This reporter has picked up exactly where ROBBIE'S version left off, now doing a walk-and-talk (a walk-and-ski, in this case) up Main Street, toward the town hall.

> WOMAN TV REPORTER
> (LINOGE)
> Police continue to assure reporters that a solution will be found, but even they are not able to deny one essential fact: hope is dimming for the missing residents of Little Tall Island.

She skis on toward the town hall, which is also buried in drifts.

> WOMAN TV REPORTER
> (LINOGE)
> Evidence suggests that most or all of the islanders spent the first and worst night of the storm here, in the basement of the Little Tall Island Town Hall. After that . . . no one knows. One wonders if there was anything they could have done to change their strange fate.

She skis onto what would be the town hall lawn in summer, toward the little cupola with the bell inside. THE CAMERA REMAINS STATIONARY now, watching her go.

214    INTERIOR: DAVEY HOPEWELL, CLOSE-UP.

Sleeping uneasily. Eyeballs moving. Dreaming while the WIND SHRIEKS OUTSIDE.

215   EXTERIOR: IN FRONT OF THE TOWN HALL—DAY.

The **REPORTER** in the purple ski suit reaches the cupola, and even with his back to us, we can tell that DAVEY'S version of the REPORTER is a man. He turns. He is BALDING, BESPECTACLED, wearing a MUSTACHE . . . but it's LINOGE again.

> TV REPORTER
> (LINOGE)
> One wonders if, in their insular selfishness and Yankee pride, they refused to give something . . . some simple thing . . . that would have changed matters for them. To this reporter, that seems more than possible; it seems *plausible*. Do they regret it now? (pause) Are any of them *alive* to regret it? What really happened in Roanoke, in 1587? And what happened here, on Little Tall Island, in 1989? We may never know. But I know one thing, Davey—you're too damn short to play basketball . . . and besides, you couldn't throw it in the ocean.

DAVEY'S version of the REPORTER makes a half-turn and reaches into the shadowy cupola. Here is the memorial bell, only in DAVEY'S dream, it's not a bell. What the REPORTER brings out is a BLOOD-STAINED BASKETBALL, and he heaves it DIRECTLY INTO THE CAMERA. As he does this, his lips part in a grin, revealing teeth that are really FANGS.

> TV REPORTER
> *Catch!*

216   INTERIOR: RESUME DAVEY, IN THE TOWN HALL BASEMENT—NIGHT.

Moaning, he turns back the other way. His hands come up briefly, as if to ward off the basketball.

> DAVEY
> No . . . no . . .

217   INTERIOR: THE TV AREA OF THE BASEMENT, FEATURING MIKE—NIGHT.

His head is dropped and limp, but his eyeballs are moving behind his closed lids, and like the others, he is DREAMING.

> PREACHER (voice)
> Be sure that your sin will find you out, and that your secrets
> will be known. All secrets will be known . . .

218   INTERIOR: PREACHER ON SNOWY TV, CLOSE-UP.

Yes, now we see it; the TV PREACHER is LINOGE, too.

> PREACHER
> (continues)
> . . . can you say "hallelujah"? Oh, brethern, can you say
> "amen"? For I ask you to behold the sting of sin and the price
> of vice; I ask you to behold the just end of those who bar the
> door to the wandering stranger who comes, asking so little.

THE CAMERA MOVES IN on the SNOWY TV. THE PREACHER melts
into DARKNESS . . . but a *snowy* DARKNESS, because the wind has
blown down the town hall antenna and there's no good reception. Only
now a PICTURE starts to appear, anyway. The snow is real snow now,
snow that's a part of the Storm of the Century, and PEOPLE are
moving in it—a dark snake-dance line of PEOPLE floundering their
slow way down Atlantic Street Hill.

219   INTERIOR: ATLANTIC STREET, CLOSER—NIGHT.

> PREACHER (voice-over)
> For the wages of lust are dust, and the wages of sin are death.

Passing us is a nightmare procession of DAZED, HYPNOTIZED
ISLANDERS in their nightclothes, oblivious of the HOWLING WIND
and SHEETING SNOW. We see ANGELA with little BUSTER in her
arms; followed by MOLLY, in her nightgown and carrying RALPHIE;
followed by GEORGE KIRBY . . . FERD ANDREWS . . . ROBERTA
COIGN . . . well, you get it. They're all here. And tattooed on each
forehead is that strange and ominous word: CROATON.

> PREACHER (voice-over)
> For if the supplicant is turned away and the seeker given no
> respite, shall not the hard-hearted be sent hence?

220   INTERIOR: MIKE, CLOSE-UP.

> MIKE
> (sleeping)
>
> Hallelujah. Amen.

221   INTERIOR: THE STUMP OF THE TOWN DOCK.

They march toward THE CAMERA—and their death in the frigid ocean—like lemmings. We don't believe it . . . and yet we do, don't we? After Jonestown and Heaven's Gate, we do.

> ROBBIE
> (first in line)
>
> I'm sorry we didn't give you what you wanted.

He topples off the jagged end of the dock and into the ocean.

> ORV BOUCHER
> (second in line)
>
> Sorry we didn't give it to you, Mr. Linoge.

He follows ROBBIE into the ocean. Next is ANGIE and BUSTER.

> ANGIE CARVER
>
> I'm sorry. We both are, aren't we, Buster?

With the child in her arms, ANGELA steps from the pier. Next is MOLLY, with RALPHIE.

222   INTERIOR: RESUME MIKE, IN THE TV AREA.

He is growing steadily more restive . . . as who would not, if subjected to such an awful dream as this?

> MIKE
>
> No . . . no, Molly . . .

> PREACHER (voice-over)
>
> For so little is asked of you, can you say "hallelujah" . . . and yet if you harden your hearts and stop up the porches of your ears, you must pay. You must be branded as one of the ungrateful and sent hence.

223   EXTERIOR: MOLLY, ON THE PIER—NIGHT.

She is as hypnotized as the rest, but RALPHIE is awake and afraid.

> MOLLY
> We hardened our hearts. We closed our ears. And now we
> pay. I'm sorry, Mr. Linoge—

> RALPHIE
> Daddy! *Daddy, help!*

> MOLLY
> —we should have given you what you wanted.

She goes over the edge and into the black water with RALPHIE
SCREAMING in her arms.

224   INTERIOR: THE TV AREA, WITH MIKE—NIGHT.

He snaps awake, GASPING. Looks at the TV.

225   INTERIOR: TV, FROM MIKE'S POINT OF VIEW.

Nothing but snow. The station has either lost its tower to the storm or
ceased broadcasting for the night.

226   INTERIOR: RESUME MIKE.

He sits upright, trying to get his breath back.

> SONNY BRAUTIGAN
> Mike?

SONNY lumbers over, looking disheveled and puffy with sleep, his hair
sticking up in the back.

> SONNY
> Man, I just had the most awful dream . . . this reporter . . .

Now UPTON BELL joins them.

> UPTON
> On Main Street . . . talkin' about how everybody was
> gone . . .

He stops. He and SONNY look at each other in mutual amazement.

SONNY
Like in this little town in Virginia, a long time ago.

MELINDA (voice)
No one knew where they went . . . and in the dream, no one
knew where *we* went.

They look toward the draw curtains. MELINDA is standing there in her
nightgown.

MELINDA
They're all dreaming it. Do you understand? *They are all
dreaming what we dreamed!*

She looks back toward:

227    INTERIOR: THE SLEEPING AREA—NIGHT.

The sleepers are in SLOW, TWISTY MOTION on their cots. They moan
and protest without waking.

228    INTERIOR: RESUME TV AREA.

MELINDA
But where could two hundred people disappear to?

SONNY and UPTON shake their heads. TESS comes halfway down the
stairs. Her hair is mussed; she still looks half asleep.

TESS MARCHANT
Especially on a little island, cut off by a big storm . . .

MIKE gets up and snaps off the TV.

MIKE
Into the ocean.

MELINDA
(shocked)
*What?*

> **MIKE**
> Into the ocean. Mass suicide. If we don't give him what he wants.

> **SONNY**
> How could he—

> **MIKE**
> I don't know . . . but I think he can.

MOLLY comes through the draw curtains, holding RALPHIE in her arms. RALPHIE is fast asleep, but she can't bear to let him go.

> **MOLLY**
> What does he want, though? Mike, what does he want?

> **MIKE**
> I'm sure we'll find out. When he's ready.

229   EXTERIOR: THE LIGHTHOUSE—NIGHT.

The light swings around and around, briefly cutting through the DRIVING SNOW on each swing. In one of the shattered windows at the top, a SHAPE stands.

THE CAMERA MOVES IN ON LINOGE, who stands looking out at the town with his hands behind his back. He has the air of a ruler surveying his kingdom. At last he turns away.

230   INTERIOR: LIGHTHOUSE CONTROL ROOM—NIGHT.

LINOGE, little more than a shadow in the RED LIGHTS of the control panels, crosses the circular room and opens the door to the stairs. THE CAMERA MOVES IN on the computer screen we saw before. Marching down from the top, replacing the storm surge warning for the morning's high tide, is this message, repeated over and over: "GIVE ME WHAT I WANT."

231   INTERIOR: THE LIGHTHOUSE STAIRCASE—NIGHT.

We're looking down this dizzying spiral at LINOGE, who is descending rapidly.

232   EXTERIOR: THE LIGHTHOUSE—NIGHT.

LINOGE comes out, wolf's head cane in hand, and moves off into the snow, headed God knows where to do God knows what mischief. We HOLD on the lighthouse, then

FADE TO BLACK. THIS ENDS ACT 6.

# Act 7

233   EXTERIOR: THE DOWNTOWN AREA—MORNING.

The snow is falling as fast and hard as ever. Buildings are half-buried. Power lines disappear into the snow. It looks like the newscast walk-and-ski we saw in the dreams, only with the storm still going on.

234   EXTERIOR: THE TOWN HALL—MORNING.

The cupola with the memorial bell in it is almost buried, and the brick town hall building itself looks ghostly. The WIND HOWLS, unabated.

235   INTERIOR: THE TOWN MEETING HALL—MORNING.

About half of the folks who took shelter in the town hall are here, sitting on the hard wooden benches with plates on their laps, eating pancakes and drinking juice. A kind of buffet has been set up at the back of the hall, with MRS. KINGSBURY (wearing a brilliant red hunter's cap with the bill turned around backward gangster-style) and TESS MARCHANT officiating. There's juice, coffee, and cold cereal in addition to the pancakes.

The folks eating breakfast are very quiet . . . not sullen, but introspective and a little afraid. All the families with small children are up—of course they are, wee folks rise and shine early—and among them we see the HATCHERS and the ANDERSONS in a sleepy morning party of six. MIKE is feeding RALPHIE bites of pancake, and HATCH is doing about the same with PIPPA. The wives drink coffee and talk quietly.

The side door OPENS, letting in a HOWL OF WIND, a SWIRL OF SNOW, and an excited JOHNNY HARRIMAN.

                              JOHNNY
         Mike! Hey, Mikey! I never seen such a storm surge in my life!
         I think the lighthouse is gonna go! I really do!

The ISLANDERS STIR and MURMUR. MIKE puts RALPHIE on

MOLLY'S lap and gets up. HATCH gets up too, and so do most of the others.

> MIKE
>
> Folks, if you go out, stay close to the building! We've got whiteout conditions, remember!

236   EXTERIOR: ANGLE ON THE HEADLAND AND THE LIGHTHOUSE— MORNING.

The tide is coming high, and huge waves pound the rocks. The headland is almost inundated with each one. The base of the lighthouse is drowned with each incoming surge of water. The lighthouse survived last night's high tide; it probably won't survive this one.

237   EXTERIOR: THE SIDE OF THE TOWN HALL—MORNING.

ISLANDERS spill out, CHATTERING, some buttoning their coats, some knotting scarves under their chins, some pulling up hoods and yanking down ski masks.

238   INTERIOR: THE TOWN MEETING ROOM—MORNING.

The last of the people going out are just slipping through the easing clog at the side door. What's left in here are a few people who don't want to quit eating, plus SEVEN MOMMIES and ONE DADDY (JACK CARVER) coping with little kids who are *exceedingly* reluctant to be left out of the excitement.

> RALPHIE
>
> Mommy, please can't I go see?

MOLLY exchanges a look with MELINDA—it's exasperated and a-mused at the same time, a look that only the parents of preschool children know.

> PIPPA
> (picking up on it)
> Please, Mommy, please can't I?

DON BEALS, meanwhile, is employing a more masterful approach with SANDRA.

DON

Put my coat on! I wanna go out! Hurry up, you slowpoke!

MOLLY
(to RALPHIE)

Oh . . . all right.

(to MELINDA)

Hey, I want to see, too.

(to RALPHIE)

Come on, Ralphie, let's find your coat.

Most of the other parents—LINDA ST. PIERRE, CARLA BRIGHT, JACK CARVER, JILL ROBICHAUX—are doing the same. URSULA GODSOE, however, is resisting SALLY'S imploring.

URSULA

Mommy can't, honey—she's too tired. I'm sorry.

SALLY

Daddy will take me . . . Where's Daddy?

URSULA can't think of an answer and is on the verge of tears. The other ladies who overhear are melting with sympathy. SALLY doesn't know yet that her father is dead.

JENNA FREEMAN

I'll take you out, hon. If it's okay with your mom.

URSULA nods gratefully.

239   EXTERIOR: THE SIDE LAWN OF THE TOWN HALL—MORNING.

About seventy ISLAND RESIDENTS are clustered in a loose line, all standing with their backs to us, all looking toward the ocean. The PARENTS come from the side door, either carrying young, bundled-up children or leading them by the hand. They occasionally sink hip deep in the new snow and have to help each other out of the drifts. There is some LAUGHTER; the excitement has helped to stir them out of their post-dream introspection.

In the foreground, the black barrel of a CANE comes down, burying itself in the snow.

240   EXTERIOR: THE REAR OF THE TOWN HALL—MORNING.

LINOGE is standing here, watching the townsfolk through the heavy snow. They don't see him, because their backs are turned.

241   EXTERIOR: HEADLAND AND LIGHTHOUSE, FROM THE TOWN HALL'S POINT OF VIEW—MORNING.

From here, the lighthouse is almost obscured by the snow . . . from time to time it *will* be obscured . . . but right now we can see both it and the GIANT WAVES surging around it.

242   EXTERIOR: MIKE AND HATCH—MORNING.

> HATCH
>
> Is it gonna go, Mike?

MOLLY and MELINDA, accompanied by RALPH and PIPPA, join their husbands. MIKE bends to pick up RALPHIE without taking his eyes off the lighthouse.

> MIKE
>
> I think it is.

243   EXTERIOR: HEADLAND AND LIGHTHOUSE, FROM THE TOWN HALL'S POINT OF VIEW.

A huge wave smacks the headland and surges around the lighthouse. Then the WIND HOWLS, the SNOW THICKENS, and the lighthouse is hardly there, only a dim white ghost in the swirling snow.

244   INTERIOR: THE LIGHTHOUSE CONTROL ROOM.

Water POURS IN through the shattered windows and inundates the electronic gear. Sparks fly; the computers SHORT OUT.

245   EXTERIOR: HEADLAND AND LIGHTHOUSE, FROM THE TOWN HALL'S POINT OF VIEW.

Except we really can't see much at all now except for a couple of houses and some ghostly trees down the hill from where the people stand. The snow has thickened and the wind is swirling it up, creating WHITE-OUT CONDITIONS.

246 EXTERIOR: THE TOWNSFOLK, A PANNING SHOT—MORNING.

We see the little family groups and clusters of friends (SONNY and UPTON BELL are together; KIRK and his younger sister, JENNA— accompanied by little SALLY GODSOE—are standing near the BEALSES), but some folks stand a bit apart from the others. Behind them all, the snow provides a SHIFTING WHITE BACKDROP. The town hall itself is only a pink shadow.

As we PAN:

> KIRK
>
> I can't see a thing!

> FERD ANDREWS
>
> It's a damn whiteout!

> DON BEALS
>
> Daddy, where's the lighthouse?

> ROBBIE
> (to DON)
>
> Wait for the wind to drop, honey.

> DON
>
> Make it drop *now!*

> DAVEY HOPEWELL
> (to MRS. KINGSBURY)
>
> Look! There's the light, just coming around! It's still there!

247 INTERIOR: LOOKING INTO THE WHITEOUT, FROM THE ISLANDERS' POINT OF VIEW—MORNING.

In all that swirling snow, the SEARCHLIGHT gleams fitfully, brightens, then revolves out of sight again. As it does, we begin to see the headland once more.

248 EXTERIOR: RESUME PANNING TOWNSPEOPLE—MORNING.

> HATCH
>
> It's lifting!

MRS. KINGSBURY is standing to the left of the HOPEWELLS, her RED HUNTING CAP now turned around so the bill faces front. BRIGHT YELLOW GLOVES (LINOGE must have had another pair of them stashed somewhere) come out of the snow. One clamps over MRS. KINGSBURY'S mouth; the other grabs her by the neck. She is JERKED BACKWARD into the whiteout. The HOPEWELLS are quite close-by, but none of them see; they are peering into the snow as hard as they can.

249   EXTERIOR: HEADLAND AND LIGHTHOUSE, FROM THE TOWN HALL'S POINT OF VIEW.

A GIGANTIC WAVE smashes into the headland, humps up, and CRASHES INTO THE LIGHTHOUSE. And now we can see it beginning to TILT.

250   EXTERIOR: SONNY BRAUTIGAN AND UPTON BELL.

> SONNY
> She goin'! Holy God, she surely goin'!

Near them is a MALE RESIDENT bundled up in a grease-stained parka with "ISLAND E-Z PUMP" written on the left breast. A SHAPE— LINOGE—looms behind him. It pauses for a second or two, and then the CANE comes down across MR. E-Z PUMP'S throat, gripped at either end by BRIGHT YELLOW GLOVES. MR. E-Z PUMP is yanked backward into the whiteout. Neither SONNY nor UPTON notice; they are thrilled by the destruction taking place below.

251   EXTERIOR: THE WHITEOUT, LOOKING BACK TOWARD THE TOWN HALL.

We see TWO BLACK SHAPES—the soles of MR. E-Z PUMP'S boots. They float briefly in all that white, then disappear.

252   EXTERIOR: THE LIGHTHOUSE—MORNING.

Another of those huge waves buries the lower half. We hear the RUMBLE OF WATER and the GROAN of crumbling bricks. The lighthouse's tilt becomes more pronounced.

253   INTERIOR: THE LIGHTHOUSE CONTROL ROOM—MORNING.

It's tilting . . . tilting . . . water pouring in . . . the tilt becoming more pronounced as equipment comes unanchored and begins to slide down the steepening slope of the floor . . .

254    EXTERIOR: THE ISLANDERS OUTSIDE THE TOWN HALL—MORNING.

THE CAMERA is behind them, PANNING from left to right. From between them, or over their shoulders, we can see the tottering lighthouse.

255    EXTERIOR: JACK, ANGIE, AND BUSTER CARVER—MORNING.

JACK is highly excited. He sweeps BUSTER into his arms and lunges forward a little through the snow.

> JACK
> Look, Buster! The lighthouse is falling down!

> BUSTER
> Falling down! Lighthouse falling down!

ANGELA is about four steps behind them. Neither JACK nor BUSTER see the YELLOW GLOVES as they float out of the snow, grab her, and yank her backward into the WHITE CURTAIN.

256    EXTERIOR: RESUME LIGHTHOUSE—MORNING.

The inundating wave retreats. For a moment it seems the lighthouse might endure yet a little longer . . . and then it goes CRASHING DOWN, the light above the shattered control room still revolving valiantly. As it falls, another wave strikes, drowning the ruins.

257    EXTERIOR: THE ISLANDERS, PANNING.

They are silent, their brief excitement gone. Now that it's actually happened, they wish it had not. We end up on JACK and BUSTER.

> BUSTER
> Where's the lighthouse, Daddy? Did it go bye-bye?

> JACK
> (sadly)
> Yeah, honey, I guess so. Lighthouse went bye-bye.

(turning)
Angie, did you see it? Did you . . .

But there's no one where she was standing.

JACK
Angie? Angela?

He looks up and down the line of ISLANDERS, puzzled but not yet worried or afraid. He doesn't see her.

JACK
Hey, Ange . . .

BUSTER
Hey, Mommeee . . .

JACK looks at ORV BOUCHER, who is standing nearby.

JACK
Did you see my wife?

ORV
Gee, Jack, I didn't notice. Maybe she got cold and went back inside.

258   EXTERIOR: THE HOPEWELL FAMILY: STAN, MARY, AND DAVEY— MORNING.

DAVEY'S parents are still looking down at the place where the lighthouse stood (as if expecting an instant replay), but DAVEY is looking around, frowning.

DAVEY
Mrs. Kingsbury?

MARY HOPEWELL
(hears him)
Davey?

DAVEY
She was just here.

JACK comes slogging along, now holding BUSTER by the hand.

                              JACK
    Angie . . .?
                         (to BUSTER)
    I guess Orv's right—she must've gotten cold and gone back
    inside.

Nearby are ALEX HABER and CAL FREESE.

                              CAL
                        (looking around)
    Hey, where's old George Kirby?

259   EXTERIOR: THE ANDERSONS AND THE HATCHERS—MORNING.

Along the ragged line of ISLANDERS who have come out to watch the
lighthouse go down, CAL and ALEX are calling for GEORGE KIRBY,
JACK and BUSTER are calling for ANGELA, DAVEY HOPEWELL is
calling for MRS. KINGSBURY, and a couple of other folks are calling
for BILL—the real name of MR. E-Z PUMP, one assumes.

A kind of sick realization is dawning on MIKE'S face. He looks at
HATCH and sees much the same look there. MIKE sets RALPHIE
down and turns to the ragged line of ISLANDERS.

                              MIKE
    Back inside! Everyone back inside!

                             MOLLY
    Mike, what's wrong?

MIKE ignores her. He begins RUNNING down the line of ISLAND-
ERS, looking frantic.

                              MIKE
    Inside! Everybody! Now! And stay together!

His fear communicates itself to the ISLANDERS, who begin to turn
and go inside. ROBBIE comes over to MIKE.

ROBBIE

What the hell's this?

MIKE

Maybe nothing. For now, just go inside. Take your wife and your boy and go inside.

As he gets ROBBIE turned around and begins shepherding him back to SANDRA and DON, JACK CARVER comes floundering up through the snow, holding BUSTER.

JACK
(now beginning to be afraid)
Michael, have you seen Angela? She was right here.

ROBBIE begins to understand. He goes to SANDRA and BUSTER, suddenly not wanting them out of his sight.

MIKE

Take your boy on inside, Jack.

JACK

But—

MIKE

Go on, now. Do it.

260    EXTERIOR: HATCH, ON THE SNOWFIELD BESIDE THE TOWN HALL.

Around him, people are hurrying back to the side door. Most look fearful. HATCH ignores them, trying to look everywhere at once . . . an impossible trick, given the thick snow.

HATCH
Mrs. Kingsbury? . . . George? . . . George Kirby? . . . Bill Timmons, where you at?

He sees a BRIGHT SPLASH OF RED and goes to it. He picks up MRS. KINGSBURY'S hat, dusts the snow from it with his gloved hand, and looks at it gravely as MIKE comes up to him, herding people along. MIKE'S eyes also move everywhere. They are shepherds trying to guard a diminishing flock.

MIKE takes the hat from HATCH and looks at it for a moment.

### MIKE
*Inside! Inside now! Stick together!*

261   INTERIOR: THE TOWN MEETING HALL, FEATURES JACK AND BUSTER.

### BUSTER
Where's Mommy? We left Mommy outside! Daddy, we left Mommy outside!

### JACK
(beginning to cry)
Come on, big boy. Mommy's fine.

He almost drags BUSTER up the aisle and toward the door leading to the town office and the stairs.

262   INTERIOR: MONTAGE OF ISLANDERS, MEETING HALL—MORNING.

They shuffle up the aisles—MOLLY and RALPHIE, the STANHOPES, JOHNNY HARRIMAN, TAVIA GODSOE, KIRK and JENNA FREEMAN, all our new acquaintances—and every face is stamped with fear.

DISSOLVES TO:
263   EXTERIOR: THE TOWN HALL—AFTERNOON.

TITLE CARD: 2:00 P.M.

The snow is still SWIRLING DOWN, and the WIND is still HOWLING. Parked by the side door is the biggest Sno-Cat on the island, its engine idling.

264   EXTERIOR: THE TOWN HALL'S SIDE DOOR, CLOSER—AFTERNOON.

Bundled up in the doorway are MIKE, SONNY, HENRY BRIGHT, and KIRK FREEMAN. There to see them off, clutching sweaters against the chill, are MOLLY, HATCH, and TESS MARCHANT. Once again, they all shout to be heard over the storm.

### MOLLY
Are you sure this is necessary?

                    MIKE

No—but we're fresh out of weather forecasts, and it's best to
be safe. Besides, there's stuff at the market that'll just go over
if we don't use it.

                    MOLLY

Fresh orange juice isn't worth risking that psychopath!

                    MIKE

He's not going to take on four of us.

                    MOLLY

Promise me you'll be careful.

                    MIKE

I promise.
              (shifts his attention to HATCH)
Buddy system, right? No one gets left alone.

                    HATCH

Right. Be careful, you guys.

                    SONNY

You better believe it.

As they turn away toward the Sno-Cat:

                    MOLLY

Mike . . . since the house is right on your way . . .

She stops, a little embarrassed to ask what has come to her mind, but
his eyes are kind and encourage her.

                    MOLLY

Well . . . the kids are being as good as they can, but if you
could just maybe grab a handful of games and two or three
boxes of Slip-Stix or something, it'd be a lifesaver.

                    MIKE
              (kisses her on the cheek)
Consider it done.

He goes to the Sno-Cat and slides behind the controls. He guns the engine. They all wave, and the Sno-Cat buzzes away into the storm.

#### TAVIA
Will they be all right?

#### HATCH
Sure.

He looks worried, though. They go back inside and shut the door against the storm.

265    EXTERIOR: THE ANDERSON HOUSE ON LOWER MAIN—AFTERNOON.

The Sno-Cat pulls up in front. The picket fence is totally buried. The WEE FOLKS DAY-CARE CENTER sign is lying on top of a ten-foot drift.

266    INTERIOR: THE SNO-CAT—AFTERNOON.

#### MIKE
(to the others)
Just be a minute.

He opens the door on his side and gets out.

267    EXTERIOR: OUTSIDE THE ANDERSON HOUSE, WITH MIKE—AFTERNOON.

He slogs around the front of the Sno-Cat, bent over against the SNOW and WIND, and almost runs headlong into KIRK FREEMAN. Once more, they SHOUT over the WIND to be heard.

#### MIKE
Get back in and stay warm; I'll be fine!

#### KIRK
Buddy system, remember?

He points into the Sno-Cat at HENRY and SONNY.

#### KIRK
We buddy up in there; they buddy up out here; we all buddy up together in the market.

MIKE
Okay . . . come on.

They start slogging up what used to be a path to a porch wallowing under the drifts like a slowly sinking boat.

268    INTERIOR: CAT WITHERS, CLOSE-UP.

She sitting on a folding chair and looks pretty vacant. She's got a mug of something in one hand and a sweater pulled over her shoulders. She's still bombed on shock and tranquilizers.

In the background, children sing:

CHILDREN AND SANDRA BEALS
"I'm a little teapot, short and stout. . . ."

CAT reacts to this, but doesn't overreact; she may not remember the song. THE CAMERA PULLS BACK to show us the DAY-CARE KIDS. They are being monitored by ROBBIE and SANDRA BEALS—buddy system. SANDRA is leading the singing and trying to look vivacious. ROBBIE sits on another wooden chair, looking almost as lost as CAT.

The KIDS are being teapots—as they sing, they make handles of their arms and tug their noses to show they know where their spouts are.

Around them at this end of the common room, which is between the stairs and the wall, is a litter of makeshift amusements: books, paste, magazines with lots of cutout pictures and scraps, a few toys.

Beyond them is a closed door with a plaque on it that reads CUSTODIAN.

                    CHILDREN AND SANDRA
    "Here is my handle, here is my spout."

FERD ANDREWS comes down the stairs and stands next to ROBBIE.

                    ROBBIE
    I hate that song.

                    FERD
    Why?

                    ROBBIE
    I just hate it. How's Jack Carver?

                    FERD
    Quieted down some. It's just good the women got the kid
    away from him before he cracked.
                    (nods at BUSTER)
    There ought to be a search party made up to look for Angela
    and them others. If Alton Hatcher won't lead it, you could.

                    ROBBIE
    And if the search party didn't come back, what then? Send
    out another one?

                    FERD
    Well . . . we can't just sit here . . .

                    ROBBIE
    Sure we can. And that's just what we're going to do. Sit here
    and wait out the storm. Pardon me, Ferd. I need a coffee.

Giving FERD a contemptuous look, ROBBIE gets to his feet and heads upstairs. FERD goes after him.

                    FERD
    I was just thinkin' we ought to do somethin', Robbie . . .

THE CAMERA returns to CAT. Her eyes flicker. She sees:

269    INSERT: LINOGE'S CANE.

It SWINGS toward THE CAMERA, silver wolf's head seeming to SNARL.

270    INTERIOR: RESUME KIDS' PLAY AREA—AFTERNOON.

CAT drops her mug and puts her hands over her face, beginning to SOB. The KIDS stop singing and turn to look at her. PIPPA and HEIDI start to sniffle in sympathy.

> FRANK BRIGHT
> What's wrong with Katrina Withers?

> SANDRA
> Nothing, Frankie . . . she's just tired . . . You kids, pick up a little, okay? Mr. Anderson'll be bringing back some new things to play with, I think, so just . . .

> DON
> *I'm* not gonna pick up! My dad'll give me a doughnut!

He dashes for the stairs.

> SANDRA
> Don! Don Beals! You come back and help the others—

> RALPHIE
> We don't need him. Monkeys can't pick up.

The others SNICKER—that's a pretty good one. And when RALPHIE starts picking up the litter, the rest join in. SANDRA goes over and begins comforting CAT.

271    INTERIOR: ISOLATE ON RALPHIE.

He works his way a little apart from the others, picking up magazines. He's moving toward the door marked CUSTODIAN, and when it COMES OPEN, he looks up.

LINOGE (voice)
Ralphie! Hey, big boy!

The others do not hear, but RALPHIE does.

272   INTERIOR: WEE FOLKS DAY-CARE CENTER, WITH MIKE AND KIRK.

KIRK has an armload of games and those kid puzzles with the great big pieces. MIKE has the Slip-Stix and a few other simple crafts.

KIRK
That it?

MIKE
Yep, should do. Let's . . .

Something catches his eye. It's a scatter of alphabet blocks on a low worktable. MIKE kneels beside it, looks thoughtfully at the blocks, then begins to pull some of them together into a line.

KIRK
(over to have a look)
What you doing?

MIKE has used six of the blocks to spell out "LINOGE." He looks at them, then swaps them around to make "NILOGE." No, that's nonsense. Next comes "GONILE."

KIRK
Go Nile. Sounds like an ad for a vacation in Egypt.

273   INTERIOR: THE KIDS' PLAY AREA.

SANDRA is busy with CAT, and the other kids have grouped together around some baskets in the corner, where they stow the toys, books, and magazines. They are having a good time. No one notices RALPHIE as he gets up and walks hesitatingly toward the half-open door of the custodian's closet.

LINOGE (voice)
Got something for you, big boy—a present!

RALPHIE reaches for the door . . . then hesitates.

> LINOGE (voice)
> (teasing)

Not afraid, are you?

RALPHIE reaches for the door again, this time more decisively.

274    INTERIOR: WEE FOLKS DAY-CARE, WITH MIKE AND KIRK.

KIRK is interested now. He moves the blocks himself, making "LIN-OGE" into "LONIEG." And suddenly, MIKE sees it. His eyes WIDEN WITH HORROR.

> MIKE

Jesus and the disciples in the country of the Gadarenes. Book of Mark. Oh my God.

> KIRK

*Huh?*

> MIKE

They met a man with an unclean spirit; that's what it says in the Gospel. A man with demons inside of him. He lived among the tombs, and no man could bind him, not even with chains. Jesus cast the demons into a herd of pigs that ran into the ocean and drowned themselves. But before he cast them out, Jesus asked their names. And the thing inside said—

KIRK is watching him with increasing fright as MIKE manipulates the blocks.

> MIKE

"Our name is *Legion,* for we are many."

Now the blocks that spelled "LINOGE" spell "LEGION." MIKE and KIRK stare at each other, wide-eyed.

275    INTERIOR: OUTSIDE THE CUSTODIAN'S CLOSET.

RALPHIE opens the door and looks up at ANDRE LINOGE. In one hand, LINOGE grips his wolf's head cane. The other is behind his back. LINOGE is smiling.

### LINOGE
It's a present for the fairy-saddle boy. Come and see.

RALPHIE enters the custodian's closet. The door swings shut.

THIS ENDS PART TWO.

# PART 3
## The Reckoning

## Act 1

1   EXTERIOR: THE ISLAND MARKET—AFTERNOON.

The snow is falling as hard as ever. The porch is almost completely buried beneath one huge, dunelike drift from floor to roof overhang. Parked in front is the big Sno-Cat MIKE and the others took out on the reprovisioning expedition. From its side door to the door of the market, a notch almost like a tunnel has been dug. The four men—MIKE ANDERSON, SONNY BRAUTIGAN, HENRY BRIGHT, and KIRK FREEMAN—are just entering.

2   INTERIOR: THE MARKET, BY THE CASH REGISTERS—AFTERNOON.

The men make their way in, gasping and shedding snow. SONNY and HENRY have shovels. We can see their BREATH in the air, and the place is very dim.

SONNY

Gennie's out.
(MIKE nods)
How long, do you think?

MIKE

Hard to tell. Since morning, anyway, from the way it feels. Snow probably piled up and blocked the exhaust.

He goes to the cash registers, bends beneath one, and begins to toss out big cardboard cartons.

MIKE

Sonny, Henry. You're Meat Patrol. Get the big cuts of beef, plus the turkeys and chicken. The best stuff's back in the freezer.

HENRY

Will it still be all right, do you think?

MIKE

Are you kidding? It won't even be thawed yet. Come on, let's go. Dark's gonna come early.

SONNY and HENRY start up toward the cooler and the freezer beyond. KIRK comes over to the checkout and takes one of the cartons.

MIKE

We'll stick to the canned goods, this trip. All of us'll come back for bread, potatoes, and vegetables. And milk. Little kids have to have milk.

KIRK

You gonna tell 'em about what the guy's name spells when you move the blocks around?

MIKE

What good would it do?

KIRK

I dunno. God, Mike, that gave me a chill.

MIKE

Me, too. And for the time being, maybe we better just . . . keep the chill to ourselves. We've still got at least one more night to get through.

KIRK

But—

MIKE

Come on. Canned goods. Let's load up.

He starts up the aisle containing the overturned card table, and after a moment or two's consideration, KIRK follows.

3   EXTERIOR: THE TOWN HALL—AFTERNOON.

We can barely see it in all the snow, but at regular intervals we can hear the BLARE OF A HORN.

4   EXTERIOR: THE PARKING LOT—AFTERNOON.

The Island Services vehicle is idling here, not too far from the town hall's side door. It's not going to go anywhere—not even a four-wheel drive can move in five feet of snow—but the lights are on and we can see one man standing outside and another inside. The one behind the wheel is HATCH. The one outside, wearing his V.F.D. parka and peering anxiously into the snow, is FERD ANDREWS. The window between them is open. Snow is blowing into the cab of the truck, but at this point, neither man cares.

FERD cups his hands around his mouth and hollers into the SHRIEK-ING WIND as loud as he can.

> FERD
> *Angie Carver! Billy Timmons!*

> HATCH
> Any sign? Any at all?

> FERD
> No! Wouldn't I tell you? Keep blowin' that thing!

HATCH continues to lay on the horn in long, measured beats. FERD peers anxiously into the snow, then turns and yanks open the door.

> FERD
> You watch and let me honk—your eyes're better.

They change places.

> HATCH
> (squinting into the snow)
> *George Kirby! Janie Kingsbury! Where are you guys?*

FERD keeps blowing the horn in long, measured BLASTS.

5   INTERIOR: THE TOWN HALL'S MAKESHIFT DAY-CARE AREA—
AFTERNOON.

SOUND, MUFFLED: THE HORN CONTINUES.

The KIDS have finished picking up and don't really know what to do
with themselves now. No one has noticed that RALPHIE ANDERSON
isn't among them. SANDRA has gotten CAT quieted down and now
looks restless herself. CAT sees this and offers SANDRA a wan smile
and a pat on the arm.

> CAT
>
> I'm okay. Go on up. Find your husband and little boy.

> SANDRA
>
> But . . . the kids . . .

CAT gets up and approaches them. SANDRA watches apprehensively.
This is the young woman who beat her boyfriend to death not long ago.

> CAT
>
> Who wants to play Giant Step?

> HEIDI
>
> Yeah!

> SALLY GODSOE
>
> Me! Yayy, I do!

The kids start to line up, facing CAT. Only BUSTER CARVER lags.

> BUSTER
>
> Where's my mommy?

> SANDRA
>
> I'll just peek and see if she's upstairs, shall I? Or your daddy?

> BUSTER
>
> Yes, please, Missus Beals.

PIPPA
And send Don down! He *always* forgets to say "May I"!

The others laugh gleefully, including BUSTER.

FRANK
(takes BUSTER'S arm)
Come on, you play next to me—we'll be partners.

BUSTER
(starts, then stops)
Where's Ralphie?

There's a moment of nervousness as they all look around and realize RALPHIE isn't there. CAT turns to SANDRA, an eyebrow raised in question.

SANDRA
He probably chased upstairs after Donnie, to see if he could get a doughnut, too. I'll send them both down.

She goes upstairs. The other kids are satisfied with this explanation, except for PIPPA, who's looking around with a frown.

PIPPA
He didn't go upstairs with Donnie Beals . . . at least I don't *think* he did . . .

UPTON BELL comes over, grinning like the amiable fool he is.

SALLY GODSOE
Who's blowing that horn, Mr. Bell?

UPTON
Someone tryin' to call the snowbirds, I guess.

FRANK
What're snowbirds?

UPTON
You never heard of snowbirds?

> KIDS
> No . . . no . . . What are they? . . . Tell us!
> (etc.)

> UPTON
> Oh, big as refrigerators, they are, white as snow and tasty as
> the devil . . . but they only fly around when there's a big
> blizzard. Only time there's wind enough to give 'em the lift.
> To them a horn's just like a birdcall, but they're cussed hard
> to catch, just the same. Can I play, too?

> KIDS
> *Yeah! Yeah, all right!*
> (etc.)

PIPPA has been looking around for RALPHIE, but now she joins in,
distracted from her concern by her delight at having a grown-up who's
willing to play the game with them.

> CAT
> Get right in line, Upton Bell. Just don't be smart and don't
> forget to say, "May I." Now—here we go. Frank Bright, take
> two helicopter steps.

FRANK takes two steps forward, whirling around, flapping his arms
and making HELICOPTER SOUNDS.

> KIDS
> *You forgot to say, "May I"!*

Grinning, shamefaced, FRANK goes back. THE CAMERA moves away
from the game to the closed door marked CUSTODIAN.

6   INTERIOR: THE TOWN MEETING HALL—AFTERNOON.

SOUND, MUFFLED: THE HORN CONTINUES.

In the foreground we see MOLLY ANDERSON sitting beside JACK
CARVER on one of those hard meeting benches, trying to soothe him.
In the background, at the rear of the long room, is the buffet, where
people are coming and going, getting coffee and snacks. Some look
toward MOLLY and JACK, troubled and sympathetic, but not ROBBIE

BEALS and his son, DON. They are eating doughnuts with a remarkable lack of concern. ROBBIE has coffee; DON is slurping a Coke.

> JACK
>
> I got to find her!

He makes an effort to rise, and MOLLY puts a hand on his arm, holding him where he is for the time being.

> MOLLY
>
> You know what it's like out there.

> JACK
>
> She could be wandering around, freezing to death in a whiteout fifty yards from the building!

> MOLLY
>
> And if you go out there, you'll be lost, too. If they're there, they'll come to the horn. Same as in a fog, at sea. You know that.

> JACK
>
> I'll go out spell Ferd.

> MOLLY
>
> Hatch said—

> JACK
>
> Alton Hatcher can't tell me what to do—that's my wife out there!

She can't stop him this time, so she gets up with him. Behind them, SANDRA comes in from the town office area, looks around, spots her husband and son.

> MOLLY
>
> Go to the truck, then, but *just* to the truck. Don't go wandering off on your own.

But JACK can promise her no such thing. He's totally distracted. MOLLY watches sadly as he goes up the aisle, then follows herself. SANDRA, meanwhile, is looking around. She doesn't see MOLLY yet.

                          SANDRA
                         (to DON)
Where's Ralphie?


                           DON
                   (munching his doughnut)
I dunno.


                          SANDRA
But didn't he come upstairs with you?


MOLLY is in time to hear this and is of course immediately concerned.


                           DON
Nah, he 'us pickin up with the rest of 'em. Dad, can I have
another doughnut?


                          MOLLY
                       (to SANDRA)
He's not down there? What are you saying, that he's not with
the others?


                          SANDRA
                        (flustered)
I didn't see . . . Cat started to cry . . . she dropped her cup
and broke it . . .


                          MOLLY
You were supposed to be watching them!


SANDRA winces. She's been married to ROBBIE for ten years and is
used to being blamed when things go wrong.


                          ROBBIE
                     (the usual bluster)
I hardly think that tone is—


                          MOLLY
                        (ignores him)
        *You were supposed to be watching them!*
                  (she breaks for the stairs)
        *Ralphie! Ralphie!*

7   EXTERIOR: THE ISLAND MARKET—AFTERNOON.

The men are clustered at the Sno-Cat, handing loaded cartons to
MIKE, who stows them in the back. MIKE SHOUTS TO BE HEARD
over the storm as the last box goes in.

> MIKE
> One more trip! Sonny, you and Henry get the bread and rolls!
> Everything on the shelves! Kirk, you want to grab at least a
> hundred pounds of potatoes! I'll get the milk! Let's go—I
> want to get back as soon as we can!

They go single file into the cut in the drift, SONNY and HENRY
BRIGHT first, followed by MIKE and KIRK. SONNY and HENRY go
inside. MIKE is about to follow, then stops so suddenly that KIRK just
about runs into him.

> KIRK
What the hell?

MIKE has stopped at the mannequin set up on the porch—HATCH's
joke at ROBBIE BEALS'S expense. The mannequin is now almost
completely buried, and although the face is covered with wind-driven
snow and the figure is still dressed in the lobsterman's slicker, we can
see it's not the same figure.

MIKE brushes FROZEN SNOW away from the face. It's MRS. KINGS-
BURY. She's frozen solid. KIRK stares in dismay as MIKE digs into the
snow around the dummy's neck and pulls out a new joke sign . . . only
now the joke is on them. "GIVE ME WHAT I WANT AND I'LL GO
AWAY," it says.

The two men stare at each other in horror.

8   EXTERIOR: THE TOWN HALL—AFTERNOON.

SOUND OF HORN CONTINUES—EVEN, REGULAR BLASTS.

> MOLLY (voice-over)
> Ralphie! *Ralphie!*

9   INTERIOR: THE DAY-CARE AREA OF THE BASEMENT—AFTERNOON.

SOUND OF HORN, MUFFLED.

MOLLY is frantic, looking everywhere for RALPHIE, who isn't here. CAT
and UPTON BELL have drawn together in fright. ROBBIE, DON, TESS
MARCHANT, and TAVIA GODSOE are on the stairs. SALLY GODSOE
sees her aunt and runs to her. The other children huddle, dismayed.

> PIPPA
> I *said* he didn't go with Don—

All the other adults are gathering—some from the seats around the
now-useless TV, some from upstairs, some from the sleeping area. One
is URSULA GODSOE, looking blasted with grief.

> URSULA
> Oh, God, what now?

MOLLY ignores her. She goes to PIPPA, kneels in front of her, and
grasps her gently by the arms. She peers into PIPPA'S frightened face.

> MOLLY
> Where was Ralphie when you saw him last, Pippa?

PIPPA thinks about it, then points to the area between the stairs and
the wall. MOLLY looks in that direction, and sees the door marked
CUSTODIAN. There is TOTAL SILENCE—except for the MUFFLED,

REGULAR BLASTS OF THE HORN—as MOLLY goes toward that door, afraid of what she may find. She reaches for the knob but can't bring herself to touch it, let alone turn it.

MOLLY

Ralphie? Ralphie, are you—

RALPHIE (voice)

Mommy? Mom?

Oh, boy, the relief. It's as if somebody let the air out of everyone in the room, KIDS included. MOLLY'S reserves of strength are gone. She begins to cry as she tears the door open.

RALPHIE is standing there in the custodian's closet, happy, excited, unhurt, and unaware there's been any fuss about him. His expression turns to one of puzzlement as his mother sweeps him up into her arms. In the general excitement we may or may not notice that RALPHIE has a SMALL LEATHER BAG in one hand, the kind with a drawstring at the top.

RALPHIE

Hey, Mom—wassup?

MOLLY

What are you doing in there? You scared the *life* out of me!

RALPHIE

The man was in there. He wanted to see me.

MOLLY

Man—?

RALPHIE

The one Daddy arrested. Except I don't think he's a bad man, Mom, because—

MOLLY sets RALPHIE down and sweeps him behind her so hard and fast that he almost falls over. UPTON grabs the kid and hands him to JONAS STANHOPE and ANDY ROBICHAUX, who have pushed their way to the front of the semicircle of watching adults. MOLLY takes two steps into the doorway of the custodian's closet and looks at:

10   INTERIOR: CUSTODIAN'S CLOSET, FROM MOLLY'S POINT OF VIEW.

There's plenty of cleaning gear on the shelves, plus the usual complement of brooms, mops, extra fluorescent lightbars, and there's no other exit . . . but there's no man.

11   INTERIOR: RESUME MOLLY.

She starts to turn back to RALPHIE, then stops as something catches her eye. She goes into the closet, instead.

12   INTERIOR: THE CUSTODIAN'S CLOSET, WITH MOLLY.

In the far corner is a piece of GREEN PAPER. It's a flyer for the Anderson's Market, advertising this week's specials. She picks it up and turns it over. Printed in red letters on the back is "GIVE ME WHAT I WANT AND I'LL GO AWAY."

ANDY ROBICHAUX has stepped into the closet. She hands him the flyer.

> MOLLY
> But what does he want?

ANDY can only shake his head. MOLLY leaves the closet.

13   INTERIOR: THE BASEMENT DAY-CARE AREA.

MOLLY goes to RALPHIE, who is standing with the other kids. They shrink back from him, thinking he's in trouble. RALPHIE looks up at his mom, clutching the little drawstring bag and hoping like mad that he's *not* in trouble.

> MOLLY
> Where did he go, Ralphie? Where did the man go?

RALPHIE peers past her, into the closet.

> RALPHIE
> I don't know. He must have disappeared when I turned my back.

> DON
> (from the stairs)
> There's no door in there for a guy to go out of, dumbkins.

MOLLY

Shut up, Don Beals.

DON, unaccustomed to such real sharpness from MOLLY, shrinks back against his dad. ROBBIE opens his mouth to say something reproving, then decides this might not be the best time.

MOLLY kneels in front of her son as she did in front of PIPPA and for the first time sees what he has—a finely made little bag of chamois leather.

MOLLY

What's this, Ralphie?

RALPHIE

It's a present. He gave me a present. That's why I don't think he can be a bad man like on TV, because bad men don't give kids presents.

MOLLY looks at the bag as if it might be a bomb, but she remains calm and soothing. She has to be. RALPHIE doesn't know what the deal is here, but he can see the faces surrounding him and feel the atmosphere in the room. The poor kid is on the verge of tears.

MOLLY
(takes the bag)

What is it? Let Mommy s—

JOANNA STANHOPE
(near hysterics)

Don't open it! Don't open it, it might be a bomb, it could explode!

JONAS

Be quiet, Joanie!

Too late. A couple of the kids—HEIDI and SALLY, perhaps—start to sniffle. All the adults take a step backward. We are seeing the leading edge of an ugly, building hysteria here. But given all that's happened, who can blame these people for being a bit hysterical?

CAT

Don't, Molly—don't.

MOLLY looks at the bag. Its bottom hangs down in a teardrop shape, weighted by whatever is inside it. Perhaps she touches its lowest-hanging curve.

RALPHIE

It's all right, Mom—don't be scared.

MOLLY

You know what this is, Ralphie? You've looked?

RALPHIE

Sure! We even had a game, me and Mr. Linoge. He says those are special, the most special in the world. And he said I should share them, because they're not just for me; they're for everyone. Everyone on the island!

MOLLY takes the bag. As she starts to open the drawstring top, the man with the black shirt and turned-around collar under his sport coat steps forward and puts a hand on her shoulder. This is BOB RIGGINS, the minister.

REV. BOB RIGGINS

I don't think I'd open that, Mrs. Anderson. Given the dreams we all had last night, and the possible nature of this . . . this *man* . . .

MOLLY

No, I suppose you wouldn't, Reverend Riggins. But since he's had his filthy hands on my son *twice* . . .

She opens the bag and looks in. The others watch breathlessly. MOLLY sees a child's cap nearby and dumps the contents of the drawstring bag into it.

FRANK BRIGHT
(coming closer to peek)

Hey, neat!

Not surprising he thinks so; it's a present any little kid would like. THE CAMERA MOVES IN for a closer look. In the hat are almost a dozen stones as smooth and round as marbles. All of them are white except for one. The odd one is BLACK shot through with TWISTS OF RED, and should remind us of LINOGE'S eyes.

MOLLY looks up and meets MELINDA HATCHER'S eyes. Neither of them know what RALPHIE'S "present" means, but MELINDA pulls PIPPA closer to her, needing to be comforted by her daughter's presence.

14   EXTERIOR: THE INTERSECTION OF MAIN AND ATLANTIC—AFTERNOON.

Slowly, fighting for every foot it makes through the storm, comes the Sno-Cat, bound back to the town hall from the market.

15   INTERIOR: THE SNO-CAT—AFTERNOON.

The four men—MIKE, SONNY, HENRY, and KIRK—are wedged tightly into the cab. The groceries are in the cargo compartment behind them. The men are grim-faced, shaken by what they have seen. They ride in silence, jouncing through the drifts for a while. Then, at last:

> SONNY
> Just ole Mrs. K. None of the others. Where do you suppose they are? George and Angie and Bill Timmons?
>> (no one answers)
> How did he get her down there?
>> (no one answers)
> Where's the dummy? Anybody see that in the store?
>> (no answer)
> How'd he get her down there in *this?*

> HENRY
> Let it go, Sonny.

For a moment or two, SONNY does. Then he turns to MIKE.

> SONNY
> Why is this happening? You're lay reader for Reverend Riggins down at the Methodist church, always got a quote from the Good Book handy—you must have *some* idea why this is happening.

MIKE thinks about it, guiding the Sno-Cat through the desolate white driftscape that used to be Main Street.

>                   MIKE
> You know the story about Job? In the Bible?
>                   (SONNY and the others nod)
> Well, here's the part that never got written down. After the contest for Job's soul is over and God wins, Job gets down on his knees and says, "Why did you do this to me, God? All my life I worshipped you, but You destroyed my livestock, blighted my crops, killed my wife and my children, and gave me a hundred horrible diseases . . . all because You had a bet going with the devil? Well, okay . . . but what I want to know, Lord—all your humble servant wants to know is— *Why me?* So he waits, and just when he's about made up his mind God isn't going to answer, a thunderhead forms in the sky, and lightning flashes, and this voice calls down: *"Job! I guess there's just something about you that pisses me off."*

SONNY, HENRY, and KIRK look at MIKE, not knowing what to think. SONNY actually looks dumbfounded.

>                   MIKE
> Does that help you?
>                   (no answer from the others)
> Me, either.

SOUND, FAINT: RHYTHMIC BLASTS OF THE HORN.

>                   KIRK
> Still lookin' for 'em.

>                   SONNY
>                   (thinking of Mrs. K.)
> Good luck.

16    EXTERIOR: MAIN STREET, WITH THE SNO-CAT—AFTERNOON.

Slow but steady wins the race. They haven't reached the town hall yet, but it's starting to appear that they will make it.

SOUND: THE HORN.

17   EXTERIOR: BESIDE THE TOWN HALL, WITH THE ISLAND SERVICES
VEHICLE—AFTERNOON.

FERD is now in the passenger seat, while HATCH hits the horn in those
LONG BLASTS. JACK CARVER is lurching in frantic circles around
the truck, tumbling into drifts, picking himself up, peering into the
HOWLING BLIZZARD.

> JACK
>
> *Angie! Angie, over here!*

He has screamed himself hoarse, but he can't give up. At last he
stumbles back to the open driver's side window of the vehicle, doubled
over and gasping for breath. His face is red and running with sweat
that has already frozen to a cruel glaze from the corners of his lips all
the way down to his chin.

> HATCH
>
> Get in, Jack—warm up.

> JACK
>
> No! She's out here someplace. Keep hitting that horn!

18   INTERIOR: ANGLE ON FERD, IN THE PASSENGER SEAT.

He sits up, eyes widening, as the conversation continues to his left. He
can't believe what he's seeing.

> HATCH
>
> You better sit down before you fall down.

> JACK
> (snarling)
>
> My wife's out there and she's alive—I can feel it. So you just
> keep working that horn!

> HATCH
>
> Jack, I really don't think—

FERD raises a hand that trembles with excitement. His face is
incredulous.

FERD

Hatch . . . Jack! Look!

19   EXTERIOR: THE SNOWFIELD, FROM THE ISLAND SERVICES VEHICLE'S POINT OF VIEW.

It's a SCREAMING WHITEOUT . . . but a FIGURE is LURCHING AND STUMBLING around in the flying murk. It could be the figure of a WOMAN.

20   EXTERIOR: RESUME ISLAND SERVICES VEHICLE, WITH JACK, HATCH, AND FERD.

HATCH

Dear God. Oh, my dear God, is that one of 'em?

FERD

I can't tell.

JACK
(transported with hope)

ANGIE!!!

He begins to STUMBLE toward the looming, indistinct figure. He falls, rolls in the snow, and lunges to his feet again. Behind him, HATCH gets out of the truck. In the background, FERD is doing the same on his side.

HATCH

Jack! Wait! That might not be—

But it's useless. JACK is already melting into the snow himself, closing in on that WAVERING, STUMBLING FIGURE. HATCH starts after him. So does FERD.

21   EXTERIOR: JACK CARVER—AFTERNOON.

He somehow keeps moving forward, CRYING HIS WIFE'S NAME over and over. HATCH can't keep up, and FERD is running a dead last. But now we can see that figure *is* a woman. As JACK closes in, the WOMAN falls herself, going facedown in the snow.

JACK

Angie! Honey!

The WOMAN works to get to her feet, moving with the mechanical determination of a clockwork figure. And as she finally makes it, we see that it really is ANGIE CARVER . . . but what a change! BUSTER'S pretty mom is a thing of the past. This lurching, blank-faced creature looks seventy instead of twenty-eight, and the hair flying out behind her has GONE GRAY. Her eyes stare straight ahead through the snow, taking no notice of her husband. Her snow-coated face is PALE AND LINED.

JACK
(embraces her)

Angie! Honey! Oh, Angie, we been looking for you! Buster's so worried, honey!

He covers her face with kisses as he talks, constantly giving her little strokes and pats and touches, the way a parent will do with a child who has just had a close call. At first, JACK is so relieved that he doesn't realize she isn't responding. Then it starts to get through to him.

JACK

Angie? Honey?

He draws back, really seeing her for the first time—seeing the glazed blankness in her eyes and seeing the gray hair that used to be black. He reacts with HORROR AND AMAZEMENT.

HATCH comes stumbling up, badly winded. FERD is bringing up the rear. And now we hear the RUMBLE of the Sno-Cat, returning from its marketing expedition.

JACK

Angie, what happened to you? What's wrong?

He looks at HATCH, but there's no help there. HATCH is also stunned by the change in her; so's FERD. JACK turns back to his wife and takes her by the shoulders.

JACK

What happened, Ange? What did he do to you? Where did he take you? Where are the others, do you know?

A large YELLOW EYE looms out of the snow—the headlamp of the Sno-Cat. ANGIE sees it, and as MIKE pulls up, it seems to break her loose from the deep daze she's been in. Her gaze moves to her husband and begins to fill with frantic FEAR.

> ANGIE
>
> We have to give him what he wants.

> JACK
>
> What, honey? I couldn't hear you.

> HATCH
> (he heard just fine)
>
> Linoge?

The doors of the Sno-Cat open. MIKE and the others get out and begin floundering toward HATCH, FERD, and the CARVERS. ANGIE takes no notice. She stares only at JACK, and when she speaks, she does so with RISING HYSTERIA.

> ANGIE
>
> Linoge, yes, him. We have to give him what he wants, he sent me back to tell you. That's the only reason he didn't let me fall—so I'd tell you. We have to give him what he wants! Do you understand? *We have to give him what he wants!*

MIKE takes her by the shoulder and turns her toward him.

> MIKE
>
> What *does* he want, Angela? Did he tell you?

At first she doesn't answer. They cluster around her, waiting, anxious.

> ANGIE
>
> He said he'll tell us tonight. He said we're going to have a special town meeting, and he'll tell us then. He said that if some folks don't want to go along . . . don't want to do what's best for the town . . . that they should be reminded of the dreams we had last night. That they should be reminded of what happened in Roanoke. That they should remember Croaton, whatever that is.

                    MIKE
             (perhaps to himself)
His name, maybe. His *real* name.


                    ANGIE
              (turns back to JACK)
Take me inside. I'm freezing. And I want to see Buster.


                    JACK
Sure.


He puts an arm around her and leads her slowly back toward the town hall. MIKE goes to HATCH.


                    MIKE
Any sign of Bill Timmons or George Kirby?


                    HATCH
No. Janie Kingsbury, either.


                    MIKE
Jane Kingsbury's dead.
                 (to SONNY)
Take it in, would you?


SONNY climbs up into the cab of the Sno-Cat and revs the engine. MIKE and HATCH start to walk toward the town hall, MIKE telling HATCH about MRS. K.


22   EXTERIOR: THE SIDE OF THE TOWN HALL, HIGH ANGLE—AFTERNOON.

From here, we can barely see the line of ISLANDERS; trudging slowly back to the buildings through the drifts, they look like ants on safari across a desert of sugar. The Sno-Cat, piloted by SONNY BRAUTIGAN, drives slowly past them toward the building. We hold on this, then:

FADE TO BLACK. THIS ENDS ACT 1.

# Act 2

23  EXTERIOR: THE TOWN DOCK—VERY LATE AFTERNOON.

Well . . . where the town dock *used* to be. The tide is rising again, and MONSTER WAVES pound at the shore. We see overturned boats, splintered lobster traps, shattered chunks of piling, tattered skeins of netting.

24  EXTERIOR: THE HEADLAND—VERY LATE AFTERNOON.

The ocean ebbs and flows over the FALLEN LIGHTHOUSE. One wave ROLLS IN and deposits something beside the shattered circular window of the control room.

25  EXTERIOR: OUTSIDE THE CONTROL ROOM—LATE AFTERNOON.

It's the waterlogged body of old GEORGE KIRBY. There's a GROWING ROAR as the next wave comes in and pulls the body away.

26  EXTERIOR: THE BUSINESS SECTION OF TOWN—LATE AFTERNOON.

The storm is still howling away, and now the business buildings are buried halfway to the tops of their show windows.

27  INTERIOR: THE DRUGSTORE—LATE AFTERNOON.

The show windows are all shattered, the holes filled with avalanches of snow that stretch halfway down the aisles.

28  INTERIOR: THE HARDWARD STORE—LATE AFTERNOON.

Like the drugstore, the aisles are full of snow. Near the cash registers is a display of lawnmowers buried to their gas caps in snow. The sign in front of them is barely readable: LAWNMOWER SALE! GEAR UP FOR SUMMER NOW!

29  INTERIOR: THE ISLAND BEAUTY SHOP.

It's also full of snow. The hair dryers stand like frozen Martians.

Written across the mirror is "GIVE ME WHAT I WANT AND I'LL GO AWAY."

30   EXTERIOR: THE TOWN HALL—LATE AFTERNOON.

We can barely see it, partially because of the SCREAMING BLIZZARD, but mostly because night is getting ready to fall.

31   INTERIOR: THE BASEMENT DAY-CARE AREA—LATE AFTERNOON.

The KIDS are sitting in a circle. In the middle is CAT WITHERS, reading a book called *The Little Puppy* (a great favorite of DANNY TORRANCE'S, once upon a time).

> CAT
>
> So the little puppy said, "I know where my ball must be. That mean little boy put it in his pocket and took it away. But I can find it, because my nose is—"

> SALLY GODSOE
> (sings)
>
> "I'm a little teapot . . ."

> CAT
>
> Sally, honey, you shouldn't be singing now. This is storytime.

CAT'S a little freaked, although she can't quite remember what it is about that nonsense ditty that is so unpleasant. SALLY pays no attention to her in any case, goes right on singing. RALPHIE joins in. HEIDI adds her voice, then BUSTER and PIPPA, FRANK BRIGHT and HARRY ROBICHAUX do the same. Soon all the children are singing, even DON BEALS.

> KIDS
>
> ". . . short and stout. . . ."

They stand up. They show their handles and spouts at the appropriate moments. CAT looks at them with growing unease. JOANNA STANHOPE, MOLLY, and MELINDA HATCHER join her.

> MELINDA
>
> What's going on?

CAT

I don't know . . . I guess they want to sing.

KIDS

". . . Here is my handle, here is my spout. You can pick me
up and pour me out. . . . I'm a little teapot, short and stout."

MOLLY doesn't like it. There's a shelf with a few books on it to her
right. Also on it is the chamois bag with the MARBLES in it. MOLLY
glances at this, then goes quietly upstairs.

32   INTERIOR: THE TOWN MEETING HALL—AFTERNOON.

ANGIE CARVER is sitting on one of the front benches. She has been
bundled into a warm, quilted housecoat, and there's a towel over her
wet hair. JACK sits solicitously beside her, helping her with a cup of
steaming broth. She can't seem to manage it herself, because her hands
are shaking badly.

Sitting on the edge of the stage, facing her, is MIKE ANDERSON.
Behind them, on the other benches (and on the edge of their seats, you
could say) are most of Little Tall's storm refugees. HATCH weaves his
way to the front among them, and sits down next to MIKE. HATCH
looks pretty well exhausted.

HATCH
(eyeing the onlookers)
You want me to move them out?

MIKE

Think you could?

He's got a point, and HATCH knows it. MOLLY comes in, slips through
the crowd, goes to MIKE, and sits beside him on the stage, attempting
to have a private moment in a very public place.

MOLLY
(low)
The kids're acting funny.

                    MIKE
                  (also low)
Funny how?


                    MOLLY
Singing. Cat was reading them a story, and they just stood up
and started singing.
                (sees MIKE'S puzzlement)
I know it doesn't sound like much . . .


                    MIKE
If you say it's funny, it's funny. I'll come and take a look as
soon as I finish here.


He tips his eyes in ANGIE'S direction. ANGIE speaks . . . but not to
MIKE or JACK or anyone in particular.


                    ANGIE
Now I know how easy it is to just get . . . yanked out of the
world. I wish I didn't, but I do.


JACK offers her the cup of broth again, but when ANGIE puts her
hands on it, they're shaking so badly she spills it and CRIES OUT when
the liquid scalds her. MOLLY takes a handkerchief from her pocket,
sits down beside her, and wipes the hot broth from her fingers. ANGIE
looks at her gratefully and takes MOLLY'S hand. She grips it hard. It's
comfort she needs, not a cleanup.


                    ANGIE
I was just standing there, you see, watching the lighthouse.
And then . . . I was his.


                    MOLLY
Shhh. It's over.


                    ANGIE
I feel like I'll never be warm again. I've burned my fingers . . .
see, they're red . . . but they're still cold. I feel like he turned
me to snow.


                    MOLLY
Mike's got to ask you some questions, but it doesn't have to

be here—do you want to go somewhere more private? Because you can, if you want to.

She looks to MIKE for confirmation, and MIKE nods. ANGIE, meanwhile, gathers herself with an effort.

> ANGIE
> No . . . this is for everyone. Everyone should hear.

Fascinated and frightened at the same time, the ISLANDERS move in closer.

> REV. BOB RIGGINS
> What happened to you, Angie Carver?

During what follows, THE CAMERA PUSHES SLOWLY IN ON ANGIE, moving to CLOSE-UP. Intercut with this, let us see as many ISLANDER FACES as possible. On each we see the horror, the terror, and the growing belief in what she's saying, strange as it is. There are supposedly no atheists in the foxholes, and maybe no disbelievers when the Storm of the Century is huffing and puffing and threatening to blow the house down. This is a quasi-religious experience, and by the end we see one solidified idea that really doesn't need verbal expression: when LINOGE shows up, they'll give it to him. Whatever it is he wants, they will give it to him. "Ayuh, deah—shoah!" as the ISLANDERS themselves might say.

> ANGIE
> We were watching the lighthouse fall down, and then I went flying backward into the snow. At first I thought it was somebody's idea of a joke, but then I turned around and what had me . . . it wasn't a man. It wore a man's clothes and had a man's face, but there was just blackness where its eyes should have been—blackness and little red twisting things, like snakes on fire. And when it smiled at me and I saw its teeth . . . I fainted. First time in my life. I fainted.

She sips from the cup. The room is completely silent. MOLLY and JACK sit with their arms around her. ANGIE is still clutching MOLLY'S hand.

### ANGIE

When I came to, I was flying. I know that sounds crazy, but it's true. Me and George Kirby, we were both flying. It was like *Peter Pan*, with me as Wendy and old George as John. That . . . that *thing* had us, one under each arm. And right ahead of us, as if it was leading us or holding us up, there was a cane. A black cane with a silver wolf's head. As fast as we flew, that cane always stayed ahead of us.

MIKE and HATCH lock eyes.

### ANGIE
#### (continues)

It was the island we saw. The storm was over and the sun was out, but there were cops on snowmobiles everywhere. Mainland cops, state cops, even game wardens. News people, too, from the local stations and the networks. They were all looking for us. Only we were gone . . . gone where nobody could ever find us . . .

### ORV BOUCHER

Like in the dreams . . .

### ANGIE

Yes, like that. Then it got dark again. At first I thought it was night, but it wasn't. It was the storm clouds. They were back and the sunshine was gone. Pretty soon it started snowing again, and I understood what was happening. I said, "You showed us the future, didn't you? Like the last ghost showed Mr. Scrooge the future in *A Christmas Carol*." And he said, "Yessum, that's very smart of you. Now you best hang on tight." We started to go up, and the snow got thicker, and old George started to cry and talk about how he couldn't stand it because of his arthritis, he had to get down . . . although it wasn't cold a bit; at least it didn't seem that way to me. And then the man laughed and said that was fine, George could go down right away if he wanted to, and by the express route, too . . . because he only needed one of us, really, to come back and tell. We were just going into the clouds by then—

### JONAS STANHOPE

It was a dream, Angie; it must have been.

> ### ANGIE
> I tell you it wasn't. I could *feel* the clouds, not cold the way you'd think snow clouds would be, but damp, like wet cotton. And George saw what it meant to do, and he screamed, but the thing that had us opened its right arm . . . it had me in its left . . . and . . .

33   EXTERIOR: OLD GEORGE KIRBY—NIGHT.

He FALLS AWAY FROM THE CAMERA, SCREAMING and waving his arms. He disappears into the dark and the snow.

34   EXTERIOR: RESUME ANGIE AND THE GATHERED ISLANDERS—LATE AFTERNOON.

> ### JACK
> Then what happened?

> ### ANGIE
> He told me he was bringing me back. Back through time, and back through the storm. He was letting me live to tell you— to tell everyone—that we have to give him what he wants when he comes tonight.

> ### ROBBIE
> If we have something this man Linoge wants, why doesn't he just take it?

> ### ANGIE
> I don't think he can. I think we have to give it to him. (pause) He told me to tell you that he'll only ask once. He asked me if I'd remember Roanoke, and Croaton, and that he'll only ask once. And I said yes. Because I knew if I said no, or even asked him to explain anything, he'd drop me the way he dropped George. He didn't have to tell me. I just knew. Then we stopped going up. We did a rollover in the air, and my stomach went way up in my throat, like it was a county fair carnival ride we were on instead of being way up in the air . . . and I fainted again, I guess. Or maybe he did something to me. I don't know. The next thing I was sure of, I was stumbling around in the snow . . . the whiteout . . . and I could hear a horn . . . I thought, "The lighthouse must not have blown down after all, because I can hear the

foghorn . . ." I tried to go toward it . . . and I saw someone coming out of the snow . . . and I thought it was him . . . him again, meaning to take me back into the air again . . . only this time he'd drop me . . . and I tried to run . . . but it was you, Jack. It was you.

She puts her head against his shoulder, exhausted by the effort this has taken. There is a beat of silence. Then:

> JILL ROBICHAUX
> (shrill)

Why us? *Why us?*

Several beats of silence. Then:

> TAVIA GODSOE

Maybe because he knows we can keep a secret.

35 INTERIOR: THE BASEMENT DAY-CARE AREA—LATE AFTERNOON.

> KIDS
> (sing)

"I'm a little teapot, short and stout—"

CAT WITHERS is still standing in the middle of the circle, holding her place in *The Little Puppy*. We can see that she's freaked but is trying to hide this from the KIDS. MELINDA and JOANNA are still on the stairs. Now, joining them, is KIRK FREEMAN, still dressed for outdoors and with a pile of the toys and puzzles he and MIKE picked up at Wee Folks.

> CAT

If you want to sing, kids, maybe we could sing something else for a change? "London Bridge" or "The Farmer in the Dell" or . . .

She gives up. They're not listening. They hardly seem there. Once normal, happy preschool children, they have become spookily distant.

> KIDS
> (sing)

"—Here is my handle, here is my spout. You can pick—"

They stop on the word "pick," and they do it all at the same time, as neat as a lock of hair snipped by a barber's shears. Now they just stand in a circle around CAT.

> KIRK
> I brought these games and—What? What's going on?

36   INTERIOR: CAT AND THE CHILDREN, CLOSER—LATE AFTERNOON.

Oh, this is freaky. She looks from one to the next, and the normal vivacity of young children has left their faces; they are Cult City. Eyes like big zeros. Just standing there.

> CAT
> Buster?
>> (no answer)
> Heidi?
>> (no answer)
> Pippa?
>> (no answer)
> Ralphie? Are you all right?
>> (no answer)

MELINDA HATCHER hurries into the circle, almost knocking SALLY GODSOE and HARRY ROBICHAUX over. She kneels by PIPPA and grabs her arms.

> MELINDA
> Pippa, what's wrong, honey?

CAT bursts out of the circle. She's had enough.

37    INTERIOR: ON THE STAIRS, WITH CAT, JOANNA, AND KIRK FREEMAN.

> KIRK
> What is it? What's wrong with them?

> CAT
> (starting to cry)
> I don't know . . . but their eyes . . . oh, God, there's nothing *there.*

38    INTERIOR: MELINDA AND PIPPA, CLOSE-UP.

CAT is right—PIPPA'S eyes are scary in their emptiness, and although her mother shakes her harder and harder—this is panic, not anger—there is no result.

> MELINDA
> Pippa, wake up! Wake up!

She tries chafing PIPPA'S hands. No result. She looks around wildly.

> MELINDA
> *All of you, wake up!*

39    INTERIOR: RALPHIE, CLOSE-UP.

His head turns a little, and the life comes back into his eyes. He smiles. It's almost as if he's heard her and is responding . . . except he's not even looking in MELINDA'S direction.

> RALPHIE
> Look!

He points toward the shelf with the bag of marbles on it.

40   INTERIOR: THE BASEMENT DAY-CARE CENTER—LATE AFTERNOON.

Everyone looks. The KIDS light up, just as RALPHIE did. What are they looking at that pleases them so? The marbles? No, that doesn't seem to be it. Their eyes are fixed a little lower . . . but there's nothing there.

> HEIDI
> (delighted)
> It's got a doggy head! A silver doggy head! How *cool!*

CAT suddenly understands and is horrified.

> CAT
> (to KIRK)
> Go get Mike.

> JOANNA STANHOPE
> I don't understand—what—

> CAT
> Right now.

KIRK turns and does what she says, dropping the games and puzzles heedlessly on the stairs.

41   INTERIOR: DON BEALS, CLOSE-UP.

> DON
> A doggy head! Yeah!

42   INTERIOR: THE SHELF, FROM DON'S POINT OF VIEW.

Hanging from the shelf is LINOGE'S cane. The SILVER SNARLING WOLF'S HEAD is now a FRIENDLY, GRINNING SAINT BERNARD.

43   INTERIOR: RESUME THE CIRCLE OF KIDS.

MELINDA still kneels in front of PIPPA, but PIPPA is looking over her head, like the others.

### PIPPA
A doggy! A doggy!

Bewildered and afraid, MELINDA turns to look. Nothing there.

44    INTERIOR: THE TOWN MEETING HALL—LATE AFTERNOON.

MIKE is just getting up from the stage. The interview with ANGELA is over.

### MIKE
(to JACK)
Why don't you see if you can get her to lie down for a little while?

### JACK
That's a good—

KIRK comes bursting through the clustered ISLANDERS.

### KIRK
Mike! Mike, there's somethin' wrong with the kids!

FRIGHTENED MURMURS from the ISLANDERS . . . but some do more than just MURMUR—JILL and ANDY, MIKE and MOLLY, ROBBIE and SANDY, the BRIGHTS, HATCH, URSULA . . . the parents BOLT FOR THE STAIRS.

### ANGIE
(as if waking up)
Buster? Is something wrong with Buster? Buster! *Buster!*

She is up in a flash, knocking the cup of broth from JACK'S HAND.

### JACK
Honey, wait—

### ANGIE
(ignores him)
*Buster!*

45    INTERIOR: BUSTER, CLOSE-UP.

He breaks from the circle and runs to the shelf, where the cane hangs by the crook of its neck. He touches it . . . and crumples to the floor as if shot.

46    INTERIOR: THE DAY-CARE AREA, WIDER—LATE AFTERNOON.

The rest of the children follow BUSTER'S lead. They are laughing and excited, like kids who have just been given free all-day passes to Disneyland. They reach out to thin air . . . or to something only they can see . . . and one by one CRUMPLE TO THE FLOOR, joining BUSTER.

> CAT
>
> No! Don't let them—

A gaggle of FRIGHTENED PARENTS, led by JILL and ANDY, appear at the head of the stairs.

> ROBBIE
>
> Get out of my way!

He shoves JILL aside—would have knocked her right downstairs, if not for ANDY'S last-second grab—and goes pelting down to the basement.

CAT ignores all this and runs across the room. HARRY ROBICHAUX touches thin air and falls down with the others. Now there's only RALPHIE ANDERSON and PIPPA, who is back where the circle was. PIPPA is struggling in her mother's grip. CAT grabs RALPHIE and pulls him back as he reaches up to touch . . . well, to touch whatever it is he sees.

> PIPPA
>
> Let me go! Wanna see doggy! Wanna see *DOGGY!!*

47    INTERIOR: CAT AND RALPHIE, CLOSE-UP.

CAT doesn't see the cane hanging down from the shelf, but in this shot we do . . . and RALPHIE does, too. He reaches for it . . . almost touches it . . . and CAT pulls him back out of reach.

> CAT
>
> Ralphie, what do you see?

RALPHIE
(struggling wildly)
Let me go! Let me go!

He reaches again . . . CAT pulls him back again . . . and then ROBBIE BEALS comes cannonading into her, wanting only to reach DON, who is lying in the pile of tangled limbs with his eyes closed and doughnut crumbs still on his mouth. CAT, meanwhile, loses her grip on RALPHIE and goes sprawling.

ROBBIE
(to his knees)
Donnie!

RALPHIE is free. He lunges forward and touches the cane. For a moment we see a DEEP AND PERFECT BLISS on his face.

RALPHIE
Neat!

His eyes roll up to whites, and he sprawls with the others.

48    INTERIOR: PIPPA AND MELINDA, CLOSE-UP.

PIPPA is now the only child left. She struggles furiously with her mother, tearing her shirt in her efforts to get free, her eyes continually turning to the area above the tangle of KIDS.

MELINDA
Pippa . . . Pippa, no . . .

PIPPA
Let me go!

HATCH comes pelting down the stairs and runs toward his wife and his daughter.

HATCH
Pippa! What's wr—

MELINDA turns some of her attention toward her husband. A bad mistake. PIPPA'S sweet little face twists into an expression of rage, and she claws at her mother's cheek, drawing blood in three lines.

> PIPPA
> *Let me go you BITCH!*

Stunned both by the pain and by the word her daughter has used, MELINDA loosens her grip. Only a little, and only for a moment, but it's enough. PIPPA tears out of her grasp and races across the room.

> HATCH
> Honey, no!

He goes after her.

49   INTERIOR: PIPPA, CLOSE-UP.

HATCH loses the race. PIPPA touches the cane an instant before he can grab her around the waist. We see that same BLISSFUL EXPRESSION on her face, and then she SWOONS AWAY with the others.

> HATCH
> No! *No! NO!*

He picks her up in his arms, looks at the place where her hand touched, and sees nothing but thin air. He turns around with her, unbelieving.

50   INTERIOR: THE BASEMENT OF THE TOWN HALL—LATE AFTERNOON.

Total pandemonium—as choreographed by our fearless director—reigns as ISLANDERS continue to push down the stairs and crowd into the makeshift day-care space. The dominant note is CONFUSED TERROR.

ROBBIE is shaking DONNIE, trying to wake him up. HATCH stands up with PIPPA in his arms, beginning to WEEP. MIKE pushes through the cluster of people at the foot of the stairs and looks with unbelief at the TANGLE OF TINY BODIES.

> DELLA BISSONETTE
> They're dead! He's killed them!

URSULA
*No! Oh, God, please no! Not Sally! Not my Sally!*

She pushes her way through the people in her way, actually knocking a couple of them over. She is maddened with grief and terror . . . this lady lost her husband just the day before, remember.

Shoving down the stairs—almost *moshing* down the stairs—comes ANDY ROBICHAUX, dragging JILL by the hand. ANDY knocks old BURT SOAMES down on the stairs. There's a CRUNCH as BURT'S ARM BREAKS. The old guy SCREAMS WITH PAIN.

BETTY SOAMES
(shrieking)
*You're trampling him! Stop! You're killing him!*

ANDY and JILL take no notice. They don't care about BURT SOAMES; they care about HARRY, who is lying with the others.

Meanwhile, DELLA'S hysterical cry has been picked up by the others, and it jumps from person to person like a virulent flu germ: they're dead; the kids are dead; LINOGE has somehow killed the children.

51   INTERIOR: MIKE, MOLLY, RALPHIE.

As MOLLY arrives, CRYING WITH TERROR, MIKE is gently lifting RALPHIE into a sitting position and dropping one ear to the boy's face and chest.

MOLLY
Is he—

MIKE takes her hand and holds it in front of RALPHIE'S nose and mouth. She feels his breath going in and out. An expression of deep relief comes over her face. Her shoulders sag.

MOLLY
Thank God. Is he asleep, or—

MIKE
I don't know.

He scoops RALPH into his arms and stands up.

52    INTERIOR: THE BASEMENT DAY-CARE AREA, ANGLE ON THE STAIRS.

ROBBIE has DONNIE in his arms now. He runs for the stairs, with his
BEWILDERED, TERRIFIED wife tumbling along in his wake. His way
is blocked by the SOAMESES; BETTY is just helping BURT to his feet.
Also nearby are JOHNNY HARRIMAN, SONNY BRAUTIGAN, and
UPTON BELL. But the SOAMESES, unlucky parents of the late
BILLY, are ROBBIE'S first obstacle.

> ROBBIE
> (no great diplomat he)
> Outta my way!

He shoves BURT, whose broken arm smashes against the side of the
stairs. BURT SCREAMS AGAIN, and BETTY grabs him again. JOHN-
NY, outraged, blocks ROBBIE'S path.

> JOHNNY HARRIMAN
> Here, here, now! That's an old man you're pushing around!
> Where do you think you're going, anyway?

> ROBBIE
> Let me by! I have to get him to a doctor!

> SONNY
> Good luck to you, Robbie Beals—closest one's across the
> reach in Machias, and the wind's blowin' a hurricane.

ROBBIE looks at him, wide-eyed, some semblance of sanity dawning.
SONNY is right, of course. SANDRA joins ROBBIE and brushes
DONNIE'S hair gently back from his brow. BETTY SOAMES, hugging
her WEEPING HUSBAND, glares at them.

53    INTERIOR: THE BASEMENT DAY-CARE AREA, ANGLE ON THE ANDERSONS.

MIKE is aware of the panic in the parents, which is bad, and the panic
of the ISLANDERS in general, which could be even worse. He draws in
a deep breath, and lets loose the LOUDEST SHOUT he can manage.

> MIKE
> *Everybody JUST . . . SHUT . . . UP!!!*

Some people in their immediate vicinity quiet down . . . and that quiet SPREADS OUTWARD. Only ROBBIE BEALS doesn't turn toward the constable, and by now that shouldn't much surprise us.

> ROBBIE
> Where's Ferd? He's got EMT training, at least . . . Ferd Andrews, where the hell are you?

> FERD
> (lost in the back of the crowd)
> Here—

We see him struggling to get through.

> ROBBIE
> Get your ass down here! Folks, let him pass! My boy—

> HATCH
> That's enough. Shut up.

> ROBBIE
> Don't you tell me to shut up, fatso. I've had all the crap out of you I'm going to take.

The two men face each other, each with an UNCONSCIOUS CHILD in his arms, but ready to brawl, just the same.

> MIKE
> Stop it. Both of you. Robbie, I don't think Don's in any immediate danger. Or Pippa, or Ralphie, or any of them.

URSULA has been kneeling over SALLY, keening to her. Now MOLLY whispers something in her ear, and URSULA stands up.

> MARY HOPEWELL
> Then . . . they're not dead?

The ISLANDERS are all quiet now, watching and hoping. ANDY has got his son HARRY in his arms. JILL is standing next to them. Nearby, JACK is holding BUSTER while his wife—the haggard, newly gray-haired ANGIE—kisses the boy's cheek and whispers in his ear.

ANDY

I think . . . he's sleeping.

URSULA

This isn't sleep. If they were asleep, we could wake them up.

FERD
(finally at the front of the crowd)
Then what is it?

MIKE

I don't know.

He looks down into RALPHIE'S serene face, as if trying to read whatever is happening behind the boy's closed eyes. THE CAMERA FOLLOWS HIS GAZE, moving in and in on RALPHIE'S face, from MEDIUM SHOT to CLOSE-UP, from CLOSE-UP to EXTREME CLOSE-UP. And as it does, we:

SLOWLY DISSOLVE TO:
54   EXTERIOR: BLUE SKY, WHITE CLOUDS—DAY.

The sky above is that DEEP, PENETRATING BLUE that we see only from airplanes. We are at about 22,000 feet above the surface of the earth. Below us, at 21,000 or so, is a WIDE DECK OF CLOUD—an enormous ballroom floor in the sky. We can see tendrils of cloud smoking off the top of this deck and into the blue. Up where we are, all is sunlit and serene. Below, still driving like hell, is the Storm of the Century.

A V-SHAPE becomes visible through the clouds, grayish against the white. It's like watching a submarine running just below the surface, or a plane about to break into the clear. You'd think "plane," given our location, but it isn't.

The V-SHAPE rises out of the clouds. At the tip of the V is LINOGE, dressed in his watch cap, pea coat, blue jeans, and yellow gloves. Ahead of him, leading the way like a lodestar, is the CANE. LINOGE holds his hands out to either side, slightly spread. Clinging to one is PIPPA HATCHER. Clinging to the other is RALPHIE ANDERSON. Clinging to the hands of these two are HEIDI and BUSTER; clinging to HEIDI'S and BUSTER'S are SALLY and DON; clinging to their hands and bringing up the rear are HARRY and little FRANK BRIGHT. Their hair flies back from their foreheads. Their clothes ripple. They are totally blissed out.

> LINOGE
> (calls back)

Having fun, kids?

> KIDS

*Yeah . . . yeah . . . Cool . . . This is great!*
> (etc.)

55   EXTERIOR: LINOGE, CLOSE-UP.

His eyes are BLACK, shot with TWISTING RED VEINS. When he smiles, he once more reveals those SHARPENED FANGS. The shadow of the CANE lies on his face like a scar. The KIDS think they have gone flying with a fabulous friend. We know the truth: they are in the grip of a monster.

FADE TO BLACK. THIS ENDS ACT 2.

# Act 3

56   EXTERIOR: THE TOWN HALL—NIGHT.

It's still almost blotted out by the snowstorm, its few lights flickering bravely.

57   EXTERIOR: THE GENERATOR SHED BEHIND THE TOWN HALL—NIGHT.

It's barely visible, almost buried by drifts, but it's impossible to mistake the ENGINE ROAR. Then the ENGINE COUGHS . . . SPUTTERS . . .

58   EXTERIOR: THE TOWN HALL—NIGHT.

The lights flicker on and off . . .

59   INTERIOR: THE TOWN HALL KITCHEN—NIGHT.

TESS MARCHANT, TAVIA GODSOE, and JENNA FREEMAN are taking BOXES OF CANDLES out of the supply closet adjacent to the pantry and stacking them on the kitchen counter. The overhead lights CONTINUE TO FLICKER. TAVIA and JENNA look up, nervous.

> TAVIA GODSOE
> (nervously, to TESS)
> Are we going to lose the generator, do you think?

> TESS
> Ayuh. It's a miracle it's run as long as 't 'as, with no one able to keep it dug out. Wind must have kept the exhaust pipe clear, but now it's shifted. In a way, that's good news. Means the storm's almost over.

She hands several stacked boxes of candles to JENNA and gives more to TAVIA. She takes a third stack for herself.

> JENNA
> Main meeting hall?

### TESS

Ayuh, shoah—Mike wants that ready first. There's a couple of emergency lights in there, but that isn't enough for him. Let's get as much done as we can while we can still see to do it, ladies.

60    INTERIOR: A CORRIDOR LEADING TO THE FRONT OF THE TOWN HALL.

Up ahead are URSULA GODSOE'S glassed-in office and the stairs going down to the basement. To the right is the main meeting hall, visible through the corridor windows. Through these we can see perhaps a hundred and twenty ISLANDERS, some grazing the buffet (scant provisions there by now), most sitting on benches and talking as they drink coffee.

There are chairs lining the corridor; these are used in less disastrous times by people waiting their turn to do some bit of town business— licensing a car, a dog, a boat; paying property tax; checking the voter rolls; perhaps renewing a commercial fishing or clamming permit. In these are sprawled another two dozen ISLANDERS, some talking quietly, some dozing. It's the storm they're waiting on now.

TESS, TAVIA, and JENNA come hurrying along with their bounty of candles. Up ahead, HATCH comes out of URSULA'S office.

### HATCH

I just caught a little bit of the latest NWS bulletin on the shortwave. They say we may see the moon tonight.

### TAVIA GODSOE

That's wonderful.

Those sitting in the hall like patients in a doctor's waiting room think so, too—MANY APPLAUD, waking the dozers, who look around and ask what's up.

### TAVIA

Where's Ursula, do you know?

### HATCH

Downstairs, with Sally and the others. Sleeping, the last I saw. (pause) But not like the kids're sleeping. You know?

                              TAVIA
Yes . . . but I'm sure they'll be all right. They'll wake up and
be just fine.

                              HATCH
I hope you're right, Tavia Godsoe. *Pray* you're right.

He goes downstairs. The THREE WOMEN watch him with deep
sympathy, then go on their way. As they reach the stairs and turn right
to go into the meeting hall, JOANNA STANHOPE comes up the stairs.

                       JOANNA STANHOPE
Can I help?

                              TAVIA
Go down to the kitchen and get the rest of the candles, if you
want. I'm afraid we're going to lose the generator.

TAVIA, TESS, and JENNA go into the town meeting hall. JOANNA
(who has gotten over the shock of her unpleasant mother-in-law's
death in record time) heads down to the kitchen.

The overheads FLICKER, go out, then COME BACK ON again. The
ISLANDERS sitting in the chairs along the walls of the corridor look
up and MURMUR QUIETLY.

61   INTERIOR: THE KIDS' SLEEPING AREA OF THE BASEMENT—NIGHT.

Except now it looks like Intensive Care in a children's hospital; this
could be the aftermath of some hideous tragedy, like the shooting of all
those kids in Scotland.

URSULA has drawn a cot up next to SALLY'S and sleeps, holding both
her daughter's hands in both of her own. MIKE and MOLLY are with
RALPHIE, and MELINDA is with PIPPA, brushing her hair back from
the child's brow. The ROBICHAUXES are with HARRY, the CARVERS
are with BUSTER, the BRIGHTS are with FRANK, LINDA ST.
PIERRE is with HEIDI. Next to her, also alone, is SANDRA BEALS.
She's got a washcloth and is gently and lovingly wiping the doughnut
crumbs from around DON'S mouth. Fast asleep as they are, you'd think
them heaven's smallest angels. Even DON.

Sitting in the corner, hands clasped and PRAYING UNOBTRUSIVELY, is REV. BOB RIGGINS.

HATCH slips through the makeshift draw curtains, then stops and looks up as the LIGHTS FLICKER AGAIN. They come back, and he comes over to the KIDS and PARENTS.

> HATCH
> (to MELINDA)
> Any change?
> (she shakes her head)
> Any change in any of them?

> MELINDA
> (soft, despairing)
> No.

> MOLLY
> But their respiration is normal, reflexes are normal, and if you roll back an eyelid, their pupils react to light. All that's good.

HATCH sits next to MELINDA and looks closely into PIPPA'S face. He sees her eyelids TWITCH and MOVE.

> HATCH
> She's dreaming.

> MIKE
> They all are.

MIKE and HATCH exchange a look, then HATCH glances toward SANDRA.

> HATCH
> Where's Robbie, Sandra?

> SANDRA
> Don't know.

"And don't care," her tone implies. She goes on wiping at DONNIE'S mouth. The crumbs are all gone now; she's only caressing him, loving him as best she can.

62   INTERIOR: A TOWN MEETING HALL BENCH, WITH ROBBIE BEALS— NIGHT.

He's sitting by himself—elected official or not, few people care for ROBBIE on a personal level. In the background, people TALK TO-GETHER. Some are helping TAVIA, TESS, and JENNA put up candles in the ornamental holders along the walls. ROBBIE is wearing a sport coat. Now he reaches into the right-hand pocket and brings out the PISTOL we saw in his possession in Part One. He holds it in his lap, looking at it thoughtfully.

The overhead lights FLICKER OFF. The emergency lights on the walls FLICKER ON in corresponding pulses. People LOOK UP NERV-OUSLY. The three WOMEN go a little faster with their candle place-ment. More folks drift over to help.

ROBBIE isn't in a helpful mood and doesn't react to the imminent departure of the electric lights. He's off in his own little world, where thoughts of revenge are all that matter. He looks at the little gun a second or two longer, then tucks it back into his jacket pocket, where it will be near to hand. Then he goes on sitting and staring off into space. Just a pissed-off town manager waiting for LINOGE to show up.

63   INTERIOR: THE TOWN HALL KITCHEN.

JOANNA STANHOPE comes in and LOOKS UP UNEASILY as the LIGHTS FLICKER.

64   EXTERIOR: THE GENERATOR SHED—NIGHT.

The engine COUGHS . . . SPUTTERS . . . and this time doesn't catch again. It CHOKES AWAY TO SILENCE, leaving only the HOWL OF THE WIND.

65   INTERIOR: THE KIDS' SLEEPING AREA—NIGHT.

The overhead LIGHTS GO OUT. After a moment of BLACK, one FEEBLE EMERGENCY LIGHT comes on, shining from a box mounted high up on the wall at the very back of the room.

MIKE
(to HATCH)
Want to help with the candles?


HATCH

Honey?


MELINDA

Go ahead.


MIKE and HATCH get up and leave.

66 INTERIOR: THE TV AREA OF THE TOWN HALL BASEMENT—NIGHT.

MIKE and HATCH come out through the makeshift draw curtains and head for the stairs.


HATCH

Radio says the storm'll be pretty much over by midnight. If Linoge intends to do something—


MIKE

I think you can pretty much count on that.

67 INTERIOR: THE TOWN HALL KITCHEN, WITH JOANNA—NIGHT.

The kitchen is VERY DIM: there are two battery-powered emergency lights, but one is not working at all and the other is putting out the thinnest possible thread of YELLOW GLOW. As JOANNA starts across the room, it goes out entirely.

JOANNA, now just a shadow among other shadows, makes her way past the table in the middle of the room to the counter. She bumps her hip and CRIES OUT SOFTLY—more in impatience than in pain. She reaches the counter and takes one of the candles out of its box. There are also stacks of boxed wooden matches beside a cluster of candle-holders, and she uses a match to light her candle. When the flame is high, she takes a holder and sticks the base of the candle on the prong.

She takes the rest of the candles, stacking the boxes carefully in the crook of one arm, and turns. Lying on the table, which was all cleaned up for the night and quite bare when she came into the room, is LINOGE'S wolf's head cane.

JOANNA GASPS, TURNS . . . and LINOGE is standing right there, his smiling face underlit by her candle. It looks like the face of a goblin. She gasps, INHALING A SCREAM, and all the candles—the lit one and the boxes of unlit ones—drop from her hands. The lit one WHIFFS OUT, leaving her (and us) in SHADOWY DARKNESS once more.

> LINOGE
>
> Hello, Joanna Stanhope. Glad the old bitch is dead, aren't you? I did you a favor there, oh, ayuh. You kept a straight face, but inside you were dancing a jig. I know; I can smell it on you like musk.

JOANNA begins to SCREAM—this time the right way, with the breath going out. Then she claps both hands over her mouth before she can do more than get started. Above them, her eyes bulge in terror, and we know she didn't shut herself up of her own free will.

> LINOGE
> (tenderly)
>
> Shhhh . . . Shhh . . .

68   INTERIOR: THE TOWN HALL CORRIDOR, FEATURING MIKE AND HATCH.

The place is dim, lit by a couple of underpowered emergency lights on the wall, plus a few candles, flashlights . . . maybe even an upheld cigarette lighter or two. Through the windows, we can see the women lighting the meeting hall.

> STAN HOPEWELL
>
> What about the generator, Mike?

> FIRST ISLANDER
>
> Is the power off for the rest of the storm, do you think?

> SECOND ISLANDER
>
> What about heat? They took the damn woodstove out three years ago! I told 'em it was a mistake, they'd want it come blizzard season either one year or the next, but nobody listens to the old-timers no more—

MIKE
(not stopping)
We'll have plenty of light and heat, don't worry. And the worst of the storm will be over by midnight. Right, Hatch?

HATCH
Right.

REV. BOB RIGGINS has followed MIKE and HATCH, falling a little behind on the stairs (RIGGINS is a portly soul) but now catching up.

REV. BOB RIGGINS
It's not light or heat these good people are worried about, Michael, and you know it.

MIKE pauses in his march toward the kitchen and turns. All the WHISPERED CONVERSATIONS in the hallway cease. RIGGINS has touched a bare nerve, is speaking for everyone, saying what the rest can't, and MIKE knows it.

REV. BOB RIGGINS
When this fellow comes, Michael, we must give him what he wants. I've prayed on it, and this is the guidance the Lord has—

MIKE
We'll listen and then decide . . . all right?

A DISAPPROVING MURMUR greets this.

ORV BOUCHER
How can you say that when your own kid—?

MIKE
Because I don't believe in blank checks.

He turns to go.

REV. BOB RIGGINS
There's a time to be stubborn, Michael . . . but there's also a time to let go of the reins and look toward the greater good, hard as that may be. "Pride goeth before destruction, and a haughty spirit before a fall." Book of Proverbs.

> MIKE

"Render therefore unto Caesar the things which are Caesar's, and unto God the things that are God's." Book of Matthew.

REV. BOB RIGGINS is angry that MIKE would try to outscripture him. When he moves to follow, and perhaps continue the argument, MIKE shakes his head.

> MIKE

Stay here, please—we've got this under control.

> REV. BOB RIGGINS

I know you believe that . . . but not all of us are convinced.

> ORV BOUCHER

You want to remember that this is still a democracy, Michael Anderson! Storm or no storm!

MURMURS OF APPROVAL.

> MIKE

I'm sure that if my memory wavers, you'll refresh it, Orv. Come on, Hatch.

69   INTERIOR: THE KITCHEN DOORWAY, WITH MIKE AND HATCH—NIGHT.

They start inside, then stop, HORRIFIED AND AMAZED.

> LINOGE (voice)

Come in! Come in!

70   INTERIOR: THE KITCHEN—NIGHT.

Lighted candles stand on the table and the counter. We can see LINOGE, looking dapper with his cane planted before him and his hands (the yellow gloves have disappeared again, for the time being) folded over the wolf's head. We can also see JOANNA STANHOPE. She is floating against the far wall, with her head almost touching the ceiling and her feet dangling down on thin air. Her arms are outstretched so that her hands are on a level with her hips—a posture that does not quite mimic crucifixion but at least suggests it. In each fisted hand, JOANNA holds a LIGHTED CANDLE. The melting wax has run down over her fingers. Her eyes are wide open. She can't move, but she's aware . . . and she's terrified.

Across the room, MIKE and HATCH stand right where they are.

> LINOGE
> Come in, boys. Do it now and do it quietly . . . unless you want me to make this bitch burn her face off.

He raises the cane slightly. When he does, JOANNA raises one of the candles in corresponding fashion toward her head.

> LINOGE
> All that hair! Shall we watch it burn?

> MIKE
> No.

He comes into the room. HATCH follows, with a glance back down the hall. There, BOB RIGGINS is talking to the ISLANDERS. Impossible to tell what he's saying, but he's got quite a few of them agreeing with him, from the look.

> LINOGE
> Having a little trouble with the local witch doctor, are you? Well, here's something you might want to file away for later, Constable . . . always assuming there *is* a later, of course. The Reverend Bobby Riggins has got a couple of nieces over in Castine. Eleven and nine they are, cute little blondies. He likes them a lot. Too much, probably. They run and hide when they see his car turn into the driveway. In fact—

> MIKE
> Let her down. Joanna, are you all right?

She doesn't answer, but her eyes ROLL IN TERROR. LINOGE frowns.

> LINOGE
> If you don't want to see Mrs. Stanhope's impression of the world's biggest birthday candle, I advise you not to speak again until you're invited to. Hatch, close the door.

HATCH closes it. LINOGE watches, then turns his attention back to MIKE.

> LINOGE

You don't like knowing, do you?

> MIKE

Not your brand of it, no.

> LINOGE

Well, that's too bad. A real shame. Perhaps you don't believe me?

> MIKE

I believe you. The thing is, though, you know all the bad and none of the good.

> LINOGE

That's so inspirational it brings tears to my eyes. But by and large, Constable Anderson, the good's an illusion. Little fables folks tell themselves so they can get through their days without screaming too much.

> MIKE

I don't believe that.

> LINOGE

I know. A good boy to the end, that's you . . . but I think you're going to find yourself on the short end this time.

He looks at JOANNA. He raises his cane . . . then SLOWLY LOWERS IT. As he does, she SLIDES down the wall. When her feet touch the floor, LINOGE purses his lips and makes a little PUFF. A wind STIRS THROUGH THE ROOM. The flames of the candles on the table and counter flicker; those in JOANNA'S hands WHIFF OUT. When they do, the spell holding her breaks. She drops the candles and runs to MIKE, SOBBING. She CRINGES AWAY from LINOGE when her cross takes her nearest to him. He smiles at her in fatherly fashion as MIKE puts an arm around her.

LINOGE

Your town is full of adulterers, pedophiles, thieves, gluttons, murderers, bullies, scoundrels, and covetous morons. I know every one of them, too—born in lust, turn to dust. Born in sin, come on in.

JOANNA
(sobbing)

He's the devil! He's the devil! Don't let him near me again, I'll do anything, just don't let him near me again!

MIKE

What do you want, Mr. Linoge?

LINOGE

Everybody on those benches an hour from now—that'll do to start with. We're going to have a little unscheduled town meeting, at nine o'clock PM, prompt. After that . . . well . . . we'll see.

MIKE

See what?

LINOGE crosses the room to the back door. He holds up his cane, and the door SWINGS OPEN. The storm's wind BLOWS IN, dousing all of the candles. The SHAPE that is LINOGE turns in the doorway. In the silhouette of his head, we can see the TWISTING RED LINES that light his eyes.

> LINOGE

If I'm through with this town . . . or only just beginning. Nine o'clock, Constable. You . . . him . . . her . . . Reverend Bobbie . . . Town Manager Robbie . . . *everyone.*

He goes out. The door SLAMS SHUT behind him.

71   INTERIOR: THE KITCHEN, WITH MIKE, HATCH, AND JOANNA—NIGHT.

> HATCH

What do we do?

> MIKE

What *can* we do? Listen to whatever else he wants. If there's another choice, I don't see it. Tell Robbie.

> HATCH

What about the kids?

> JOANNA

I'll watch them . . . I don't want to be where he is, anyway. Not ever again.

> MIKE

No, that won't do. He wants everyone, and that includes you, Jo.
> (thinks)
We'll bring them upstairs. Cots and all. Put them in the back of the meeting hall.

> HATCH

Yeah. That'll work.
> (as MIKE opens the door again)
I've never been so scared in my life.

> MIKE

Me, either.

They go out to tell the storm survivors about the meeting.

72   EXTERIOR: THE FRONT OF THE TOWN HALL—NIGHT.

The little cupola with the memorial bell inside it is almost swallowed in snowdrifts. Standing on one of those drifts—a trick almost as miraculous as walking on water—is ANDRE LINOGE. His cane is planted neatly between his feet. He is watching the town hall . . . guarding it . . . biding his time.

FADE TO BLACK. THIS ENDS ACT 3.

# Act 4

73   EXTERIOR: THE INTERSECTION OF MAIN AND ATLANTIC—NIGHT.

The WIND is still blowing, sending sheets of snow down Main and continuing to build up the drifts, but the SNOW itself has almost stopped.

74   EXTERIOR: THE REMAINS OF THE TOWN DOCK—NIGHT.

The waves continue CRASHING IN against the seawall, but not as hard as before. There's an overturned fishing boat lying at the foot of Atlantic Street, with its prow smashed through the display window of Little Tall Gifts and Antiques.

75   EXTERIOR: THE SKY—NIGHT.

At first we see only BLACKNESS AND CLOUDS, but then there is a lightening, a silvering. We see the troubled, smoky shapes of the clouds more clearly in this light, and then, for just a moment or two, the FULL MOON shines through before disappearing again.

76   EXTERIOR: THE TOWN HALL—NIGHT.

The building, visible through WHIRLING MEMBRANES OF SNOW, still looks a bit like a mirage. In the shelter of its cupola, the memorial bell swings back and forth, being GENTLY RUNG by the wind.

77   INTERIOR: OLD-FASHIONED REGULATOR CLOCK, CLOSE-UP.

It's TICKING LOUDLY. WHEN the minute hand reaches straight-up nine, the regulator begins to CHIME THE HOUR. As it does, THE CAMERA PULLS BACK AND TURNS, giving us the town meeting hall of Little Tall Island.

It is a spectral and beautiful sight. Every member of the community that we have met is sitting there, plus all the other ISLANDERS—two hundred, in all. They look eerie by candlelight, like villagers from an earlier time . . . the time of Salem and Roanoke, let us say.

Sitting in the front row are MIKE and MOLLY; HATCH and ME-
LINDA; REV. BOB RIGGINS and his wife, CATHY; URSULA GODSOE
and SANDRA BEALS. ROBBIE BEALS is up on the stage, at a small
wooden table to the left of the podium. Before him on the table is a
little plaque that reads TOWN MANAGER.

At the rear of the room, eight cots have been set up in one corner. On
these, the children are sleeping. Sitting on folding chairs to either side
of this little enclave are ANGIE CARVER, TAVIA GODSOE, JOANNA
STANHOPE, ANDY ROBICHAUX, CAT WITHERS, and LUCIEN
FOURNIER. They are trying as best they can to guard the children.

The last BONGS of the regulator clock die away to the SOUND OF THE
WIND whining around outside the building. People look around
nervously for any sign of LINOGE. After a moment or two, ROBBIE
gets up from his little table and approaches the podium, tugging fussily
at the hem of his sport coat.

ROBBIE
Ladies and gentlemen . . . like you, I'm not sure what we're
waiting for, but—

JOHNNY HARRIMAN
Then why don't you sit down and wait like the rest of us,
Robbie?

NERVOUS LAUGHTER greets this. ROBBIE frowns at JOHNNY.

> ROBBIE
> I only wanted to say, Johnny, that I'm sure we'll find our way through this . . . *situation* . . . if we stick together, as we have always stuck together on the island . . .

78   INTERIOR: THE TOWN HALL'S FRONT DOOR—NIGHT.

It SMASHES OPEN with a LOUD, ECHOING BOOM. Outside, standing in the snow on the stoop, we see LINOGE'S boots and the black shaft of LINOGE'S cane.

79   INTERIOR: ROBBIE BEALS.

He stops talking and looks toward the door. His face is just *pouring* sweat.

80   INTERIOR: MONTAGE OF ISLANDERS.

TAVIA . . . JONAS STANHOPE . . . HATCH . . . MELINDA . . . ORV . . . REV. BOB RIGGINS . . . LUCIEN . . . others. All looking toward the door.

81   INTERIOR: TOWN HALL CORRIDOR—NIGHT.

The boots step onto the black-and-white-checked tiles. The cane keeps pace, coming down at regular intervals. We TRACK WITH THE BOOTS until they reach the door that gives upon the meeting hall. Then THE CAMERA BOOMS UP to the double doors with their glass panels. Written across them is LITTLE TALL ISLAND TOWN MEETING HALL. And, below that, LET US TRUST IN GOD AND EACH OTHER. We can see the ISLANDERS looking out toward the visitor, their eyes wide and AFRAID.

Hands clad in BRIGHT YELLOW GLOVES come up and grasp the two doorknobs. They open the doors toward THE CAMERA . . .

82   INTERIOR: THE TOWN MEETING HALL DOORWAY, REVERSE—NIGHT.

LINOGE stands there in pea jacket and yellow gloves, his cane tucked beneath one arm. He is smiling, eyes more or less normal, his MONSTER TEETH prudently hidden. He strips off his gloves and tucks them into his jacket pockets.

Slowly, and in a SILENCE so thick it's deafening, LINOGE enters the room. The only SOUND is the STEADY TICK of the regulator clock.

83    INTERIOR: THE TOWN MEETING HALL—NIGHT.

LINOGE walks slowly along the aisle that runs behind the benches and in front of the crumb-strewn tables where the buffet was set up. All of the ISLANDERS, but especially those occupying the last two or three rows of benches (those closest to him, in other words) turn to look at him, their eyes distrustful and afraid.

When LINOGE nears the little grouping of cots and the SLEEPING CHILDREN, the self-appointed guardians draw together, creating a barrier between LINOGE and the KIDS.

LINOGE reaches the place where a right turn will take him down the center aisle to the stage. For a moment he stands there, SMILING BENIGNLY, obviously enjoying the FEAR AND DISTRUST swirling in the silent room. Feeding on it, likely.

We INTERCUT this with all the ISLANDERS we have come to know. CAT is defiant: "you'll take these kids only over my dead and dismembered body," her face says. HATCH'S ROUND, HONEST FACE is full of tension and determination; MELINDA'S, full of FEAR AND DISMAY. We see others, too: JACK CARVER . . . FERD ANDREWS . . . UPTON BELL . . . all afraid, all awed by the presence of the supernatural . . . and he *is* supernatural; they feel it.

Last of all, we look at ROBBIE, whose face is DRENCHED WITH SWEAT and whose hand is plunged deeply into the coat pocket where he has hidden his gun.

LINOGE taps his cane first against the bench to his left and then the bench to his right, just as he tapped at the sides of MARTHA'S gate. There is a HISSING SOUND; smoke drifts up from the CHARRED SPOTS that are left by the cane's touch. Those sitting closest to the aisles on these two sides SHRINK AWAY. It's the HOPEWELL FAMILY on the right—STAN, MARY, and DAVEY. LINOGE SMILES at them, this time parting his lips enough to show the tips of his FANGS. All three HOPEWELLS see and react. MARY puts an arm around her son's shoulders and looks fearfully at LINOGE.

> LINOGE

Hello, Davey—your day off from school would make quite an English composition, wouldn't it?

DAVEY doesn't reply. LINOGE looks at him a moment longer, still smiling.

> LINOGE

Your father's a thief—over the last six years or so he's stolen more than fourteen thousand dollars from that marine supply company he works for. He gambles with it. (And, confidentially:) He loses.

DAVEY turns and shoots a STARTLED, INCREDULOUS GLANCE at his father. "I don't believe it," that look says, not *my* dad, never *my* dad—but for just an instant he sees NAKED GUILT and TRAPPED PANIC on STAN'S face. Only an instant, but enough to deeply shake a boy's trust in his previously idolized father.

> DAVEY

Dad—?

> STAN HOPEWELL

I don't know who you are, mister, but you lie. (pause) You *lie.*

It's good, but not quite good enough. No one, including his own son and wife, believes him. LINOGE grins.

> LINOGE

Born in vice, say it twice . . . eh, Davey? At least twice.

His work with the HOPEWELLS done, a family's lifetime of trust ruined in seconds, LINOGE starts slowly down the center aisle toward the stage. Every eye that attempts to meet his falters and turns away; every cheek grows pale; every heart recalls its mistakes and deceptions. When he reaches JOHNNY HARRIMAN, LINOGE stops and smiles.

> LINOGE

Well, Johnny Harriman! The fellow who burned down the planing mill across the reach there in Machias!

### JOHNNY HARRIMAN
I . . . you . . . I never did!

### LINOGE
(smiling)
Of course you did! Two years ago, right after they fired you!
(switches to KIRK FREEMAN)
And Kirk helped . . . didn't you? Of course you did—after
all, what are friends for?
(back to JOHNNY)
Seventy men lost their jobs, but you got your payback, and
that's what matters, isn't it? Ayuh—shoah, deah!

ISLANDERS are staring at JOHNNY as if they have never seen him
before . . . and at KIRK. JOHNNY shrinks under that gaze until he's
about a foot high.

### KIRK
(to JOHNNY)
There now, you dope. Lookit the trouble you got us into!

### JOHNNY
Shut up!

KIRK does, but it's too late. Smiling, LINOGE walks on toward the
stage. Each person he looks at cringes like an oft-kicked dog. No eye
will meet his. Every ISLANDER hopes LINOGE will not stop and speak
to him or her, as he did to STAN and JOHNNY HARRIMAN.

LINOGE stops one more time, when he reaches JACK CARVER. JACK
is sitting flanked by the two men LINOGE also mentioned in connec-
tion with the assault on the young gay man. JACK looks up quickly at
LINOGE, then looks away. ALEX HABER and LUCIEN FOURNIER
are equally uncomfortable.

### LINOGE
You boys really ought to go see that gay fellow you beat up.
You'd get a kick out of the eye patch he wears. That paisley
eye patch.

84   INTERIOR: ANGIE CARVER.

Frowning, curious. What is LINOGE saying about her husband . . . that he beat someone up? JACK wouldn't do something like that. Would he?

85   INTERIOR: RESUME CENTER AISLE OF TOWN MEETING HALL.

> JACK
> (hardly more than a whisper)
>
> Shut up.

> LINOGE
>
> Fellow's in one of those walk-ups on Canal Street, right behind Lisbon. I could give you the address. I don't know, maybe the three of you would like to take away the rest of his light. What do you think, Lucien, want to poke out his other eye? Finish the job?
>
> (LUCIEN looks down, says nothing)
>
> Alex?
>
> (ALEX is also mum)
>
> Born in sin, come on in.

LINOGE leaves them, walking toward the front of the hall again.

86   INTERIOR: ROBBIE BEALS.

He's standing between his little town-manager's table and the stage, face still running with sweat, the collar of his shirt now drenched, as well. He is seeing:

87   INTERIOR: THE MEETING HALL, FROM ROBBIE'S POINT OF VIEW.

Coming slowly up the aisle to the stage, still wearing the hospital johnny, her wild white hair spraying out all around her head, is the FALSE MOTHER. It's still LINOGE, of course, and he's still clutching the wolf's head cane.

> FALSE MOTHER
> Robbie, why did I have to die among strangers? You still
> haven't explained that. Why did I have to die calling for you?
> All I wanted was a kiss—

88   INTERIOR: THE MEETING HALL, ANGLE ON THE STAGE.

As LINOGE (he *is* LINOGE, in this shot) approaches, ROBBIE yanks the pistol from his pocket and points it at him.

> ROBBIE
> Stay away! I'm warning you, stay back!

> LINOGE
> Oh, put that down.

ROBBIE'S hand opens. We can see him struggling to keep this from happening, but it's as though a bigger hand—one we can't quite see—has grabbed his and is bending the fingers back one by one. The pistol THUMPS TO THE STAGE FLOOR just as LINOGE mounts the stairs at center stage.

89   INTERIOR: THE FRONT OF THE STAGE, FROM ROBBIE'S POINT OF VIEW.

It's the FALSE MOTHER mounting those steps, with the hospital johnny flapping around her scrawny body. She points the tip of the cane at ROBBIE; her rheumy old eyes FLASH MALEVOLENTLY.

> FALSE MOTHER
> Why don't you tell these people where you were and what
> you were doing when I died, Robbie? I think your wife would
> be especially interested, don't you?

90  INTERIOR: ANGLE ON ROBBIE, LINOGE, AND THE FIRST FEW ROWS
BELOW.

ROBBIE

You keep your mouth shut! Sandra, don't listen to him! It's
all lies!

SANDRA BEALS, puzzled and afraid, starts to get up. URSULA seizes
her wrist and gets her to sit down again.

On stage, LINOGE reaches one hand out toward ROBBIE'S face,
clutching with the fingertips.

LINOGE

Your eyes . . .

91  INTERIOR: THE FALSE MOTHER, FROM ROBBIE'S POINT OF VIEW.

FALSE MOTHER

I'll eat your eyes right out of your head . . .

The bony old hand not holding the cane continues to make CLUTCH-
ING GESTURES.

92  INTERIOR: THE STAGE.

ROBBIE stumbles backward, trips over his own feet, and FALLS
DOWN. He skitters backward from LINOGE/MOM on his butt, pushing with his feet, finishing up crouched beneath his own small town-
manager's table. There he stops, GIBBERING SOFTLY. His gun lies
forgotten on the stage some five feet away.

The ISLANDERS MURMUR, FRIGHTENED, as LINOGE steps behind
the podium and grips its sides like a confident politician about to orate.

LINOGE

Not to worry, folks—he'll recuperate just fine, I'm sure. And
in the meantime, it's sort of nice to have him under the table
instead of pounding on it, wouldn't you say? Sort of restful.
Come on. Tell the truth . . .
(he pauses; smiles)
. . . and shame the devil.

They look at him silently, fearfully. He looks back, smiling.

> LINOGE
> So now we come to it, don't we? I'll lay things out for you,
> then go downstairs and wait for you to take your decision.

93    INTERIOR: THE ISLANDERS.

SONNY BRAUTIGAN stands. He's scared but determined to speak.

> SONNY
> Why did you come here? *Why us?*

94    INTERIOR: MIKE AND MOLLY, CLOSE-UP.

> MIKE
> (low; almost to himself)
> I guess there's just something about us that pisses him off.

MOLLY takes his hand. MIKE folds his fingers over hers, raises her
hand to his cheek, and rubs it there, taking comfort from her touch.

95    INTERIOR: ANGLE ON THE STAGE AND THE HALL, FEATURES LINOGE

> LINOGE
> I'm here because island folks know how to pull together for
> the common good when they need to . . . and island folks
> know how to keep a secret. That was true on Roanoke Island
> in 1587, and it's true on Little Tall in 1989.

> HATCH
> (stands)
> Tell us. Quit dancing around it. Tell us what you want.

HATCH sits down. LINOGE stands at the podium with his head bent,
as if in thought. The ISLANDERS wait breathlessly for him to go on.
Outside, the WIND MOANS. At last, the stranger raises his head and
looks at his audience.

> LINOGE
> Your children are here with you . . . but they're not. It's the
> same with me, because part of me is with them.

He points to his right, where the room's outer wall is lined with windows. On a nice day, these would give a western view of the slope that runs down to the docks, the reach, and the mainland. Now the windows are DARK . . . except when LINOGE raises his other hand and points the wolf's head of his cane in that direction.

The windows fill with BRIGHT BLUE LIGHT. The ISLANDERS murmur in FEAR and WONDER. Several of them actually shade their eyes.

> LINOGE
>
> Look!

THE CAMERA MOVES IN on the center window. We see BLUE SKY . . . we see the CLOUDS BELOW . . . we see what could be a V-formation of birds (ducks, perhaps?) winging their way above the clouds. Except those aren't ducks or geese . . . those are . . . are . . .

96    INTERIOR: THE "KIDS' CORNER" OF THE MEETING HALL.

ANDY ROBICHAUX lurches to his feet, eyes never leaving the GLOW-ING WINDOWS. His face is filled with dismay.

> ANDY
>
> Harry . . . oh, my God, that's Harry!

He looks wildly at his sleeping son, reassuring himself that the boy hasn't disappeared, then back at the image in the window. And now ANGIE gets to her feet beside him.

> ANGIE
> (screams)
>
> *Buster! Jack, that's Buster!*

97    INTERIOR: LINOGE, CLOSE-UP.

> LINOGE
>
> That's *all* of them.

98    EXTERIOR: LINOGE AND THE CHILDREN, FLYING—DAY.

LINOGE is in the lead as he was before, just behind the FLYING CANE. He is holding hands with PIPPA and RALPHIE as before, and the other kids string out behind them, making that V. The kids are laughing, happy, TOTALLY BLISSED OUT. Until—

> LINOGE (voice)
> And if I drop them *there*—

LINOGE opens his hands, letting go of RALPHIE and PIPPA. Their expressions of happiness immediately turn to terror. SHRIEKING, unlinking from each other, the EIGHT CHILDREN tumble downward and are swallowed in the floor of clouds beneath them.

99   INTERIOR: LINOGE, CLOSE-UP.

> LINOGE
> —they die *here.*

100   INTERIOR: RESUME STAGE AND AUDIENCE, FEATURING LINOGE.

LINOGE lowers his cane, and the BRIGHT BLUE LIGHT leaves the windows; they FADE TO BLACK. The ISLANDERS are terribly shaken by what they have seen. None, quite understandably, are more shaken than the parents.

> LINOGE
> You'll see it happen. They'll puff out . . .

He turns slightly to his left, PUFFS WITH HIS LIPS, and several candles (eight, in fact) mounted along the wall GO OUT.

> LINOGE
> (smiling, continues)
> . . . like candles in the wind.

URSULA GODSOE totters to her feet. Her once-pretty face is now battered and twisted with grief. She sways and almost falls. MELINDA HATCHER rises and steadies her. URSULA pleads with all her heart.

> URSULA
> (through tears)
> Please don't hurt my Sally, mister. She's all I got left, now that Peter's gone. We'll give you what you want, if we have it to give. I swear we will. Won't we?

101   INTERIOR: TOWN HALL MONTAGE.

CAT WITHERS . . . SONNY . . . DELLA BISSONETTE . . . JENNA
FREEMAN . . . JACK, LUCIEN, and ALEX HABER in a guilty little
huddle . . . they all nod and MURMUR AGREEMENT. Yes, they will
give LINOGE what he wants. They are ready to do that.

102   INTERIOR: THE FRONT ROW.

HATCH
(stands beside his wife)
What is it? Tell us.

103   INTERIOR: RESUME STAGE AND AUDIENCE, FEATURING LINOGE.

LINOGE
I've lived a long time—thousands of years—but I'm not a
god, nor am I one of the immortals.

LINOGE holds his cane in the middle, raises it above his head, then
brings it down horizontally in front of his face. A faint shadow, thrown
by CANDLELIGHT, crosses his face from the forehead down. As it
does, the strong and handsome features of a man in early middle age
CHANGE . . . AGE. LINOGE'S face becomes the lined and sagging
countenance of a man who is not just old but ANCIENT. The eyes peer
out of sagging sockets and from beneath puffy eyelids.

The AUDIENCE GASPS AND MURMURS. Once more, the director
will intercut the faces he wants, getting reactions. We see ANDY
ROBICHAUX, for instance, sitting beside his son, holding and stroking
the boy's small hand.

LINOGE
So you see me as I really am. Old. And sick. Dying, in fact.

LINOGE raises his cane again, and as the shadow goes back up,
LINOGE'S YOUTH RETURNS. He waits as the AUDIENCE MURMURS.

LINOGE
By the standards of your mayfly existences, I have long to live
yet—I'll still be walking the earth when all but the freshest
and newest among you . . . Davey Hopewell, perhaps, or
young Don Beals . . .

We INTERCUT SHOTS of DAVEY with his parents and DON sleeping on his cot.

LINOGE
(continues)

. . . have gone to your graves. But in terms of my own existence, time has grown short. You ask me what I want?

104    INTERIOR: MIKE AND MOLLY ANDERSON.

MIKE already knows, and his face is filling with HORROR and FURIOUS PROTEST. When he begins speaking, his voice rising from a WHISPER TO A SCREAM, MOLLY seizes his wrist . . .

MIKE

No, no, no, *no* . . .

105    INTERIOR: LINOGE, AT THE PODIUM.

LINOGE
(ignores MIKE)

I want someone to raise and teach; someone to whom I can pass on all I have learned and all I know; I want someone who will carry on my work when I can no longer do it myself.

106    INTERIOR: MIKE.

He rises to his feet, dragging MOLLY with him.

MIKE

*No! No! Never!*

107    INTERIOR: LINOGE.

LINOGE
(ignores MIKE)

I want a child. One of the eight sleeping back there. It doesn't matter which one; all are just as likely in my eyes. Give me what I want—give it freely—and I'll go away.

108   INTERIOR: THE STAGE AND THE AUDIENCE, ANGLE ON MIKE AND
LINOGE.

MIKE

*Never! We'll never give you one of our children! Never!*

He pulls away from MOLLY and lunges for the stairs leading to the
stage, meaning to tackle LINOGE. In his fury, any doubts he might
have had about his ability to prevail over LINOGE'S supernatural
powers have disappeared.

LINOGE

Grab him! Unless you want me to drop the children! And I
will! I promise you I will!

109   INTERIOR: THE "KIDS' CORNER"

The KIDS are MOANING AND TURNING on their cots, their serenity
broken by some interior fear . . . or something that's happening to
them FAR AWAY and HIGH ABOVE.

JACK CARVER
(horror and panic)
Get him! Stop him! For God's sake, stop him!

110    INTERIOR: RESUME STAGE AREA.

REV. BOB RIGGINS throws his arms around MIKE'S shoulders before
MIKE can do more than reach the foot of the stairs. HATCH joins him
and also grabs hold before MIKE can throw off RIGGINS, who is big
but a touch on the blubbery side.


                            HATCH
        Mike, no—we've got to hear him out—at least hear him out—


                            MIKE
                         (struggling)
        No, we don't! Let me go, Hatch! Dammit—

He almost gets free, but then he's swamped by LUCIEN, SONNY,
ALEX, and JOHNNY. Big boys all, they drag him back to his seat in the
first row. We can see they're embarrassed to be doing it, but we can
also see that they're determined.

                            JOHNNY
        You just sit tight for a bit, Michael Anderson, and let him
        have his say. We'll hear him out.

                            LUCIEN
        We got to.

                            MIKE
        You're wrong. Listening to him is the worst thing we can do.

He looks to MOLLY for help and support, and what he sees there stuns
him . . . a KIND OF DESPERATE UNSURETY.

                            MIKE
                         (horrified)
        Molly? *Molly?*

                            MOLLY
        I don't know, Mike. I think we better listen.

                            MELINDA
        Surely it can't hurt to listen.

SONNY

He's got us over a stump.

They turn back to LINOGE.

111   INTERIOR: THE ISLANDERS.

All of them turn back to LINOGE, waiting for the bottom line.

112   INTERIOR: RESUME LINOGE.

As he speaks, THE CAMERA MOVES SLOWLY IN TO CLOSE-UP.

LINOGE

In a matter such as this, I cannot take . . . although I can punish; I assure you I can punish. Give me one of the babies sleeping yonder to raise as my own and I'll leave you in peace. He or she will live long—long after all the others sleeping there are gone—and see much. Give me what I want and I'll go away. Refuse me, and the dreams you shared last night will come true. The children will fall from the sky, the rest of you will walk into the ocean, two by two, and when the storm ends, they will find this island as they found Roanoke Island. Empty . . . deserted. I'll give you half an hour. Discuss it . . . isn't that what a town meeting is for? And then . . .

He pauses. We have reached EXTREME CLOSE-UP.

LINOGE

Choose.

FADE TO BLACK. THIS ENDS ACT 4.

# Act 5

---

113   EXTERIOR: THE LITTLE TALL ISLAND TOWN HALL—NIGHT.

The wind is still blowing the snow around, but the stuff falling from the sky has stopped. The Storm of the Century—Mother Nature's version, anyway—has ended.

114   EXTERIOR: THE SKY—NIGHT.

The clouds have begun to tatter and pull apart. This time when the FULL MOON appears, it remains in view.

115   INTERIOR: THE TOWN MEETING HALL, FROM THE CORRIDOR.

We're looking in through the glass doors, and running across the bottom of our view, like a super on a newscast, is that motto: LET US TRUST IN GOD AND EACH OTHER.

We can see ROBBIE BEALS getting to his feet (his hair is still mussed from hiding under the table) and crossing slowly toward the podium.

116   OMIT.

117   INTERIOR: THE TOWN MEETING HALL—NIGHT.

[The director will shot-block the following as he/she desires, but it should play almost as one big master, which is how it's mostly written.]

ROBBIE reaches the podium and looks out over the silent, waiting audience. Below him, on the first bench, MIKE remains seated, but thrums almost visibly, like a high-tension wire. HATCH sits on one side of him, and MOLLY on the other. MIKE is holding her hand, and she is looking at him anxiously. Sitting behind him on the next bench are LUCIEN, SONNY, ALEX, and JOHNNY—self-appointed sergeants-at-arms. If MIKE tries to interfere with the decision-making process, they will restrain him.

At the rear of the room, where the KIDS are sleeping, the circle of adults has grown. URSULA has joined TAVIA near SALLY GODSOE; both ANDY and JILL are with HARRY; JACK has joined ANGIE to be close to BUSTER . . . although when JACK tries to put an arm around his wife, ANGIE dips her shoulders and slips away from his touch. "Jackie, you got some 'splainin' to do," as Ricky Ricardo might have said. MELINDA is sitting by PIPPA, and next to her, SANDRA is sitting by DON. CARLA and HENRY BRIGHT sit at the foot of FRANK'S cot, holding hands. LINDA ST. PIERRE is with HEIDI. The attention of all the parents is not on their sleeping children, however, but on ROBBIE, the self-appointed moderator . . . and on their fellow ISLANDERS, who will decide the fate of their children.

Making a tremendous effort to get his act together, ROBBIE looks beneath the podium and brings out a GAVEL—old and heavy, a relic that has been handed down from the seventeenth century. ROBBIE looks at it for a moment as if he's never seen it before, then brings it down with a HARD BANGING SOUND. Several people jump.

> ROBBIE
> I call the meeting to order. I think it'll be best if we deal with this matter the way we would any other piece of town business. After all, that's what it is, isn't it? Town business?

SILENCE and strained faces greet this. MIKE looks as if he would like to respond, but doesn't. MOLLY continues to look at her husband ANXIOUSLY and to caress his hand, which is tightly (painfully, one would think) enfolding hers.

> ROBBIE
> Any objection to that?

SILENCE. ROBBIE brings the gavel down again—*WHACK!*—and once again, people jump. Not the KIDS, though. They are deeply asleep again. Or comatose.

> ROBBIE
> The item on the floor is whether or not to give this . . . this thing that's come among us . . . one of our children. He says he'll go away if we give him what he wants, and kill us all— the kids included—if we don't. Have I stated it fairly?

SILENCE.

> ROBBIE

All right. How say you then, Little Tall? Will you speak of this?

SILENCE. Then CAL FREESE gets slowly to his feet. He looks around at his fellow ISLANDERS.

> CAL

I don't see what choice we have, if we believe he can do what he says he can do.

> ROBERTA COIGN

Do you believe him?

> CAL

First thing I asked myself. And . . . ayuh, I do. I've seen enough to convince me. I think we either give him what he wants or he'll take everything we have . . . includin' our kids.

CAL sits down.

> ROBBIE

Roberta Coign's got a good point, though. How many of you think Linoge is telling the truth? That he can and will wipe out everyone on the island, if we go against him?

SILENCE. They all believe it, but no one wants to be first to hoist his or her hand.

> DELLA BISSONETTE

We all had the same dream . . . and they weren't regular dreams. I know that. We all know that. He's given us fair warning.

She raises her hand.

> BURT SOAMES

There's nothin' fair about it, but—

One of BURT'S arms is in a makeshift sling, but he raises his unhurt one in the air. Others follow suit, at first just a few, then more, then almost all of them. HATCH and MOLLY are among the last to raise their hands. Only MIKE sits grimly where he is, keeping the hand MOLLY'S not holding in his lap.

> MOLLY
> (low, to MIKE)
> It's not a question of what we're going to do, Mike . . . not yet. It's just whether or not we believe—

> MIKE
> I know what the question is. And once we start down this road, every step gets easier. I know that, too.

> ROBBIE
> (lowering his own hand)
> All right, I guess we believe him. That's one issue out of the way. Now, if there's any discussion of the main question—

> MIKE
> (to his feet)
> I have something to say.

> ROBBIE
> That's fine. You're a taxpayer, sure enough. Have on.

MIKE walks slowly up the stairs to the stage. MOLLY watches apprehensively. MIKE doesn't bother with the podium; he simply turns to his fellow ISLANDERS. We take several beats to FOCUS and build tension as he thinks about how to begin.

> MIKE
> No, he's not a man. I didn't vote, but I agree with that, just the same. I've seen what he did to Martha Clarendon, what he did to Peter Godsoe, what he's done to our kids—and I don't believe he's a man. I had the same dreams that you had, and I understand the reality of what he's threatening as well as you do. Better, maybe—I'm your constable, the man you elected to enforce your laws. But . . . folks . . . we don't give our kids away to thugs. Do you understand that? *We don't give away our children!*

At the back of the room, where the children are, ANDY ROBICHAUX steps forward.

ANDY
What's the choice, then? What do we do? What *can* we do?

A DEEP MURMUR OF AGREEMENT greets this, and MIKE is troubled, we can see that. Because the only answer he has makes no sense. It has only the virtue of being right.

MIKE
Stand against him, side by side and shoulder to shoulder. Tell him *no* in one voice. Do what it says on the door we use to get in here—trust in God and each other. And then . . . maybe . . . he goes away. The way storms always do, when they've blown themselves out.

ORV BOUCHER
(stands)
And if he starts pointing his cane around? What then? What about when we start to drop like flies on a windowsill?

MURMUR OF AGREEMENT is louder.

REV. BOB RIGGINS
(stands)
"Render therefore unto Caesar the things which are Caesar's." You said that to me yourself, Michael, not an hour ago. Book of Matthew.

MIKE
"Get thee behind me, Satan, for thou savorest not the things that be of God." Book of Mark.
(looks around)
Folks . . . if we give up a child—one of our own—how will we live with each other, even if he lets us live?

ROBBIE
Very well, that's how.

MIKE turns to look at him, stunned. At the back of the room, JACK CARVER comes forward to the head of the center aisle. When he speaks, MIKE turns back that way. He's being bombarded from all directions.

> JACK

We've *all* got things we live with, Mike. Or maybe you're different.

That hits home. We see MIKE remembering.

He addresses JACK and all of them.

> MIKE

No, I'm no different. But this isn't like trying to live with a test you cheated on, or a one-night stand, or the memory of somebody you hurt when you were drunk and in an ugly frame of mind. *This is a child.* Don't you understand that, Jack?

He's maybe getting to them . . . then ROBBIE speaks up.

> ROBBIE

Suppose you're right about being able to send him away—suppose we just put our arms around each other, gather our will, and give out a big collective "NO!" Suppose we do that and he just disappears? Goes back to wherever he came from?

MIKE looks at him warily, waiting for the hook.

> ROBBIE

You saw our children. I don't know what he's actually done with them, but I have no doubt that flying high over the earth is an accurate representation of it. They can fall. I believe that. All he has to do is wave that cane of his, and they fall. How do we live with ourselves if that happens? Do we tell ourselves that we killed all eight of them because we were too good, too holy, to sacrifice one of them?

> MIKE

He could be bluffing—

> MELINDA
> (sharp; unfriendly)

He's not, Michael, and you know it. You *saw* it.

TAVIA GODSOE comes hesitantly forward to the head of the center aisle, which seems to be the preferred speaking position for the ISLANDERS. She talks hesitantly at first, then with growing confidence.

> TAVIA
>
> You speak as though he were going to kill the child, Michael . . . as though it were some kind of . . . of human sacrifice. It sounds more like an adoption to me.

She looks around, smiling tentatively—if we have to do this, let's make the best of it. Let's look on the bright side.

> JONAS
>
> And a long life, as well! (pause) If you believe him, that is. And after seeing him, I . . . actually, I guess I do.

MURMURS of agreement. And approval.

> MIKE
>
> Linoge beat Martha Clarendon to death with his cane! Knocked the eyes right out of her head! We're debating whether or not to give a child to a monster!

SILENCE greets this. Folks drop their eyes to the floor, cheeks red, ashamed. REV. BOB RIGGINS sits down again. His wife puts a hand on his arm and looks at MIKE resentfully.

> HENRY BRIGHT
>
> Maybe that's so, but what about the rest of the kids? Do we say no and then watch them die right in front of us?

> KIRK
>
> Yeah, Mike—what happened to the good of the most?

MIKE has no real answer for this.

> MIKE
>
> He could be bluffing about the kids, too. Satan's the father of lies, and this guy has got to be a close relation.

> JILL ROBICHAUX
> (shrill and angry)

Is that a risk you want to take? Fine . . . but take it with *your* son, not mine!

> LINDA ST. PIERRE

My sentiments exactly.

> HENRY BRIGHT

You want to know the worst thing I can think of, Michael? Suppose you're half right? Suppose *we* live . . . and *they* die.
> (points to the KIDS)

How will we look at each other then? How will we live with each other then?

> JACK

And how would we ever live with you?

UGLY ASSENTING MURMURS to this. JACK the gay-basher goes back to his sleeping little boy and sits down beside him. MIKE has no real answer for this, either. We can see him floundering for one and not finding it.

ROBBIE looks at the clock. It's 9:20.

> ROBBIE

He said half an hour. That leaves us ten minutes.

> MIKE

We can't do this! Can't you see? Don't you understand? We can't allow him to—

> SONNY
> (not unkindly)

I think we've heard your side of it, Mike. Take a seat, why don't you?

MIKE looks at them helplessly. He's not stupid, and he can see which way the wind is blowing.

MIKE

You need to think about this, folks. You need to think about
it very carefully.

He goes back down the steps and sits beside MOLLY. He takes her
hand. She lets him hold it for a second or two, then draws it away.

MOLLY

I want to sit with Ralphie, Mike.

She gets up and goes down the center aisle to where the KIDS are
sleeping on their cots. She disappears into the circle of parents without
a look back.

ROBBIE

Do you have more, folks? What's your pleasure?

A moment of SILENCE.

URSULA
(steps forward)
God help us, but let's give him what he wants. Give him what
he wants and send him on his way. I don't care about my life,
but the children . . . even if it's Sally. Better she should live
with a bad man than . . . than die . . .
(she looks around, weeping)
*My God, Michael Anderson, where's your heart? They're chil-
dren! We can't let him kill the children!*

She goes back to the kids. MIKE, meanwhile, is being isolated in a
circle of hostile eyes.

ROBBIE
(glances at the clock)
Anyone else?

MIKE starts to get up. HATCH puts his hand on his arm and squeezes.
When MIKE looks at him, surprised and questioning, HATCH gives a
tiny shake of the head. "Stop," that small headshake says; "you've done
all you can do."

MIKE shakes him off and stands up again. He doesn't use the stage this time, but addresses his fellow ISLANDERS from where he is.

> MIKE
>
> Don't. Please. The Andersons go back to 1735 here on Little Tall. I ask you as an islander and as Ralphie Anderson's father—don't do this. Don't give in to this. (pause) This is damnation.

He looks around desperately. None of them, not even his own wife, will meet his eyes. SILENCE descends again. It's broken only by the WHINE OF THE WIND outside and the TICK OF THE REGULATOR CLOCK.

> MIKE
>
> All right, I move to restrict the vote. Let the parents vote, and the parents only. They're all residents—

> LINDA ST. PIERRE
>
> No, that's not fair.

She touches her sleeping daughter's brow with gentle love.

> LINDA ST. PIERRE
>
> I've raised her by myself—oh, with plenty of help from folks on the island, including you and your wife, Mike—but mostly by myself. I shouldn't have to make a decision like this all by myself. What's a community for, if it isn't to help people when something terrible happens? When none of the choices look good?

> ANDY
>
> Couldn't have said it better myself, Lin.

> MIKE
>
> But—

> MANY VOICES
>
> Sit down . . . Call the question . . . Let's vote!
>
> (etc.)

ROBBIE

Will somebody move the question of who can vote? It's probably not parliamentary, but we have to move on. I'd prefer to hear from one of the parents.

A moment of TENSE SILENCE, then:

MELINDA HATCHER

I move everybody votes.

CARLA BRIGHT

I second it.

MIKE

This isn't—

ANGIE

Shut up! You've had your say, now just shut up!

ROBBIE

It's been moved and seconded that everyone be allowed to vote on whether or not to give Mr. Linoge what he has demanded. Those in favor?

Every hand goes up except for MIKE'S. He sees that MOLLY has also raised her hand, sees she won't look at him, and something in him dies a little.

ROBBIE

Those opposed?

Not a single hand goes up. MIKE simply sits in the front row, his head dropped.

ROBBIE
(whacks the gavel)

The motion carries.

TESS MARCHANT

Call the question, Robbie Beals. The real question.

118  INTERIOR: THE BASEMENT, WITH LINOGE.

He looks up at the ceiling, EYES GLEAMING in the gloom. They're going to vote, and he knows it.

119  INTERIOR: RESUME TOWN MEETING HALL—NIGHT.

#### JOANNA
For God's sake—let's vote and have done!

#### MIKE
My son isn't a part of this. Let's understand that, all right? He's not a part of this . . . obscenity.

#### MOLLY
Yes. He is.

UTTER SILENCE greets this. MIKE stands up and looks unbelievingly at his wife. They face each other that way across the length of the meeting hall.

#### MOLLY
We've never shirked our duty, Michael, we've taken part in all the life of this island, and we'll take part in this.

#### MIKE
You don't mean it—you can't mean it.

#### MOLLY
I do.

#### MIKE
It's insane.

#### MOLLY
Maybe—but it's not an insanity we made. Michael—

#### MIKE
I'm leaving. Screw this. Screw all of you. I'm taking my son and leaving.

He gets about three steps before the self-appointed sergeants-at-arms grab him and yank him back to his seat. MOLLY sees MIKE struggling, sees how rough they're being—they don't like his disapproval of this highly questionable decision—and runs down the aisle toward him.

> MIKE
>
> Hatch! Help me!

But HATCH turns away, FACE FLUSHING WITH EMBARRASS-MENT. And when MIKE lunges in his direction, LUCIEN smashes him in the nose. Blood flows.

> MOLLY
>
> Stop it! Stop hurting him! Mike, are you all right? Are you—

> MIKE
>
> Get away from me. You want to do it before I lose control of myself and spit in your face.

She takes a step back from him, eyes huge and shocked.

> MOLLY
>
> Mike, if you'd only see . . . this isn't our decision to make alone. This affects the whole town!

> MIKE
>
> I know it does—what else have I been saying? Get away from me, Molly.

She backs away, GRIEVING and SORROWFUL. SONNY BRAUTIGAN hands MIKE a handkerchief.

> MIKE
>
> You can let go. I'll sit.

They let go, but warily. On the podium, ROBBIE looks on with unmistakable satisfaction. "This may be a bad situation," his face says, "but at least our self-righteous prick of a constable is taking a face-washing, and that's something."

MOLLY, meanwhile, backs away from MIKE, who won't look at her. Her face twists and crumples. WEEPING, she walks toward the back of the room. People sitting on the aisle pat her hands and WHISPER COMFORTS and ENCOURAGEMENTS as she goes—"That's all right, deah" . . . "He'll come around" . . . "You're doing the right thing." At the back of the room, MELINDA, JILL, and LINDA ST. PIERRE enfold her.

HATCH slides close to MIKE, almost humming with shame.

> ### HATCH
> Mike, I—

> ### MIKE
> (doesn't look at him)
> Shut up. Get away from me.

> ### HATCH
> When you've had a chance to think about it, you'll under-stand. You'll come around. It's the only thing we can do. What else is there? Die for a principle? Every one of us? Including those who're too young to understand *why* they're dying? You need to think about it.

MIKE at last looks up.

> ### MIKE
> And if it's Pippa that Linoge ends up taking?

A long silence as HATCH thinks. Then he meets MIKE'S eyes.

> ### HATCH
> I'll tell myself she died as an infant. That it was a crib death, something no one could help or foresee. And I'll believe it. Melly and me, we'll both believe it.

ROBBIE hammers on the podium some more with the gavel.

> ### ROBBIE
> Oyez, oyez—this question has been called. Do we or do we not give Mr. Linoge what he has asked for, pursuant to his promise that he will leave us in peace? How say you, Little Tall? Those in favor, signify in the usual way.

There is a moment of BREATHLESS SILENCE, and then, at the back of the room, ANDY ROBICHAUX raises his hand.

ANDY

I'm Harry's father, and I vote yes.

JILL ROBICHAUX

I'm his mother, and so do I.

HENRY

Carla and I vote yes.

LINDA ST. PIERRE raises her hand. So does SANDRA BEALS, and at the podium, ROBBIE raises his.

MELINDA
(raises her hand)

Yes. We have no choice.

HATCH

No choice.

He raises his hand.

URSULA

I vote yes—it's the only way.

She raises her hand, and so does TAVIA.

JACK

Got to.

Up goes his hand. ANGELA takes a long, loving look at the sleeping BUSTER, then raises her own.

The eyes of everyone in the room turn to MOLLY. She kneels, kisses RALPHIE on the fairy saddle on his nose, then rises to her feet. She speaks to them all . . . but in a way, she speaks only to MIKE, her face pleading for understanding.

MOLLY

To lose one in life is better than to lose them all in death. I vote yes.

She raises her hand. Soon other hands go up. THE CAMERA RANGES AMONG all the folks we have come to know, watching as every hand goes up . . . save one.

ROBBIE draws the moment out, looking at the forest of raised arms and solemn faces. To give these people the credit they're due, they have made a terrible decision . . . and know it.

> ROBBIE
> (soft)
> Those opposed?

The raised hands go down. MIKE, still looking at the floor, hoists his hand high in the air.

> ROBBIE
> I count all in favor save one. The motion is carried.

120   INTERIOR: THE REGULATOR CLOCK, CLOSE-UP.

The minute hand reaches 9:30, and the CLOCK CHIMES ONCE.

121   INTERIOR: RESUME TOWN MEETING HALL—NIGHT.

The doors open. LINOGE steps in, his cane in one hand, the small chamois bag in the other.

> LINOGE
> Folks, have you reached your decision?

> ROBBIE
> Yes . . . we've voted in favor.

> LINOGE
> Excellent.

He walks along the back row, then pauses when he reaches the center aisle. He looks at the parents.

> LINOGE
> You've made the right choice.

MOLLY turns away, sickened by this smiling monster's approval. LINOGE sees her revulsion, and his smile broadens. He makes his way slowly down the center aisle, holding the bag of marbles out before him.

He mounts the steps, and ROBBIE moves away from him rapidly, his face full of terror. LINOGE stands by the podium, looking at his hostages with a kindly smile.

#### LINOGE
You've done a hard thing, my friends, but despite what the constable may have told you, it's also a good thing. The right thing. The only thing, really, that loving, responsible people *could* have done, under the circumstances.

He holds out the bag by the drawstring, so it hangs down from his hand.

#### LINOGE
These are weirding stones. They were old when the world was young, and used to decide great issues long before Atlantis sank into the African Ocean. There are seven white stones in here . . . and one black one.

LINOGE pauses . . . smiles . . . a smile that shows the tips of his fangs.

#### LINOGE
You're eager for me to be gone, and I don't blame you. Will one parent of each child come forward, please? Let's finish this up.

122   INTERIOR: THE ISLANDERS.

Realizing for the first time on a gut level what they have done. Realizing also that it's too late to turn back.

123   INTERIOR: LINOGE, CLOSE-UP.

Smiling. Showing the tips of his fangs. And holding out the bag. It's time to choose.

FADE TO BLACK. THIS ENDS ACT 5.

# Act 6

124   EXTERIOR: THE REACH—NIGHT.

The snow has stopped, and now MOONLIGHT beats a gilded track across the reach toward the mainland.

125   EXTERIOR: MAIN STREET—NIGHT.

Snow-clogged and silent.

126   EXTERIOR: THE TOWN HALL—NIGHT.

Dark on the right, BRIGHTLY CANDLELIT on the left, where the meeting hall is.

127   INTERIOR: THE MEETING HALL—NIGHT.

Slowly, slowly, the parents come down the center aisle: JILL, URSULA, JACK, LINDA, SANDRA, HENRY, and MELINDA. At the rear of the group is MOLLY ANDERSON. She looks pleadingly at MIKE.

### MOLLY
Mike, please try to understand—

### MIKE
Do you want me to understand? Go back and sit with him, then. Refuse to take part in this obscenity.

### MOLLY
I can't. If you could only see . . .

MIKE is looking down between his legs at the floor. He doesn't want to look at her, doesn't want to look at any of it. She sees this and goes on, sorrowfully, up the steps.

The PARENTS range themselves in a line on the stage. LINOGE looks at them with the benign smile of a dentist assuring a child that this won't hurt, this won't hurt at all.

LINOGE

It's perfectly simple. You each draw a stone from the bag. The child whose parent draws the black stone comes with me. To live long . . . see far . . . and know much. Mrs. Robichaux? Jill? Would you start us, please?

He offers her the bag. At first it seems she won't reach into it . . . or can't.

ANDY

Go on, honey—do it.

She gives him a haunted look, then reaches into the bag, feels around, and comes out with her hand tightly clasped around a stone. She looks as though she might faint.

LINOGE

Mrs. Hatcher?

MELINDA takes a stone. SANDRA is next. She reaches toward the bag . . . then draws away.

SANDRA

Robbie, I can't! You!

But ROBBIE doesn't want to be that near LINOGE.

ROBBIE

Go on! Draw!

She does, and stands back, little mouth quivering, her hand clasped so tightly around the stone that the fingers are white. Next is HENRY BRIGHT, feeling around a long time, rejecting one (or two) in favor of another. Then JACK. He chooses fast, then steps back and gives ANGIE a desperate, hopeful smile. LINDA ST. PIERRE draws one. That leaves URSULA and MOLLY.

LINOGE

Ladies?

URSULA

You go first, Molly.

MOLLY

No. Please. You.

URSULA plunges her hand into the bag, takes one of the two remaining stones, then steps back, fist clenched. MOLLY steps forward, looks at LINOGE, and takes the last stone. LINOGE tosses the empty bag aside. It flutters toward the stage . . . then DISAPPEARS IN A DIM BLUE GLOW before it ever reaches the boards. No reaction from the ISLANDERS; their silence is so thick and tense you could cut it with a knife.

LINOGE

All right, my friends; so far it's done very well. Now, who has the courage to show first? To put fear aside and let sweet relief rush in to take its place?

No one responds. They stand, eight parents with their hands clenched before them, each in utter white-faced terror.

LINOGE
(genial)
Come, come—have you never heard that the gods punish the fainthearted?

JACK
(cries out)
Buster! I love you!

He opens his hand. The marble he holds is WHITE. The AUDIENCE MURMURS.

URSULA steps forward. She holds out her closed, trembling fist. She nerves herself up, and her hand springs open. This marble is also WHITE. The AUDIENCE MURMURS AGAIN.

ROBBIE

Let's see, Sandra. Show it.

SANDRA

I . . . I . . . Robbie, I can't . . . I know it's Donnie . . . I *know* it is . . . I've never been lucky . . .

Impatient with her, contemptuous of her, in a frenzy to know one way or the other, he goes to her, seizes her hand, and pries the fingers open. We can't see, and at first we can read nothing from his face. Then he seizes what she holds, and lifts it up so they can all see. He's GRINNING SAVAGELY; looks like Richard Nixon at a political rally.

> ### ROBBIE
> White!

He tries to embrace his wife, but SANDRA pushes him away with an expression beyond disgust—this is outright revulsion.

Now it's LINDA ST. PIERRE's turn to step forward. She holds out her closed hand, looking down at it, then closes her eyes.

> ### LINDA ST. PIERRE
> Please, God, I beg of you, don't take my Heidi away.

She opens her hand, but not her eyes.

> ### ANOTHER VOICE
> *White!*

The AUDIENCE MURMURS. LINDA opens her eyes, sees the stone is indeed WHITE, and begins to WEEP, closing her hand again and holding the precious stone to her breasts.

> ### LINOGE
> Jill? Mrs. Robichaux?

> ### JILL ROBICHAUX
> I can't. I thought I could go through with it, but I can't. I'm sorry—

She heads for the stairs, still holding her clenched fist in front of her. Before she can get there, LINOGE points his cane her way. She is driven back at once. LINOGE now dips the silver wolf's head at her hand. She tries to hold the fingers closed and can't. The stone drops to the stage, rolls like a marble (which is what the stones look like), and

THE CAMERA TRACKS IT. It finally stops, resting against one of the legs of the town manager's table. It's WHITE.

JILL collapses to her knees, SOBBING. LINDA helps her to her feet and embraces her. Now there is only HENRY, MELINDA, and MOLLY. One of them has the black stone. We INTERCUT their spouses. CARLA BRIGHT and HATCH are watching the stage with passionate, terrorized fascination. MIKE is still looking at the floor.

> LINOGE
> Mr. Bright? Henry? Will you favor us?

HENRY steps forward and slowly opens his hand. The stone is WHITE. He all but deflates in his relief. CARLA looks at him, smiling through her tears.

Now it's down to MOLLY and MELINDA, RALPHIE and PIPPA. The two mothers look at each other with LINOGE smiling in the background. One of them is about to cease being a mother, and both of them know it.

128    INTERIOR: MOLLY, CLOSE-UP.

She's imagining:

129    EXTERIOR: BLUE SKY—DAY.

Flying high above the clouds is LINOGE, but now the V is very short. Of the eight children, only RALPHIE and PIPPA are left, each gripping one of LINOGE'S hands.

130    INTERIOR: RESUME STAGE—NIGHT.

> LINOGE
> Ladies?

MOLLY looks a thought at MELINDA. MELINDA catches it and nods slightly. The women hold out their closed fists, hand to hand. They look at each other, frantic with love, hope, and fear.

> MOLLY
> (very soft)

Now.

131    INTERIOR: THE CLOSED HANDS, CLOSE-UP.

They open. In one is a white "marble"; in the other is a black. There are
MURMURS, GASPS, and CRIES OF SURPRISE from the audience . . .
but *we* can't tell—not yet. We see only the stones lying on the open palms.

132    INTERIOR: MOLLY'S FACE, EXTREME CLOSE-UP.

Wide eyes.

133    INTERIOR: MELINDA'S FACE, EXTREME CLOSE-UP.

Wide eyes.

134    INTERIOR: HATCH'S FACE, EXTREME CLOSE-UP.

Wide eyes.

135    INTERIOR: MIKE, EXTREME CLOSE-UP.

Head down . . . but he can't keep it that way, despite his intention not to
participate in this, even passively. He raises his face and looks toward
the stage. And we must read the loss of his son first on this man's face—
we see incredulity, then the dawn of a terrible understanding.

MIKE
(to his feet)

*NO!!! NO!!!*

SONNY, LUCIEN, and ALEX grab him when he tries to lunge forward, and wrestle him back to his seat.

136   INTERIOR: MOLLY AND MELINDA, ON STAGE.

They continue to face each other, almost forehead to forehead, frozen, their hands—now open—held out. In MELINDA'S is the seventh white stone. In MOLLY'S is the black one.

MELINDA'S face breaks in delayed reaction. She turns, blinded by tears, and walks toward the edge of the stage.

> MELINDA
> Pippa! Mummy's coming, love—

She stumbles on the stairs and would go headlong, if not for HATCH, who is there to catch her. MELINDA, hysterical with relief, doesn't even notice. She fights free of her husband's arms and runs up the center aisle.

> MELINDA
> Pippa, honey! It's all right! Mummy's coming, sweetheart, mummy's coming!

HATCH turns to MIKE.

> HATCH
> Mike, I—

MIKE only looks at him—a look of pure, poisonous hate. "You condoned this, and it has cost me my son," that look says. HATCH cannot bear it. He goes after his wife, almost slinking.

MOLLY has been stunned through all of this, looking down at the BLACK MARBLE, but now she begins to realize what has happened.

> MOLLY
> No. Oh, no. This isn't . . . This can't be . . .

She throws the stone away and turns to LINOGE.

MOLLY

It's a joke! Or a test? It's a test, isn't it? You didn't really mean . . .

But he did really mean it, *does* really mean it, and she sees that.

MOLLY

You can't have him!

LINOGE

Molly, I feel your grief keenly . . . but you agreed to the terms. I'm sorry.

MOLLY

You fixed it somehow! You wanted him all along! Because . . . because of the fairy saddle!

Is this true? We will never know if we imagined the FLICKER in LINOGE'S eyes . . . or actually saw it.

LINOGE

I assure you that's not so. The game, as you'd say, was straight. And since I believe that long, drawn-out farewells only add to the pain—

He starts toward the stairs, on the way to claim his prize.

MOLLY

*No, no, I won't let you—*

She tries to attack him. LINOGE gestures with the cane, and she is flung backward, hitting the town manager's table and rolling over it. She lands in a SOBBING HEAP on the floor.

LINOGE, at the lip of the stage and the top of the stairs, regards the ISLANDERS—who look like people waking up from a communal nightmare in which they have done some terrible, irrevocable thing—with BEAMING, SARDONIC PLEASURE.

LINOGE

Ladies and gentlemen, residents of Little Tall, I thank you for
your attention to my needs, and I declare this meeting at an
end . . . with a suggestion that the less you say to the outside
world about our . . . our arrangement, the more happy you
are apt to be . . . although such matters are, of course,
ultimately up to you.

Behind his back, MOLLY gets to her feet and comes forward. She looks
all but insane with shock, grief, and incredulity.

LINOGE
(pulls on gloves, watch cap)

With that, I'll take my new protégé and leave you to your
thoughts. May they be happy ones.

He starts down the stairs. His path to the center aisle brings him close
to where MIKE sits. MOLLY rushes forward to the edge of the stage,
her eyes so big they seem to fill the whole top half of her face. She sees
that MIKE'S guards are no longer doing their job; LUCIEN, SONNY,
and the others are sitting back, looking at LINOGE, their jaws agape.

MOLLY
(shrieking)
*Mike! Stop him! For God's sake, stop him!*

MIKE knows what will happen if he goes for LINOGE; a single wave of
the cane, and he will be peeling himself off one of the walls. He looks
up at his wife—his *estranged* wife now, one supposes—with HORRI-
BLE DEAD EYES.

MIKE

Too late, Molly.

She reacts first with dismay, then with CRAZED DETERMINATION. If
MIKE will not help her right the mistake they've made, she will do it
herself. She looks around . . . and sees ROBBIE'S little pistol, now
lying on the podium. She seizes it, whirls, and plunges down the steps
to the floor.

MOLLY

Stop! I'm warning you!

LINOGE sweeps on, and A CHANGE IS TAKING PLACE as he walks: the pea coat is becoming a robe of royal silver-blue, decorated with suns and moons and other symbols of cabalistic design. The watch cap is becoming the tall, pointed hat of a SORCERER or WIZARD. And the cane is becoming a SCEPTER. The wolf's head is still there, but now it tops a GLOWING WAND worthy of Merlin.

MOLLY either doesn't see or doesn't care. All she wants to do is to stop him. She steps to the head of the center aisle and levels the pistol.

MOLLY

Stop, or I'll shoot!

But SONNY and ALEX HABER crowd into the aisle, blocking her off from LINOGE. LUCIEN and JOHNNY HARRIMAN grab her . . . and HATCH plucks the gun neatly from her hand. During all this, MIKE only sits with his head down, unable to look.

LUCIEN

Sorry, Missus Anderson . . . but we made a deal.

MOLLY

We didn't *understand* the deal! We didn't understand what we were doing! Mike was right, we didn't . . . didn't . . . Jack, stop him! Don't let him take Ralphie! *Don't let him take my son!*

JACK

I can't do that, Molly.
                    (then, with some resentment)
And you wouldn't be screaming like that, either, if it'd been me with the black marble.

She looks at him, unbelieving. He holds her eyes for a moment, then wavers. But ANGELA is there to put her arm around him, and ANGIE looks at MOLLY with bright hostility.

ANGIE

Can't you be a good loser?

MOLLY

This isn't a . . . a *baseball game!*

137    INTERIOR: THE KIDS' CORNER, WITH LINOGE.

He is now a WIZARD from head to toe, wrapped in a BRIGHT BLUE AURA. We once more see his GREAT AGE. The other parents and friends surrounding the sleeping children draw back from him in fear. He pays them absolutely no notice. He bends down, picks RALPHIE ANDERSON up in his arms, and gazes at the boy raptly.

138    INTERIOR: THE FOOT OF THE CENTER AISLE, WITH MOLLY.

In her hysteria, she almost succeeds in struggling free from the big men holding her. She faces LINOGE along the length of the aisle with HYSTERICAL DEFIANCE.

MOLLY

You tricked us!

LINOGE

Perhaps you tricked yourselves.

MOLLY

He'll never belong to you! Never!

LINOGE lifts the sleeping boy up like an offering. The BLUE GLOW around him INTENSIFIES . . . and now it begins to STEAL OVER RALPHIE, as well. LINOGE'S age is not kindly but cruel, a thing to be feared. And his smile is horrible in its triumph . . . a thing to haunt our dreams.

LINOGE

But he will. He'll come to love me. (pause) He'll come to call me Father.

There is an awful truth to this against which MOLLY cannot hold out. She slumps in the hands holding her back, ceasing to resist. LINOGE holds her gaze a moment longer, then turns, the hem of his silk robe flaring out. He strides for the door. Everyone turns to watch him.

139   INTERIOR: MIKE.

He gets up. That **DEAD LOOK** is still on his face. HATCH reaches for him.

> HATCH
>
> Mike, I don't think—

> MIKE
> (pushes his hand off)
> Don't touch me. Don't ever touch me again. Not any of you.
> (looks at MOLLY)
> Not *any* of you.

He walks up the side aisle. No one stops him.

140   INTERIOR: THE CORRIDOR OF THE TOWN HALL.

MIKE steps out of the meeting hall just in time to see the hem of LINOGE'S robe going out the front door and into the night. He pauses, then goes after.

141   EXTERIOR: THE FRONT STEPS OF THE TOWN HALL—NIGHT.

MIKE comes out and stands looking, his breath PUFFING SILVER in the moonlight.

142   EXTERIOR: LINOGE AND RALPHIE IN FRONT OF THE TOWN HALL—NIGHT.

LINOGE is still **GLOWING BRIGHT BLUE. THE CAMERA TRACKS WITH HIM** as he carries RALPHIE down the slope toward the street . . . the shore . . . the reach . . . the mainland . . . and all the leagues of Earth beyond. We see LINOGE'S tracks, first quite heavy . . . then light . . . then just faint prints.

As LINOGE passes the cupola with the memorial bell inside, he begins rising into the air. Only an inch or two at first, but the distance between him and the earth is growing. It's almost as if he's climbing stairs we can't see.

143   EXTERIOR: MIKE, ON THE TOWN HALL STEPS—NIGHT.

He cries out after his son, putting all his grief and loss into that one shouted word:

MIKE
*Ralphie!*

144    EXTERIOR: LINOGE AND RALPHIE—NIGHT.

RALPHIE opens his eyes and looks around.

RALPHIE
Where am I? Where's my daddy?

MIKE (voice, growing faint)
*Ralphie . . .*

LINOGE
It doesn't matter, fairy-saddle boy. Look down!

RALPHIE looks down. They are flying over the reach now. Their shadows flee across the waves, etched in moonlight. RALPHIE smiles, delighted.

RALPHIE
Whoa! Neat! (pause) Is it real?

LINOGE
Real as rhubarb.

RALPHIE looks back at:

145    EXTERIOR: LITTLE TALL ISLAND, FROM RALPHIE'S POINT OF VIEW—NIGHT.

This is almost a negative image of our introduction to the island—night instead of day, going away instead of approaching. In the moonlight, Little Tall looks almost like an illusion. Which, to RALPHIE, it will soon be.

146    EXTERIOR: RESUME LINOGE AND RALPHIE—NIGHT.

RALPHIE
(very impressed)
Where we going?

LINOGE tosses his scepter into the air ahead of him. It rises and resumes the position it held in the visions of LINOGE and the FLYING CHILDREN. Its shadow, now thrown by the moon instead of by the sun, lies across LINOGE'S face. He bends and kisses the fairy saddle on RALPHIE'S nose.

> LINOGE
> Anywhere. Everywhere. All the places you ever dreamed of.

> RALPHIE
> What about my mom and dad? When are they coming?

> LINOGE
> (smiling)
> Why don't we worry about them later?

Well, he's the grown-up . . . and besides, this is fun.

> RALPHIE
> Okay.

LINOGE turns—banks like an airplane, almost—and flies away from us.

147    EXTERIOR: MIKE, ON THE TOWN HALL STEPS—NIGHT.

He's weeping. JOANNA STANHOPE comes out and puts a hand on his shoulder. She speaks to him with infinite kindness.

> JOANNA
> Mike. Come in.

He ignores her, going down the steps and stumbling his way into the new snow. It's tough going for folks who aren't wizards, but he flounders ahead just the same, even though it's waist deep at times. He follows LINOGE'S footprints, and THE CAMERA TRACKS WITH HIM, watching as the impressions grow lighter and lighter, less and less tied to the earth where mortals must live.

Past the memorial bell, there is one more faint imprint . . . then nothing. Just acres of virgin snow. MIKE collapses beside that last print, CRYING. He holds his hands up to the EMPTY SKY, the GLOWING MOON.

> MIKE
> (low)

Bring him back. Please. I'll do anything if you bring my son back. Anything you want.

148   EXTERIOR: THE DOORS TO THE TOWN HALL—NIGHT.

They are crowded with ISLANDERS who stand there, silently watching. JOHNNY and SONNY, FERD and LUCIEN, TAVIA and DELLA, HATCH and MELINDA.

> MIKE (pleading voice)

*Bring him back!*

The faces of the ISLANDERS do not change. We may see sympathy, but we will see no mercy. Not here; not among these. What's done is done.

149   EXTERIOR: RESUME MIKE, ON THE SNOWFIELD—NIGHT.

He huddles in the snow beyond the cupola holding the memorial bell. Holds his arms out to the moon and the light-drenched water one final time, but without hope.

> MIKE
> (whispers)

Please bring him back.

THE CAMERA begins to PULL UP AND AWAY. Little by little, MIKE loses his human dimension and becomes just a black speck on a VAST WHITE SNOWFIELD. Beyond is the headland, the tumbled lighthouse, and the waves of the reach.

FADE TO BLACK.

> MIKE (voice)
> (a final whispered plea)

I love him. Have mercy.

THIS ENDS ACT 6.

# Act 7

150   EXTERIOR: THE REACH—A SUMMER MORNING.

The sky is bright blue, and so is the reach. Fishing boats chug stolidly; pleasure boats dash, dragging wakes and whooping water-skiers. Overhead, gulls SWOOP AND CRY.

151   EXTERIOR: A SEACOAST TOWN—MORNING.

TITLE CARD: MACHIAS, SUMMER OF 1989.

152   EXTERIOR: A SMALL CLAPBOARD BUILDING ON MAIN STREET—MORNING.

The sign out front reads SEACOAST COUNSELING SERVICES. And, below this: THERE IS A SOLUTION. WE'LL FIND IT TOGETHER.

THE CAMERA MOVES IN on a side window. A WOMAN sits there, looking out. Her eyes are red, her cheeks wet with tears. Her hair is gray, and at first we do not recognize MOLLY ANDERSON. She has aged twenty years.

153   INTERIOR: THE COUNSELOR'S OFFICE—MORNING.

MOLLY sits in a bentwood rocker, looking out at summer and CRYING SOUNDLESSLY. Sitting across from her is her COUNSEL-OR, a professional woman in a light cream-colored summer skirt and silk summer blouse. Nicely coiffed, nicely turned out, and looking at MOLLY with that kind of sympathy good psychologists show—often helpful, but scary in its distance.

The silence spins out. The COUNSELOR is waiting for MOLLY to break it, but MOLLY only sits in the rocker, looking out at summer with her streaming eyes.

COUNSELOR

You and Mike haven't slept together in . . . how long?

361

MOLLY
(looking out the window)
Five months. Give or take. I could tell you exactly, if you thought it would help. The last time was the night before the big storm came. The Storm of the Century.

COUNSELOR
When you lost your son.

MOLLY
Correct. When I lost my son.

COUNSELOR
And Mike blames you for that loss.

MOLLY
I think he's going to leave me.

COUNSELOR
You're very afraid of that, aren't you?

MOLLY
I think he's running out of ways to stay. Do you understand what I mean by that?

COUNSELOR
Tell me again what happened to Ralphie.

MOLLY
Why? What good will it do? For God's sake, what good *can* it do? He's gone!

The COUNSELOR makes no response. After a bit, MOLLY sighs and gives in.

MOLLY
It was the second day. We were in the town hall—where we took shelter, you know. The storm . . . you can't believe how bad it was.

COUNSELOR
I was here. I went through it.

MOLLY
Yes—you were *here*, Lisa. On the mainland. It's different on
the island. (pause) Everything's different on the island.
(pause) Anyway, Johnny Harriman came rushing in while we
were having breakfast and said the lighthouse was going
over. Everyone wanted to see, of course . . . and Mike . . .

154   EXTERIOR: THE ANDERSON HOUSE—SUMMER MORNING.

There's a SMALL WHITE CAR at the curb with the trunk lid up. There
are two or three suitcases in it. Now the door opens and MIKE comes
out, carrying two more. He closes the door, descends the porch steps,
and goes down the walk. Every motion and gesture, every look back,
tells us that this is a man who is leaving for good.

MOLLY (voice-over)
Mike told us it was whiteout, and to stay close to the
building. Ralphie wanted to see . . . Pippa and all the kids
wanted to go out and see . . . and so we took them. God help
us, we took them.

MIKE stops by the WEE FOLKS DAY-CARE sign. It's still chain-hung from
a low branch of the yard maple, but now it looks dusty, somehow.
Forgotten. Of no importance. MIKE yanks it down, looks at it, then
turns and throws it back at the porch, momentarily FURIOUS.

MOLLY (voice-over)
It was a mistake for any of us to go out, especially the
children. We underestimated the storm. Several people wandered away and were lost. Ralphie was one of them. Angie
Carver found her way back. None of the others did.

MIKE looks at the porch, where the sign has landed, then turns and
walks down to his car. He puts the last couple of bags in and slams the
trunk. As he starts around to the driver's side, digging the keys out of
his pocket:

HATCH (voice)
Mike?

MIKE turns. HATCH, looking strange in a T-shirt and Bermuda shorts, walks up to where he stands. He looks painfully unhappy to be here. MIKE looks back at him coolly.

### MIKE

If you've got something to say, best say it. Ferry leaves at 11:10, and I don't intend to miss it.

### HATCH

Where you going?
(silence from MIKE)
Don't, Michael. Don't leave.
(silence from MIKE)
Would it do you any good to tell you I haven't had a decent night's sleep since February?
(no answer from MIKE)
Would it do any good to tell you that . . . we might have been wrong?

### MIKE

Hatch, I have to get going.

### HATCH

Robbie says to tell you the constable's job is yours again whenever you want it. All you have to do is ask.

### MIKE

Tell him where he can park his job. I'm done here. I've tried until I can't try anymore.

He starts for the driver's door, and just before he swings in, HATCH touches his arm. MIKE whirls at that touch, eyes burning, as if he means to punch HATCH'S lights out. But HATCH doesn't flinch. Maybe he thinks he deserves it.

### HATCH

Molly needs you. Have you seen the way she is, now? Have you even looked?

### MIKE

You look for me. Okay?

HATCH
(drops his eyes)
Melly isn't doing very well, either. She takes a lot of tranquilizers. I think she might be hooked on them.

MIKE
Too bad. But . . . you've got your daughter, at least. You may
not sleep so well, but you can go into Pippa's bedroom and
watch *her* sleep any night you want. Can't you?

HATCH
You're as self-righteous as ever. Can't see it any way but your
way.

MIKE swings behind the wheel and looks bleakly up at HATCH.

MIKE
I'm not anything. I'm empty—scooped out as a gourd in
November.

HATCH
If you could just *try* to understand—

MIKE
I understand that the ferry leaves at 11:10, and if I don't get
moving now, I'm going to miss it. Good luck, Hatch. Hope
you catch up on your sleep.

He slams the car door, starts the engine, and pulls out onto Main
Street. HATCH helplessly watches him go.

155    EXTERIOR: THE LAWN OF THE TOWN HALL—MORNING.

THE CAMERA looks down toward Main Street and picks up MIKE'S
car, heading toward the docks where the interisland ferry is backed up,
ENGINE RUMBLING. We HOLD for a moment, then PAN LEFT, to
the cupola and the memorial bell. A second plaque has been added, to
the right of the war dead. Heading it is this: THOSE LOST IN THE STORM
OF THE CENTURY, 1989. Below are the names: MARTHA CLARENDON,
PETER GODSOE, WILLIAM SOAMES, LLOYD WISHMAN, CORA STANHOPE, JANE
KINGSBURY, WILLIAM TIMMONS, GEORGE KIRBY . . . and, at the very
bottom, RALPH ANDERSON.

THE CAMERA MOVES IN ON HIS NAME.

156   INTERIOR: THE COUNSELOR'S OFFICE—MORNING.

MOLLY has stopped talking and just looks out the window. Fresh tears well in her eyes and spill down her cheeks, but her weeping REMAINS SILENT.

> COUNSELOR
>
> Molly . . . ?

> MOLLY
>
> He wandered away into the whiteout. Maybe he wound up with Bill Timmons, the gas station man. I like to think so; that he was with somebody at the end. They must have lost their bearings completely and gone into the water. They were the two who were never found.

> COUNSELOR
>
> There's a great deal of this story you haven't told me, isn't there?
>
> (silence from MOLLY)
>
> Until you do, until you tell someone, it will keep festering.

> MOLLY
>
> It will fester no matter what I do. Some wounds can never be cleaned out. I didn't understand that . . . before . . . but now I do.

> COUNSELOR
>
> Why does your husband hate you so, Molly? What really happened to Ralphie?

CAMERA MOVES IN ON MOLLY. She is still looking out the window. It's sunny in the COUNSELOR'S yard; the grass is green and there are flowers . . . but it's SNOWING. The snow falls thickly, coating the grass and the walks, heaping on the leafy branches of the trees.

We MOVE IN ON MOLLY, MOVE IN TO EXTREME CLOSE-UP as she looks out on the falling snow.

MOLLY

He wandered away. People do, you know. They get lost. That's what happened to Ralphie. He was lost in the white-out. He was lost in the storm.

DISSOLVE TO:

157 EXTERIOR: THE FERRY—MORNING.

It's trudging its way across the reach to Machias. The cars are parked on the apron at the back, MIKE'S among them. MIKE himself stands alone at the rail, his face up, the ocean breeze blowing his hair back from his forehead. He looks almost at peace.

MIKE (voice-over)

Nine years ago, that was. I just gassed my car and left on the 11:10 ferry. I've never been back.

DISSOLVE TO:

158 INTERIOR: THE COUNSELOR'S OFFICE—MORNING.

MOLLY'S session is over. The clock on the wall reads 11:55. She stands at the COUNSELOR'S desk, writing a check. The COUNSELOR looks at her with a troubled expression, knowing that she has lost, and once again the island has won. The secret—whatever it is—has been kept.

Neither of them see MIKE'S little white car go by.

MIKE (voice-over)

I didn't think about where I was going, at first—I just drove.

159 EXTERIOR: MIKE, THROUGH THE WINDSHIELD OF HIS CAR—SUNSET.

He's wearing dark glasses against the BRIGHT ORANGE GLOW. Reflected in each lens is a SETTING SUN.

MIKE (voice-over)

All I cared about was that I had to wear sunglasses every night when the sun went down. That every mile on the odometer was a mile further away from Little Tall.

160 EXTERIOR: THE AMERICAN DESERT—MIDDAY.

Two-lane blacktop runs through the middle of the frame. The white car enters, moving fast, and THE CAMERA SWINGS TO FOLLOW.

MIKE (voice-over)

The divorce was no-fault. Moll got the bank accounts, the insurance, the store, the house, and a little piece of land we had in Vanceboro. I got the Toyota and the peace of mind. (pause) What was left of it.

161    EXTERIOR: THE GOLDEN GATE BRIDGE—TWILIGHT.

MIKE (voice-over)

I wound up here . . . back on the water again. Ironic I guess, huh? But it's different, somehow, the Pacific. It doesn't have that hard glow when the days start to run down toward winter. (pause) And it doesn't have the same memories.

162    EXTERIOR: A SKYSCRAPER ON MONTGOMERY STREET, SAN FRANCISCO—DAY.

MIKE comes out—an older MIKE, with gray at his temples and lines on his face—but one who looks as if he's made his peace with the world. Or found some. He wears a suit (casual, no tie) and carries a briefcase. He and the man with him walk to a sedan parked at the curb. It pulls out into traffic, swinging around a cable car. Over this, MIKE talks.

MIKE (voice-over)

I went back to school, got a degree in law enforcement and another one in accountancy. Thought about going after a law degree . . . and then thought again. Started out keeping store on an island off the Maine coast and wound up a federal marshal. How do you like that?

163    EXTERIOR: MIKE, THROUGH THE WINDSHIELD—DAY.

His partner is driving. MIKE sits quietly in the shotgun seat, his eyes distant. It's the look of a man visiting along memory lane.

MIKE (voice-over)

Sometimes the island seems very far away, and Andre Linoge just a bad dream I had. Sometimes . . . when I wake up late at night, trying not to scream . . . it seems very close. And, as I said way back at the beginning, I keep in touch.

164   EXTERIOR: THE LITTLE TALL GRAVEYARD—DAY.

MOURNERS move between the gravestones toward a newly dug grave, bearing a coffin (we see this from the middle distance). Fall leaves rush past in RATTLING BURSTS OF COLOR.

> MIKE (voice-over)
> Melinda Hatcher died in October of 1990. The local paper said it was a heart attack; Ursula Godsoe sent me the clipping. I don't know if there was more to it or not. Thirty-five's young for your pump to quit, but it happens . . . ayuh. Shoah, deah.

165   EXTERIOR: THE LITTLE TALL METHODIST CHURCH—DAY.

It's late spring. Cheerful flowers shout color along the walk leading from the front door. Faintly, we can hear the TRIUMPHAL ORGAN STRAINS of "The Wedding March." The doors burst open. Out comes MOLLY, laughing and radiant in her wedding dress. There are still lines on her face, but her graying hair is hidden. Beside her, dressed in a morning coat and clasping her waist, is HATCH. He looks as happy as she does. Behind them, holding up MOLLY'S train with one hand and clutching a bouquet in the other, is PIPPA, now bigger and with beautiful long hair. Her days of getting her head stuck between the banister posts are pretty well behind her. People follow, FLINGING RICE. Among them, smiling like a proud papa, is REV. BOB RIGGINS.

> MIKE (voice-over)
> Molly and Hatch married in May of '93. Ursula sent me that clipping, too. From what I hear, they've been good for each other . . . and for Pippa. I'm glad. I wish the three of them every happiness. I mean that with all my heart.

166   INTERIOR: A CHEESY RENTED ROOM—NIGHT.

> MIKE (voice-over)
> Not everyone from Little Tall's been so lucky.

THE CAMERA TRACKS ACROSS THE ROOM, past a rumpled, unmade bed that looks like it has seen its share of bad dreams. The bathroom door is ajar, and THE CAMERA PUSHES THROUGH.

> MIKE (voice-over)
> Jack and Angie Carver divorced about two months after
> Hatch and Molly got married. Jack fought for custody of
> Buster—it was pretty bitter, I guess—and lost. He moved
> off-island, to Lewiston, rented a room, and killed himself
> there one night in the late summer of 1994.

The bathroom window is OPEN. Through it, FAINTLY, we can hear
the SOUND of a bar band lashing its way through "Hang On Sloopy."
JACK CARVER is lying in a dry bathtub with a plastic bag pulled down
over his head. THE CAMERA MOVES IN RELENTLESSLY . . . until
we can see the paisley eye patch over one eye.

> MIKE (voice-over)
> He left what little he had to a fellow named Harmon
> Brodsky, who lost an eye in a barroom fight back in the
> eighties.

167   EXTERIOR: LITTLE TALL ISLAND, FROM THE REACH—MORNING.

It's still—except for the SLOW TOLL OF A BELL BUOY—and a little
ghostly, misted in shades of gray. We can see that the town dock has
been rebuilt, and there's a fish warehouse there, as well . . . only it's a
different color from PETER'S, and the sign along the side reads BEALS
FANCY FISH instead of GODSOE FISH & LOBSTER.

Now, as THE CAMERA BEGINS TO PULL BACK, we also hear THE
LAP OF WATER against the side of a boat. It comes into view—a small
rowboat riding on the swell. During this:

> MIKE (voice-over)
> Robbie Beals rebuilt the old fish house on the town dock,
> and hired Kirk Freeman to work there. Kirk said Robbie's
> wife Sandra came down there one early morning in the
> spring of 1996, dressed in her yellow slicker and red boots,
> and told him she wanted to go for a little row. Kirk made
> her put on a life-preserver . . . he said he didn't like the
> way she looked.

THE CAMERA reaches the boat and RISES, showing us the prow.
Neatly folded there is a yellow fisherman's slicker. A pair of red

galoshes stand beside it, and placed around their toes like a collar is a Mae West.

> MIKE (voice-over)
> He said it was like she was dreaming with her eyes open . . . but what could he do? It was a mild morning, no wind, not much of a swell . . . and she was the boss's wife. They found the boat, but they didn't find Sandy. There was one strange thing . . .

CAMERA SLIPS ALONG the length of the boat. Written across the rear seat in either red paint or lipstick is a single word: "CROATON."

> MIKE (voice-over)
> . . . but they didn't know what to make of it. There were people on the island who maybe could have helped them a little there . . .

168   INTERIOR: THE TOWN OFFICE, WITH URSULA—DAY.

A couple of STATE POLICEMEN are talking to her (we don't need to hear them; this can be MOS [without sound]), no doubt asking questions, and she is shaking her head politely. Sorry, officers . . . nope . . . can't imagine . . . and so on.

> MIKE (voice-over)
> . . . but island folk can keep a secret. We kept our share back in 1989, and the people who live there keep them still. As for Sandra Beals, she's presumed drowned, and her seven years are up in 2003. Robbie'll no doubt have her declared officially dead as soon as '03 comes around on the calendar. Tough, I know, but . . .

169   EXTERIOR: LITTLE TALL ISLAND, FROM THE OCEAN—DAY

> MIKE (voice-over)
> (continues)
> . . . this is a cash-and-carry world, pay as you go. Sometimes you only have to pay a little, but mostly it's a lot. And once in a while it's all you have. That's a lesson I thought I learned nine years ago, on Little Tall, during the Storm of the Century . . .

SLOW DISSOLVE TO:

170    EXTERIOR: SAN FRANCISCO, STOCK SHOT—DAY.

> MIKE (voice-over)
>
> . . . but I was wrong. I only started learning during the big blow. I finished just last week.

171    EXTERIOR: A BUSY DOWNTOWN STREET—DAY.

Lots of folks are shopping. We MOVE IN on an upscale deli one or two storefronts up from the corner, and MIKE comes out. It's his day off, and he's dressed casually—light jacket, jeans, and a T-shirt. He's got a couple of shopping bags in his arms, and he juggles them, trying to snag his keys out of his pants pocket as he angles toward the curb and his car.

Coming in the other direction, entering the frame with their backs to us, are a MAN and a TEENAGE BOY. The MAN is dressed in a gray topcoat and homburg hat. He carries a cane with a silver wolf's head. The BOY with him is wearing an Oakland As jacket and jeans. MIKE will pass them on the way to his car, but he takes no particular notice of them at first. He's gotten his keys out; now he's trying to peer at them over one of his bags just enough so he can see which one will unlock the door. Then, just as the MAN and TEENAGE BOY reach MIKE:

> LINOGE
> (sings)
> "I'm a little teapot, short and stout. . . ."

> BOY
> (joining in)
> "Here is my handle, here is my spout. . . ."

MIKE'S face fills with terrible recognition. The keys fall from his fingers and the shopping bags SAG in his arms as he turns and sees:

172    EXTERIOR: LINOGE AND THE BOY, FROM MIKE'S POINT OF VIEW (SLOW MOTION)—DAY.

They are already passing MIKE, and there's only time for a glimpse, even in SLOW MOTION. Yes, it's LINOGE beneath the homburg, now looking not like a psychotic fisherman but like a ruthless businessman, and not thirty-five but sixty-five.

The BOY with him—smiling up at him and HARMONIZING PRET-TILY on the well-loved old nonsense-jingle—is a handsome child of fourteen. His hair is MOLLY'S shade. His eyes are MIKE'S shade. And lying across his nose, faint but still visible, is the fairy-saddle birthmark.

> LINOGE AND RALPHIE
> (echoing dreamlike voices)
> "You can pick me up and pour me out. . . . I'm a little teapot, short and stout!"

During this, we lose our angle on their faces—which we have seen for only that heartbreakingly brief moment, anyway. Now they are only a pair of backs: a well-dressed man and the child of his late middle age, heading for the corner. And beyond the corner, for anywhere.

173   EXTERIOR: RESUME MIKE—DAY.

He stands where he is, BAGS SAGGING IN HIS ARMS, thunderstruck. His mouth opens and closes soundlessly . . . and then, at last, a whisper comes out . . .

> MIKE
> Rah . . . Rah . . . Ralphie . . . *Ralphie? RALPHIE!*

174   EXTERIOR: LINOGE AND RALPHIE—DAY.

They are beyond the deli. Almost to the corner. They stop. And look back.

175   EXTERIOR: RESUME MIKE—DAY.

He drops the bags from his arms—stuff inside smashes—and RUNS.

> MIKE
> *RALPHIE!*

176   EXTERIOR: LINOGE AND RALPHIE—DAY.

RALPHIE'S mouth opens; he HISSES LIKE A SNAKE. His good looks are gone in an instant, as the FANGS beneath his lips are revealed. His eyes DARKEN and become BLACK, shot through with WRITHING RED LINES. He raises hands that are hooked into talons, as if to claw MIKE'S face open.

LINOGE puts an arm around his shoulders and (without taking his eyes away from MIKE) urges RALPHIE to turn. Then they sweep around the corner together.

177   EXTERIOR: RESUME MIKE—DAY.

He stops outside the deli, his face filled with DISMAY and SICKENED HORROR. Pedestrians stream around him, some looking at him curiously, but MIKE takes no notice.

> MIKE
> Ralphie!

He dashes for the corner and goes around.

178   EXTERIOR: MIKE—DAY.

He comes to a stop, eyes searching.

179   EXTERIOR: THE STREET, FROM MIKE'S POINT OF VIEW—DAY.

People come and go on the sidewalks, or dart across the street, or hail taxis, or get newspapers from curbside vending machines. There is no man in a gray topcoat. There is no boy in an Oakland As jacket.

180   EXTERIOR: RESUME MIKE.

> LINOGE (voice-over)
> He'll come to love me. (pause) He'll come to call me Father.

MIKE slumps against the wall and closes his eyes. From beneath one of those closed lids, a single tear slips. A YOUNG WOMAN comes around the corner and looks at him with cautious sympathy.

> YOUNG WOMAN
> Mister, are you all right?

> MIKE
> (doesn't open his eyes)
> Yes. I just need a minute.

> YOUNG WOMAN
> You dropped your groceries. Some of it's probably okay, but some of the stuff broke.

MIKE now opens his eyes and does his best to smile at her.

> MIKE
> Ayuh, some of the stuff broke. I heard it.

> YOUNG WOMAN
> (smiling)
> What kind of accent is that?

> MIKE
> The kind you learn on the other side of the world.

> YOUNG WOMAN
> What happened? Did you trip?

> MIKE
> I thought I saw someone I knew, and I just kind of . . . lost
> my grip for a second there.

He looks down the street one more time. He reached the corner seconds after LINOGE and RALPHIE turned it, they should be right there, but they're not . . . and MIKE isn't really surprised.

> YOUNG WOMAN
> I could help you pick up the stuff that's still okay, if you
> wanted. Look, I got this.

She reaches into her coat pocket and brings out a crumpled-up net shopping bag. She holds it out to him, smiling tentatively.

> MIKE
> That would be very kind.

They go around the corner together.

181   EXTERIOR: MIKE AND THE YOUNG WOMAN, A HIGH ANGLE—DAY.

As they approach his car and the spilled groceries, we see them from above . . . then BOOM HIGHER YET, TURNING AND LOSING THEM. Now we see the bright blue sky and water of San Francisco Bay, with the bridge spanning it like a dream that has begun to rust a little around the edges.

There are swooping gulls . . . we track one of them . . . we:

DISSOLVE TO:
182   EXTERIOR: SWOOPING GULL—DAY.

We follow it, then **BOOM DOWN** to discover Little Tall Island, and the town hall. There's a car parked at the curb. Three people walk toward the cupola that holds the plaques and the memorial bell. One—a WOMAN—walks ahead of the other two.

> MIKE (voice-over)
> I could have written Molly and told her. I thought about it . . . I even prayed about it. When every choice hurts, how do you tell which one's the right one? In the end, I kept silent. Sometimes, mostly late at night when I can't sleep, I think that was wrong. But in daylight, I know better.

183   EXTERIOR: THE CUPOLA ON THE TOWN HALL LAWN—DAY.

MOLLY approaches it slowly. In her hands she has a bouquet of flowers. Her face is serene and sad and quite beautiful. Behind her, HATCH and PIPPA stand at the edge of the grass, HATCH with his arm around his daughter's shoulders.

MOLLY kneels at the base of the plaque commemorating those lost in the Storm of the Century. She puts her flowers at the base of this plaque. She is crying a little now. She kisses her fingers, then presses them to her son's name.

She gets up and walks back to where HATCH and PIPPA wait. HATCH puts his arms around her and hugs her.

184   EXTERIOR: LITTLE TALL ISLAND, LONG—DAY.

> MIKE (voice-over)
> In daylight I know better.

FADE TO BLACK.